DADA CULTURE
CRITICAL TEXTS
ON THE AVANT-GARDE

AVANT-GARDE
CRITICAL STUDIES

18

DADA CULTURE
CRITICAL TEXTS
ON THE AVANT-GARDE

Edited by
Dafydd Jones

Amsterdam - New York, NY 2006

Cover image: Tim Long 2006

Cover design: Aart Jan Bergshoeff

All titles in the Avant Garde Critical Studies series (from 1999 onwards) are available to download from the Ingenta website http://www.ingenta.com

The paper on which this book is printed meets the requirements of "ISO 9706: 1994, Information and documentation - Paper for documents - Requirements for permanence".

Transferred to digital printing 2010

ISBN 13: 978-90-420-1869-3
ISBN 10: 90-420-1869-0
Editions Rodopi B.V., Amsterdam - New York, NY 2006
Printed in The Netherlands

CONTENTS

IV. Thinkers on Stage

V. Philosophy, Theory and the Avant-Garde

VI. Dada Critical Bibliography

Short preface

Critically thinking the currency of Dada in the twenty-first century –
like Peter Sinfield's schizoid man – is imperative if Dada is to secure
any continuity and relevance beyond its narrow, if not parenthetic,
historical moment at the start of the twentieth. Moving towards realisation of such a project, the present volume was first conceptually
outlined as part of a presentation addressing theoretical virtuality in
visual culture (instanced, on that occasion, in the 1930s' drawings and
relief constructions of British modernist and Surrealist Ceri Richards –
works that made a marked impression on Hans Arp when he visited
Richards's London studio in 1937) during an otherwise fruitless visit
to the University of Leeds in late 2002. The following summer, a
number of papers addressing Dada and the idea of the avant-garde directly, and attempting a critical recontextualising of Dada, were presented at the Sixth International Literature and Humanities Conference at Eastern Mediterranean University in Famagusta, signalling
how the address of twenty-first century Dada would necessarily and
simultaneously come from a range of disciplines within the humanities. Prompted by Dietrich Scheunemann – to whom, in his absence,
this volume is heavily indebted – the guiding principle of Klaus
Beekman at Rodopi Verlag served then to direct a body of work that
in the twelve months following had diversified and at once clarified
the terms, range and ultimately limit of the scope here presented, and
which now constitutes part of the ongoing response to the call for

> a new approach towards a comprehensive assessment of the
> avant-garde ... [which will] confront more clearly the complex
> and often contradictory nature of the avant-garde's manifestations
> and its theoretical discourses ... [in the] attempt to provide initial
> outlines of alternative approaches and put forward first proposals
> of a revised practice of interpretation. (Scheunemann 2000: 9-10)

The birth of two daughters to the Jones household during the two
years outlined above not only confirmed the theory that "dada" (and
"mama" too) is indeed a developmental milestone linguistically, but
proved also a constant reminder that there was a book on Dada pressing. The book, in turn, owes to individuals whose participation has
been both directly and indirectly foundational. I most sincerely wish

to express my gratitude for the ready participation of the individual contributors, and to thank especially Clive Cazeaux, Jonathan Clarkson, Andrew Furey, Manon Gallet, the International Dada Archive at the University of Iowa, Dvora Janco, Alun Jones, Geinor Jones, Duncan Large, Jean-Jacques Lecercle, Tim Long, Nicola Pearce at DACS, Hywel Pennar, Marieke Schilling, Christopher Short, Julio Sims at the Getty Research Institute, the Société Serneriste and, inevitably, Swansea religious bookseller Gareth Rees, whose pursuit of the internationally mobile Knights Templar inside and outside the precinct of Famagusta made the summer of 2003 a blast. (Incidentally, it's the books that are religious, not necessarily the seller.)

My invariable debt comes last, outstanding as it always will be to my mother and father who are both present in every independent thought. And when the work is done, the best part of the day is to come home to revolutionary joy with Denise, Lleucu and Gwen.

DJ
Cardiff, 24 April 2006

Scheunemann, Dietrich (ed.). 2000. *European Avant-Garde: New Perspectives*, Avant Garde Critical Studies 15. Amsterdam and Atlanta: Rodopi.

Introduction

der Holzweg der Holzwege

Perhaps the falsest of all false paths was the narrow thoroughfare Spiegelgasse.

Lenin made his distinction clear, on more than one occasion, between "freedom" as symptomatic of bourgeois-anarchist individualism, and the *real* freedom he believed would be actualised through revolutionary thought breaking out of bourgeois slavery and merging with "the movement of the really advanced and thoroughly revolutionary class" (1967). His distinction drew on Dietzgen's hostility to the materialist theory of knowledge embodied in "free-thinkers" who, together, constituted a reactionary mass in relation to social democracy.[1] For Lenin, what opposed "free thinkers" were "integral people ... who do not separate theory from practice" (1962: 340-41), whose system is inscribed in their practice, even, indeed and perhaps surprisingly argued when such a system is an opiate religious one. To believe that we are free in our liberal democratic society is our delusion; it demonstrates our failure to *see* our structural accommodation and containment, and our failure to admit the painful truth, as Lenin understood it, that there can be "no real and effective 'freedom' in a society based on the power of money" (1967). The admission, if conceded, is at least productive; to recognise Lenin's comparison of a living movement with a mechanism is to make the structure visible – and if nothing else this much subsequently redeems the structuralist's position. Once the structure is visible, we can begin to *think* our relation to it; if we cease to think that relation, the structure again recedes into invisibility and resumes its unchallenged and effectively uninterrupted repressive exercise.

To think – and to think about thinking – is to participate in a common activity, and thought is a public matter that everybody, it is argued, should be required to attend to. Thinking takes the specific instance to construct a generalisation, but the general proves of little consequence unless, as Dietzgen cautions, it is "conceived in its relation to its special [specific] forms" (1906: 357). Thus read, thinking is a contradictory process, necessarily struggling between generalisation and specialisation, but *not* necessarily working towards synthesis and resolution (although Dietzgen suggests that it is in the nature of the mind to seek to "harmonise" the contradictions of the world, to relativise and equate them) – precisely the opposite on occasion, to capitalise on contradiction and conflict, and actively to counter any potential synthesis or resolution. It becomes instructive, especially when we attempt to work through the bluffs and counter-bluffs of twentieth-century avant-garde strategies, to return to Dietzgen's early observation that reason develops its understanding out of contradictions, an observation which, though central to his dialectical thought, can help us move away from too close and strict a conformity with dialectical materialism (which, we note, Dietzgen had identified independently of Marx and Engels) and the not always helpful bog standard form of the dialectic that charts passage from thesis and antithesis to synthesis – in Engels's words the "continual conflict of the opposites and their final passage into one another" (1940); in Tzara's words "an amusing mechanism which guides us ... to the opinions we had in the first place" (1989: 79). Presented as a way of understanding reality, dialectical materialism is flawed by its privileging of synthetic resolution above antithetic irreconcilability; its more productive potential resides perhaps in capitalising upon the latter, and certainly in its declared resistance to a sense of the eternal, the final, the sacred, with its deliberate insistence on transience and on the absence of absolute boundaries.

The "free thinkers" that Lenin, following Dietzgen, singled out and named for criticism were the professors of philosophy, "muddled idealists" who exercised a tortuous idealism and whose very vocation – philosophy – became the object of sustained and critical interrogation for the proletarian militant committed to following a "true" path in the late nineteenth and early twentieth centuries. The contradiction is again evident, that "in order to follow a true path it is necessary to *study* philosophy, which is '*the falsest of all false paths*'

… [and this means] that there can be no true path … without a study, and, eventually a *theory of philosophy as a false path*" (Althusser 1971: 31). In advancing his position, Lenin duly isolated himself and became tarred as "philosophically intolerable" – Althusser argues this – wilfully conceding to the vague and unpolished nature of his own formulations in the face of the philosophers' sophisticated ruminations. The distinction was an important one to draw, however, historically specifically at the time of writing in pre-dada 1908; "[n]ot only do I not 'philosophise' with their philosophy", wrote Lenin, "I do not 'philosophise' like them at all". The resistance here is to more than western philosophical conclusions: "I treat philosophy differently, I *practise* it" (1908). The integrity of cultural activity that practices its principles appears to have been of no less pressing concern at the start of the twentieth century than it continued to be throughout, and than it remains today; to put itself into practice, and to actualise a procedural "truth" by directly engaging that which is false (but which masquerades as truth), even in consciousness that problematically yet necessarily remains captive to its own falsity.

1. Spiegelgasse 1, Zürich

The revolution would, did, and will occur *inside* ideology. It may or may not be televised, but the next one will be live; we will be extremely unlucky if we miss it on simultaneous webcast; and "*Marxism Today* will produce T-shirts decorated with tanks and warning us against provocateurs" (Imrie 1987) – still, we need not begin to re-hearse Althusser here. It is, needless to say, the radical form of revolutionary action that points to its eventual stake and outcome. For the structuralist marxist, if a radicalism is not a *marxist* radicalism, its direction in the service of the revolution is not necessarily bound to the destruction of state apparatuses, but rather defaults as anything but revolutionary, and duly relegates itself to self-indulgence for the "radical" protagonist. Revolution is nothing of the sort when it condemns the system and then asks the system it has condemned for acceptance; more than once during the twentieth century, it was forcefully and sometimes violently demonstrated that people involved in a revolution do not become part of systems, but that they *destroy* systems. How we invoke the idea of revolution in view of this requires a deliberate revision of readings that have hitherto dominated art historically, prescriptive (and predictable) readings of Dada during the period 1916–1922, which characterise it as anarchic, a nihilist gesture, a negative act of cultural destruction offering nothing to replace what it set about destroying (and therefore, strictly speaking, *not* revo-lution). According to the binary schema of revolution that accom-panies this characterisation, the task of instituting a new order in place of what Dada laid waste, that is to say a new order diametrically opposed to the old, fell to the movement's supercedent (in Paris at least), the Surrealist Revolution of 1924. But does "revolution" thus read actually change anything? Well, the suggestion is that little alters beyond appearances when one order is replaced by its opposite and the cultural, political, social or economic logic is simply inverted; the logic remains the same, it remains intact, and its inversion fuels its reproduction.

    If, however, we read revolution as committed to breaking down systems in all their forms, the revolutionary increasingly assumes the recognisably destructive, anarchic and nihilist traits previ-ously ascribed to the Dadaist (art historically *contra* the Surrealist), abandoning binary schemata and engaging cultural logic – revolution, therefore, that does not define itself by preemptive conclusions. Such, potentially, becomes revolution *without* a goal, but revolution *with* effect; not revolution as Lenin envisaged it emanating to Russia and beyond from its filterbed in neutral Switzerland (Lenin arrived in Zürich in February 1915, remaining there for the year of the Cabaret Voltaire, before his return to Russia in 1917 and the next big thing), but revolution revised practically and theoretically throughout the twentieth century in reflection upon the sobering aftermath and ultimate failure of October 1917. The Spiegelgasse, it has been said, became "the epitome of the violent, the double, *the waking and the dreamt revolution*" (Weiss 1978: 59), simultaneously one and the other, where Lenin studiously planned future events from his room at Spiegelgasse 14 – and, as historical anecdote records, complained about the neighbours:

> [he] hated cafés, these smoky breeding places of endless tirades, in which day and night the revolutionary "declamators" prostituted themselves. During the war a whole crowd of unfathomable foreigners had come to Zürich: adventurers, wheeler-dealers, racketeers, students, deserters, and intellectual babblers, who rebelled with philosophical manifestos and artistic protest-actions against what-not. And they all met in the cafés. (Solzhenitsyn 1976: 113)

2. Lenin, Zürich 1916

But which, indeed, were the dreaming revolutionaries – the united Bolshevik *émigrés* Lenin, Radek and Zinoviev, or the neighbours at Spiegelgasse 1, the Cabaret Voltaire players Ball, Hennings, Tzara, Huelsenbeck, Janco and Arp? The intended irony of the recollection is obvious, but we would do well to note that in Zürich, in 1916, "the Swiss authorities were much more suspicious of the Dadaists, who were after all capable of perpetrating some new enormity at any moment, than of these quiet, studious Russians" (Richter 1966: 16).

To create a new reality, Lenin conceded, the revolutionary had to be able to dream; but what does the dream of reason produce? Lenin's aversion to, indeed intolerance of, all that is "uncontrollable" – be it creativity, chance, or even chance later formulated in terms of psychic automatism (really, though, how automatic *is* automatic writing?), whatever – allied him paradoxically with the bourgeois world view, and perhaps condemned his planned revolution to failure even before it had started. His concession for the revolutionary was applicable only to assumed *meanings* of the world (pending their postrevolutionary change, of course), and it remained in practical terms for the declamators, from their "strange protectedness" in Zürich's cafés, to confound strategic coherence and in the process to revolutionise the *self*. One thing the revolutionised self was never likely to be, however, was unified – neither politically, socially, economically nor artistically – as Dada's declared need for independence and distrust toward unity bluntly made known. But unity, specifically political unity, was essential for the Bolshevik *émigrés* in the face of the divisive threat of the philosophical disputes among those "free thinkers" that made Lenin so uncomfortable. Still, in their disciplined unity, Althusser observes "a '*practice*' of philosophy, and the consciousness of the ruthless, primary fact that philosophy *divides*". Indeed, he continues, "[i]f science unites, and if it unites without dividing, [then] philosophy divides, and it can only unite by dividing" (1971: 26). The consistency of the contradiction is telling – equal to the infamous definition of Dada as that which escapes definition – and reaffirms *practice* as critically central to the revolutionary project here in question.

If, as Althusser argues, we are indebted to Lenin for contributing to the conditions that in the early twentieth century began to allow for the possibility of anticipating a non-philosophical theory of philosophy, it might be said that at least part of the task in hand for the present volume is to acknowledge an indebtedness to Dada in anticipation of a non-artistic theory of art in the west, giving centrality therefore to the idea of practice – *coherent* practice – that divides. Lenin's example demonstrates how "his political anti-spontaneism presupposes the deepest respect for the spontaneity of the masses, [and] his theoretical anti-spontaneism presupposes the greatest respect for *practice* in the process of knowledge" (Althusser 1971: 52). What prompted Lenin to laugh through the interminable headaches he suffered on Spiegelgasse was the realisation that there is no such thing as philosophical communrication or philosophical discussion; the breakdown in any sense of artistic communication was, similarly, the prompt to laughter for the Dadaists as they placed "straight-line thinking" under rigorous scrutiny. Little wonder that the quiet, studious Lenin complained of those headaches when his loud, riotous neighbours "were known, to laymen and experts alike, more by our roars of laughter than by the things we were really doing [...] we laughed and laughed" (Richter 1966: 64).

3. Spiegelgasse, Zürich

The trouble for Lenin, however, was that the laughter rising from the Cabaret Voltaire was *very* serious – the Dadaists took their laughter deadly seriously and, they believed, "laughter was the only guarantee of the seriousness with which ... [they] practised anti-art" (Richter 1966: 65). As communication (and along with communication all of its attendant assumptions, from the interiority of individual life to the given separation of private and public spheres) fell into dereliction, it seemed to drag down with it the concept of expression in its uncritical subjectivist form, repeatedly tested to destruction as it would be in the second half of the twentieth century through structuralist, poststructuralist, postmodern and post-postmodern thought. Yet today, expression remains a stubborn prop-osition that will not yield ground, and a kind of expressionism is argued even to have substituted for the now sorely crippled concept of communication as the nature of the causal link between the subject's expression and its content (or "objects") undergoes change, leading to expression's *forming* of its content. It would, indeed, be an error on our part to believe "that content determines expression by causal action, even if expression is accorded the power not only to 'reflect' content but to act upon it in an active way", as Deleuze and Guattari duly caution (1987: 89).

Reading expression, then, increasingly becomes a process of continuous revision when it disengages the link to its content as cause. Communication has traditionally demanded that causal link, which posits an objective existence for the content necessarily coming *before* the form of its expression. But what emerges theoretically in anticipation of practical instantiation is that the traditional one-way determination must be reconfigured as some kind of subject-object (or expression-content) dialectic. Representational models require that expression, in the most basic terms, reflect its content *as is*, but fail to take into account *what might be*; the latter is the role arguably given to ideology critique in its preoccupation with change. And change, in turn, can only occur if and when the expression-content symmetry is broken, and the correspondence between the two is reestablished asymmetrically, placing the emphasis on *how* the two interact and on *what* governs their dialectic, rather than on the polarities themselves. This asymmetry means that expression no longer functions un-problematically as what Huelsenbeck termed "propaganda for the soul" (1989: 244) from the moment its correspondence with the con-tent becomes imbalanced (and notwithstanding Deleuze and Guattari's eventual accounting for the return of correspondence despite every effort theoretically to preempt that return, when, beyond merely expressing the system, the subject is an expression *of* the system). The effective principle is that there is no shared form between expressions and contents, and expression itself defies ownership, eventually over-spilling and sometimes radically exceeding its own limits: "[l]anguage is not content to go from a first party to a second party, from one who has seen to one who has not, but necessarily goes from a second party to a third party, neither of whom has seen" (Deleuze and Guattari

1987: 76-77). So language, in indirect discourse, resists functioning as expression that is attributable to a particular speaker, and we consequently move away from the subjective mode now to read "expressive qualities ... [as] auto-objective" (1987: 317).

4. Spiegelgasse 14, Zürich

This move is critical if Dada is to break its cultural accommodation and containment. To be able to think in terms of expression as agency without an agent, or as a subjectless subjectivity, or indeed to advance the notion of the autonomy of expression, is to reposition the emphasis in all of this from the actions themselves and onto the *effect* that Dada actions had (and arguably continue to have) upon their public. The effect, as Benjamin still felt it some twenty years after the event, was akin to that of a missile, an instrument of ballistics, "[i]t jolted the viewer, taking on a tactile [*taktisch*] quality" (2003: 267). What "happened" left the spectator, or reader, dazed and confused, the shocked victim reeling at the sustained intensity of Tzara's manifesto writing, for instance:

> I write a manifesto and I want nothing, yet I say certain things, and in principle I am against manifestos, as I am also against principles [...] I am against action; for continuous contradiction, for affirmation too, I am neither for nor against and I do not explain because I hate common sense. [...] *Order = disorder; ego = non-ego; affirmation = negation:* [...] I proclaim bitter destruction with all the weapons of DADAIST DISGUST [...].
> (1989: 76-81)

The manifesto writer disembodies the critique of its history and content, yet deliberately retains the myth of cultural critique among those privileged concepts of the culture that he rejects. If the manifesto reader expects ABC, just as the writer conventionally wants it, Tzara's anticipation and logical countering of that same expectation is what makes his use of the genre in 1918 incendiary – it becomes something that "happens" to the reader (rather than its responding to and realising any expectation upon it as a socially instrumental text), and the reader eventually ends up with anything – *everything* – but ABC. The event, and its very physical effect, is theatrical within what Stephen C. Foster has more broadly argued to be Dada's "theatre of radicalism" – the event as that which "happens" critically understood, "adopted as a theoretical reference point, or *medium* of artistic action" (1994). The *form* of the event – here the specifically linguistic undermining of the function of the manifesto – marks Dada's turn into the "radical subjectivity" that Leah Dickerman has now most recently named, constituting to that extent "an assault on the public, communicative functions of language, [and] on its socially binding character as a collective system governed by laws" (2003: 11). The erasure of language, as Ball famously observed, now demanded its reinvention (1974: 56).

5. *"Manifeste Dada 1918"*, Dada *no. 3, Zürich, December 1918*

The radicalism of historical Dada remained always within the delineation of western culture; culture in its depravity and bankruptcy was indeed what Dada routed upon, yet it retained and maintained culture's privileging function of art and its reception, as well as what was (and remains) perpetually categorised under the forces of culture, in unashamed mercenary fashion, whenever such categorisation proved useful for Dada engagement. To this extent, Foster argues, "art was necessitated by the situation ... and became, ironically enough, the legitimate stage for a Dada critique that could not function *except* on a theatricalised basis". Hence the artistic and political legitimacy for Tzara of using forms that he is at least theoretically opposed to, and the acute increase in their destructive potential, when they are put into operation from those theatrical sites that Dada itself created, those very places that "put, or kept Dada squarely 'inside' culture, or better yet, inside 'culturing'". Foster has consistently returned to the case for such a transactional functioning of culture for the Dadaists, as opposed to their wholesale rejection of culture, emphasising in the event these cultural outsiders' acceptance of "a position on the inside, a position that was tenuous and momentary, an impermanent configuration from which one could continue the process of culture" and, to repeat, what is engaged (and engaging) is always process rather than product.

By that very continuation, however, conventional readings of Dada demand revision in order somehow to contain the resistance to control and governability that, nonetheless, remains Dada's distinctive characteristic; such revision allows the seemingly resigned subjectivity of individual players – Jacques Vaché, for example, who ranks art historically among the "proto-dadaists" – to be understood as a culturally critical and subversive move. Vaché deliberately assumed his role, playing his part as an army officer in the First World War, but brought to this role what he described as "a total indifference decorated with a quiet farce", dreaming as he did so of "some amusing deception that would result in lots of deaths, everything performed while wearing very light athletic-style form-fitting costumes, you know, with wonderful open-topped canvas shoes" (1995: 213, 231). It is Foster's point precisely that the (occasionally exaggerated) projection of roles is not done as a means of explaining something so much as a means of creating or configuring something; Vaché, among others, declared in non-negotiable terms that *the consequences don't matter*, inversely effecting the notion of agency without an agent, or, to return to the earlier proposition, expression conceptually disengaged from any causal subject. So the invocation of no less a thinker than Nietzsche:

> It is ... only owing to the seduction of language (and of the fundamental errors of reason that are petrified in it) which conceives and misconceives all effects as conditioned by something that causes effects, by a "subject" ... [that] the popular mind separates lightning from its flash and takes the latter for an *action*, for the operation of a subject called lightning ... as if there were a neutral substratum behind [it] ... But there is no such substratum; there is no "being" behind doing, effecting, becoming ... the deed is everything. (1967: 45)

Reference to a causal subject before or behind the deed (the event), neutral or otherwise, is aborted. Just as Nietzsche's critique rounds upon the concept of cause, Vaché's resistance is clearly to the privileging of consequence (or product). Crucially, the theoretical taxation of a position which maintains that the consequences of actions don't matter can critically be worked through, recognising that "consequences" and "effects" are distinctly not the same thing. What is argued here – the idea that revolution *without* a goal can still be revolution *with* effect – becomes a socially practical and immediate proposition when we make our historical reference to Dada's instigation of what now proves to be ongoing radicalised cultural practice.

*

My knowledge of the world, it has been said, has no value except when I act to transform it (Vaneigem 1967). The deliberate attempt at transformation carried by Dada was, and continues to be, a spontaneous act which necessarily locates itself in the immediate extension of lived experience, and in the event struggles with a theoretical pessimism that rounds on and relocates the contests that take place at the edges of discourse to the very heart of the mechanism of authoritarianism. The first named field of battle was, as we know, in Zürich at the Cabaret Voltaire, and it is to that field that the first two essays in this volume orient themselves. With a nod to Foster's "theatre of radicalism", 1916 was the year of the cabaret of radicalism and mercenary deployment of cabaret as form and forum; the opening essay, "The Mysterious Moment: early Dada performance as ritual" by Cornelius Partsch, makes central the fluidity of the performative Dada events of early 1916 and the necessary transience of the "complex synaesthetic processes" put into effect at the Cabaret Voltaire. The problematic of the avant-garde, however, is well rehearsed; Mann, for instance:

> [t]he avant-garde is one mechanism of a general organisation of social forces that operates in large part by means of the careful distribution of differences, imbalances, oppositions, and negations, and that regulates them through a variety of more or less effective discursive agencies in the so-called public sphere and along the margin itself. (1991: 113)

The question of the viability of avant-garde practice from its position of marginality, always seemingly compromised if not condemned by its cultural accommodation, must therefore be taken as a point of departure. In response to it, Partsch engages "ritual" first as an instructive, structural component in opening up the spaces which then come to constitute the field of radicalism, where text, noise, violence and transgression feed into defining what become Dada's dynamic and liminal sites of cultural contestation. Those sites and spaces emerge as fully consistent with Dada (anti)logic, situating themselves at once as the positive, tangible stages for Dada rituals, and as the negatively defined interstices, or *in-betweens*, where Dada occurs. So Partsch:

> [i]n the course of ritual, a state of liminality, a middle space in which to mediate and explore for pleasure those interactions that are potentially most disruptive, takes the actors and participants to the threshold of culture's inside/outside and lets them experience a dramatic and paradoxical confrontation with the marginalised or repressed other.

It is this simultaneity, the possibility of being at once inside and outside, at once *one* and *other*, which makes effective and sustains conflict, intimating progress therefore through the antithetic irreconcilability observed at the beginning of this introduction. For Partsch, the ritualised performance space, with its dual structured and structuring function, counts visibly among those spaces resident always inside culture or, better still as Foster tells us, inside "culturing".

6. Littérature *no. 17, Paris, December 1920*

The performative dimension of ritual makes central the body, that old chestnut (or kernel) of philosophy. Its linkage in later twentieth century thought to language, and its resulting consignment to representation or trace, is where "The Body of the Voice: corporeal poetics in Dada" by John Wall and Dafydd Jones, begins. Posing a new riddle of the sphincter as it moves towards a dialectical theory of body and language, this essay critically foregrounds the corporeal dimension in Dada writings and the presence of the body (or parts of the body, dismembered and re-membered) in dramatic, if not ritual, performance. Attention to certain positions verbalised and written, in particular by Tzara and Serner during the phase of Zürich Dada, here allows both the temporal dialectic of open-ended identity *and* a concrete and elemental dialectic of body and representation to be taken into account; the subsequent invocation of Merleau-Ponty's "incarnate logic" is drawn to the lower bodily stratum and, as Wall has commented, the arse in this essay is not just a concept introduced to subvert a few others and direct discourse towards a theory of language, but rather it has a performative element – this begins with Sloterdijk's dialectical arse and Tzara's vindication of gas. The interruptive force of the arse always pulls the hermeneutics and theorising of the essay back to a mode where disputation is stripped of abstraction and is forced to confront a convergence of the comical, serious and repressed, and poses a certain correspondence to the existentialist notion of a "concrete universal", which, nonetheless, delights in the embarrassed denial of its universal application.

Section two in this volume, "Dada and Language", restates the import of thought (as Dietzgen once stressed) and the responsibility that each one of us has to work towards our own definition of truth and order – truth and order, therefore, as something that we *make* – rather than simply clinging on for preservation like the needy man to "that immense framework and planking of concepts … [which is in fact] nothing but a scaffolding and toy for the most audacious feats of the liberated intellect" (Nietzsche 1994: 89-91); it is to such audacious feats that the two essays in this section most immediately direct us. The first, "The Language of 'Expatriation'" by T. J. Demos, makes central the Dada "exemplar" (as the closing essay in this volume will argue), Marcel Duchamp and his language games during his wartime expatriation. As always, the historical incongruity of Dada in New York poses Duchamp as slightly "avant-dada" in 1915, and in artistic negotiation of individual identity his own became increasingly distinct and visible, as Demos describes, in its movement "between institutional structures and readymade forms in a perpetual counterpoint of capture and escape". The author's contextualising of the artist in relation to his early language works, to early twentieth century popular philosophy, and to the rigour of late twentieth century critical thinking, constructs what is a consistently argued claim for Duchamp's strategic "expatriation" of language and his resistance to "the repetitions of everyday life", alongside what emerges as his deliberate expansion upon the principle of indeterminate existence.

The deliberate dissolution of language is the process that provides historical focus for Anna Schaffner in the following essay, "Assaulting the Order of Signs", where late twentieth-century Baudrillard is invoked in the necessary reading of Dada through recent and into current thought. The cultural war that was waged by Dada is positioned by Schaffner as a struggle that takes place at the semiotic level, with the prioritising of signifiers at the expense of signifieds. The attack on the order of the dominant code, of course, is a perilous venture, and the marked casualty is, consistently, communication (with obvious questions to be asked of any presumed results). Mann, again, speaks of such strategies as themselves indicating

> the necessarily unresolved and unresolvable character of the
> avant-garde's relationship to … its own various ideological for-
> mulations … [and] the force of this systemic process of product-
> ive indetermination which overrides the truth or falsity of any
> position. The death of the avant-garde is precisely this recognition
> that the difference … between opposition and accommodation, is
> a matter of indifference [...]. (1991: 64)

It is precisely this paradoxical "indifference" that Schaffner interro-
gates, questioning the by now familiar condemnation of the historical
avant-garde as amounting to little more … okay, as amounting to
nothing more, than a symbolic gesture of protest. The interrogation
functions implicitly to insist that the "avant-garde" is a far from spent
force, and that there is indeed something that it can "resolve", though
admittedly it appears in dire need of revision and radical rethinking if
it is to assert itself as a continuing and viable cultural category. If we
were to remind ourselves of how Nietzsche once posed indifference to
be thought of as a power, such rethinking might well (as it does here)
exercise Baudrillard's view that *the* revolutionary strategy of today (or
at least 1993, the time of Baudrillard writing) consists of the attack on
the code itself and, as Schaffner observes, "[t]he code has to be
outwitted on its own territory and beaten with its own weapons, its
own logic must be turned against itself, its own non-referentiality
exceeded", and in this instance tested to self-destruction.

Code, therefore, has limited effect when turned on another,
opposing code; rather, maximum potential resides in turning code on
itself, when it is made to mimic itself in appropriating external
appearances as it radically reconstitutes from the inside. As a revised
way of understanding reality, we might on this occasion provocatively
(and only provocatively, I stress) suggest a reformulated dialectic for
the twenty-first century in the progression from thesis and antithesis to
prosthesis. Nice. A motley crew they may be, but Dietzgen, Marx,
Engels and Tzara would no doubt get it, and it is to the critical and
theoretical possibilities of prostheses that Martin Ignatius Gaughan
alerts us in his essay, "The Prosthetic Body in Early Modernism:
Dada's anti-humanist humanism", isolating the so-called double-logic
that again engages the notion of (expression as) agency without an
agent – the prosthetic limb which bears witness to "agency removed
from the body but simultaneously the body's functioning apparently
extended through technology". The extension is always an imaginary
one, yet in its sober rendering visually the body with its extensions is

made real – emphatically, explicitly and painfully so as a mechanical concept – though, as Gaughan notes, Sloterdijk reminds us that "the human body in the society of labour had already been an artificial limb even before one had to replace damaged parts with functioning parts" (1988: 447-48). It is Gaughan's proposition in this essay that, ultimately, these new parts, even in grotesque and exaggerated imitation of the old, damaged ones, deliberately enter into a cultural visibility in order critically to participate in denunciation of the anti-humanism of the capitalist system.

For such denunciation to be effective conventionally anticipates the notion of avant-garde oppositionality – that anything-but-unproblematic notion, which Bürger makes foundational for his *Theory of the Avant-Garde*. Bürger is well aware of the contradictory nature of the opposition here in question, which uses its apparent withdrawal from the cultural order in fact to conceal its affirmation of it, and of how the whole debate initiates the expanding complexity of a sense of the avant-garde that embraces rather than rejects what it opposes. The contradiction culminates, for Bürger, in the "failures" of the twentieth century neo-avant-garde, which, through its own cultural logic, would apparently preclude the possibility of transgression – a position further complicated by the fact that what Bürger credits as the *successes* of the historical avant-garde aren't always easily distinguishable from what he cites as the *failures* of the neo-avant-garde. Indeed, in working towards righting Bürger's concept of the dialectic, Hal Foster has hypothesised that rather than cancel the project of the historical avant-garde, the neo-avant-garde might well demonstrate a full comprehension (but critically not completion) of that project for the first time (1994: 16). If we resist the invocation of transgression as the defining characteristic of Dada, and therefore resist the historical placement that Bürger gives it, it is apposite to revisit specific instances that appear to do what we were led to believe Dada never did – not only to embrace tradition, but to continue it – and question whether those instances develop more from comprehension than misapprehension of the avant-garde project. The essay by Curt Germundson, "Montage and Totality: Kurt Schwitters's relationship to 'tradition' and 'avant-garde'", does precisely this, demonstrating the lack of correspondence between Schwitters and the idea of the historical avant-garde. In fact, Schwitters excludes himself from Bürger's category because of his adherence to concepts that are associated with the "organic" (traditional representational) work of art, but Germundson relates a certain shortfall in Bürger who "does not allow for an avant-garde art that uses montage to create a different kind of totality, one that is interactive and ever-changing". The case is well made that montage, in Schwitters's hands, functions by no means exclusively to break through the appearance of totality, but, on the contrary, continues an artistic tradition of totality and organic whole-ness that poses the problematic, intrinsic, uncomfortable yet undeni-able relationship between the avant-garde and tradition.

As a concept, "organic wholeness" undergoes as radical an overhaul as we might possibly imagine for it at this stage, in Stephen C. Foster's essay "The Mortality of Roles: Johannes Baader and spirit-ual materialism". The essay (published here for the first time in Eng-lish) is important on several counts as it develops a study of Berlin Oberdada Johannes Baader that maintains the distinction of separate, conflicting "roles" as necessary in the constitution of the person – the revolutionary cultural agent. Situating the principle in the specific in-stance, Foster exercises an approach that becomes directly applicable to the one cultural formation of the early twentieth century that is more riddled with contradiction and hostile irreconcilability than any other, outlining as he does a methodological consistency that very quickly exposes the woeful inadequacy of any standard submission to the dialectic and all subsequent attempts to locate a synthesising of "roles" in the individual. This methodology arguably underscores the thinking feeding into *Dada Culture* more generally, it should be said, where a salvaging and reassembling of positions in addressing Dada means, in Foster's words, that those same positions "sit together not as a synthesis of truths of culture but as a constitution of the truth of cul-ture". What manifests itself as "truth" is precisely the move towards a disclosure of culture in all of its aspects – overtly and covertly so – and the inclusion of Foster's essay in this volume is instructive in view of the close proximity of the principle of Architekt Baader to that of Directeur Cravan, the object of the essay that immediately follows.

The essay, "To Be or Not To Be ... Arthur Cravan", by Dafydd Jones, engages the instance of the itinerant proto-dada poet and boxer – *Hobo sapiens*, to give him his Latin appellation – whose life and "self-immolation" in 1918 secured him exemplary if not mythical status in avant-garde thought during the twentieth century, and now into the twenty-first, fuelling his most recent public appearance as the square-jawed *Mystery Man of the Twentieth Century.* (Among the supporting cast featured on the cover of this illustrated adventure, incidentally, is Trotsky, whose brief encounter with Cravan aboard the steamer *Montserrat* at the start of 1917 provides an intriguing parallel to the convergence of Lenin and the Cabaret Voltaire a year previously, and the tantalising collision of revolutionary politics, philosophy and art.) The pairing of the objects of Foster's and Jones's essays is indeed occasionally made in Dada studies – David Hopkins has stated how Baader "cultivated his megalomaniac streak to a sublimely parodic pitch, vying with Cravan in terms of sheer bravado" (Hopkins 2004: 41) – but the strategic postures of the two protagonists are broken down in these two essays in an attempt increasingly to theorise action beyond ultimately indeterminate conclusion in bravado. Jones continues here an engagement with Cravan that has already foregrounded the "highly problematised social intelligibility" of refusal (Gaughan 2003: 9), taking the poet and boxer's first published text as a starting point to read the manifesto of subject evasion that was never written, and to expand upon the constitution of new "truths" through difference and in surface appearances.

7. Cravan: Mystery Man of the Twentieth Century, *Milwaukie, 2005*

The final section of essays, titled "Philosophy, Theory and the Avant-Garde", grounds the avant-garde project as it makes itself known in Dada in a thoroughgoing and rigorous address of both the general and the particular. Joel Freeman's essay "Ernst Bloch and Hugo Ball: toward an ontology of the avant-garde" presents the case that the "Dadaist disgust" of notoriety functions not only with a particular coherence that some Dadaists would have vehemently denied, but that, moreover, the Zürich formation (particularly in the mode of Ball) functions regularly according to a philosophical system – one that is systematically open and fluid, yes, but one that is systematic nonetheless. The impulse (which I submit is consistent throughout this volume) is that "[t]o think of Dada as a system, despite itself, means simultaneously to rethink the notion of system itself". In outlining the ontological thought of Ernst Bloch (Ball's Zürich contemporary), Freeman establishes a parallel reading of the two men's ideas and written commentaries in the years 1916–19, rounding on the aesthetic as the most viable site for social rupture and for the overcoming of "the human as an alienated and subjugated being". As we remind ourselves of the way in which Dietzgen once identified the dialectic only to have to critically address the same before being able to move beyond it, we again find its reworking in Bloch's thought, freeing the dialectic from what *appears* to be the crippling effect of binary polarity, and characterising it as an "organic dialectic of self-emergence, where the subject and the object are radically inscribed in one another from the very start … [replacing] the thesis/antithesis arrangement". Such radical inscription comes about through Bloch's ontology of not-yet-being, as Freeman argues, the critical dimension of a philosophical system that is avant-garde both in content and form, though adequately to theorise content and form as avant-garde, or as Dada – or *Dada as avant-garde* – now insists that we deliberately move beyond Dada and its histories.

This last observation corresponds to David Cunningham's cautionary note in his essay, "Making an Example of Duchamp: history, theory and the question of the avant-garde", which argues for the ongoing validity of the concept of the avant-garde in relation to contemporary artistic, cultural and political concerns. The last in this volume, this essay looks forward to renewed potentiality in the way that we rethink the avant-garde, not in terms of its resistance to repetition, but more constructively in terms of its *repetition of the non-*

identical. Bloch echoes distinctly, as Cunningham asserts that "for there to be a perceivable general logic of 'avant-garde-ness', repetition of some sort, and thus critical account of the general relation between non-identical repetitions, must be possible". Duchamp reassumes centrality and *exemplarity* here, instancing repetition in the absence of any "determinate" commonality and in the presence of "the discomforting experience of uncertainty in the face of a question – 'Can one make works which are not works of "art"?' – which does not determine in advance an immediately decidable answer". The force of Cunningham's argument is to locate a "repressed futural potential" securely in the present, which in turn is conceptually to release the avant-gardist from the seduction of synthetic resolution in "the final 'unity' of art and anti-art – the identity of identity and non-identity". Reminded of Cunningham's caution, the present recovery of Dada histories, worked through Dietzgen, Lenin, Tzara, Serner et al., attests to the critical function of "something *other*, a non-identity which, in its open multiplicity, exceeds the terms of oppositionality" in radically rethought and revised revolution.

   The projection forward consolidates the present and most recent Dada studies. So, the parting shot of *Dada Culture* is the critical bibliography meticulously prepared by Timothy Shipe in documentation of the past decade of Dada scholarship, marking as it does the juncture at which this volume now appears. Dada was, and if we are to argue its continuity remains, "obsessively culture-centred" (Foster 1996: xiv), critically *practising* culture beyond its mere articulation, and making "serious and significant claims on our attention because, more than any other twentieth-century movement, it takes us most seriously" (1996: xiii). The attention returns here to engage, and in the process to dispute, the condemnation that the Dada shift may actually have been the falsest of all false paths – doomed in its consignment to "an honourable place in the avant-garde's history of unrealised humanistic visions" (1996: 1) – as demarcation continues not only of Dada's embeddedness in western culture, but precisely of *the location of Dada culture*. In the event, Shipe's bibliography covers the decade of Foster's exhaustive series on Dada, for instance, which, at its outset, stated the motive in working towards a "formulation of more rewarding ways by which to understand the Dada works in specific, and their critical activities in general" (1996: 1). The motive continues through the expanding analytical rigour which is now central to Dada studies, and through the theoretical testing that will pose the falsest of all false paths as, potentially, Dada bluff and counter-bluff. It is hoped this volume will assert the continuity.

Dafydd Jones
University of Wales

Note

[1] The principal philosophical contribution made by Joseph Diezgen (1828–1888) to marxism was the thorough exposition of epistemology. His explanation of consciousness was as an ideal product of matter, named by him the "universum" and which he considered to be eternally existing and moving. He further postulated natural and social being as the content of consciousness.

References

Althusser, Louis
    1971   *Lenin and Philosophy and Other Essays*. New York: Monthly Review Press.

Ball, Hugo
    1974   *Flight out of Time: A Dada Diary* (ed. John Elderfield, tr. Ann Raimes). New York: Viking Press.

Benjamin, Walter
    2003   "The Work of Art in the Age of Its Technical Reproducibility" (Third Version). In Howard Eiland and Michael W. Jennings (eds) and Edmund Jephcott (tr.) *Walter Benjamin: Selected Writings, vol. 4, 1938–1940*. Cambridge: Belknap Press.

Deleuze, Gilles and Guattari, Félix
    1987   *A Thousand Plateaus* (tr. Brian Massumi). Minneapolis: University of Minnesota Press.

Dickerman, Leah (ed.)
    2003   *October*, vol. 105, Summer. Cambridge: MIT Press

Dietzgen, Joseph
    1906   *The Popular Outcome of Philosophy*. Chicago: Kerr.

    1984   *The Nature of Human Brain Work*. Vancouver: Red Lion Press.

Engels, Frederick
    1940   *Dialectics of Nature*. London: Lawrence and Wishart.

Foster, Hal
    1994   "What's Neo About the Neo-Avant-Garde?". In *October*, vol. 70, Fall. Cambridge: MIT Press.

Foster, Stephen C.
    1994   "Zürich Dada: The Arts, Critique, and the Theatre of Radicalism". Unpublished keynote address to the Zürich Dada Conference, Manchester Metropolitan University, November 1994.

Foster, Stephen C. (ed.)
    1996   *Dada. The Coordinates of Cultural Politics*. Crisis and the Arts: The History of Dada vol. 1. New York: G. K. Hall.

Gaughan, Martin I. (ed.)
> 2003   *Dada New York: New World For Old.* Crisis and the Arts: The
>   History of Dada vol. 8. New York: G. K. Hall.

Greenberg, Allan C.
> 1985   "The Dadaists and the Cabaret as Form and Forum". In Stephen
>   C. Foster (ed.) *Dada/Dimensions.* Ann Arbor: UMI Research
>   Press.

Hopkins, David
> 2004   *Dada and Surrealism: A Very Short Introduction.* Oxford: OUP.

Huelsenbeck, Richard
> 1989   "Collective Dada Manifesto" (1920). In Robert Motherwell (ed.)
>   and Ralph Manheim (tr.) *The Dada Painters and Poets: An
>   Anthology.* Cambridge: Belknap Press.

Imrie, Malcolm
> 1987   "Say it with Cobblestones". Supplement to the *New Statesman*,
>   18/25 December.

Lenin, Vladimir Ilyich
> 1908   Letter to Gorky, 7 February 1908. In *Collected Works*, vol. 34.
>   Moscow: Progress.

> 1962   "Materialism and Empirio-criticism". In *Collected Works*, vol. 14.
>   Moscow: Progress.

> 1967   "Party Organisation and Party Literature" (1905). In *Lenin on
>   Literature and Art.* Moscow: Progress.

Mann, Paul
> 1991   *The Theory-Death of the Avant-Garde.* Bloomington: Indiana
>   University Press.

Nietzsche, Friedrich
> 1967   *On the Genealogy of Morals.* New York: Vintage.

> 1994   "On Truth and Lie in an Extra-Moral Sense" in Daniel Breazeale
>   (ed.), *Philosophy and Truth: Selections from Nietzsche's
>   Notebooks of the Early 1870s*, New Jersey: Humanities Press.

Richter, Hans
> 1966   *Dada: Art and Antiart.* London: Thames and Hudson.

Sloterdijk, Peter
> 1988   *Critique of Cynical Reason* (tr. Michael Eldred). London: Verso.

Solzhenitsyn, Alexander
> 1976   *Lenin in Zürich*. New York: Farrar, Straus & Giroux.

Tzara, Tristan
> 1989   "Dada Manifesto 1918". In Robert Motherwell (ed.) and Ralph Manheim (tr.) *The Dada Painters and Poets: An Anthology*. Cambridge: Belknap Press.

Vaché, Jacques
> 1995   "War Letters". In *Four Dada Suicides*. London: Atlas Press.

Vaneigem, Raoul
> 1967   *The Revolution of Everyday Life*. The Situationist International Text Library, http://library.nothingness.org/articles/SI/en/pub_contents/5

Weiss, Peter
> 1978   *Die Ästhetik des Widerstands*, vol. 2. Frankfurt am Main: Suhrkamp. Translation taken from Brigitte Pichon, 1996, "Revisiting Spie(ge)lgasse: Mirror(s) and Prism(s), Cultural and Political Stagings of Emigration and Liminality". In Stephen C. Foster, Brigitte Pichon and Karl Riha (eds), 1996, *Dada Zürich: A Clown's Game from Nothing*. Crisis and the Arts: The History of Dada vol. 2. New York: G. K. Hall.

I. Manifestos and Evenings at the Cabaret Voltaire

The Mysterious Moment:
early Dada performance as ritual

Cornelius Partsch

Abstract: With a focus on the *soirées* that took place at the Cabaret Voltaire between February and April 1916, this essay investigates the Dadaists' early performances as flawed and ferocious events illuminating, paradoxically, the possibility of a viable avant-garde practice. In engaging theories of performance and of ritual, the ritualistic patterning of the Dadaists' "services" is outlined, comprising the use of text, noise, violence, and transgression. The performances discussed here also constitute a series of conspicuously artificial, multilayered enactments of socio-cultural contestation at a moment of acute social crisis. Conscious of the fragility of their attempts to find a place for modern art at the edges of discourse and "life", the Dada performers laid claim to a moment of genuine, communal experience.

"You cannot comprehend Dada, you have to experience it. Dada is immediate and self-evident. A person is a Dadaist simply by living. Dada is the neutral point between content and form, female and male, matter and mind, because it is the apex of the magic triangle above the linear polarity of human objects and notions." – Richard Huelsenbeck

Marcel Janco's painting *Cabaret Voltaire* (1916), now extant only in photographic reproductions, provides one of the few visual traces of the unsettling and enigmatic performances of incipient Dada. It shows an animated, overcrowded and "democratic" performance space marked by minimal separation between artists and audience. The artists, Hugo Ball at the piano, Tristan Tzara wringing his hands, Emmy Hennings dancing with Friedrich Glauser, and Hans Arp, Richard

Huelsenbeck, and Marcel Janco reciting, are all positioned on a slightly raised platform. Save for a Janco mask at the back wall, the stage is
bare, constituting a non-localised performance setting. In the space
before the platform, which occupies exactly half of the painting's
frame, members of the audience can be seen displaying a variety of
reactions, ranging from disinterest to laughter and indignation. Dada's
provocative vibrancy is formally rendered through a highly kinetic
interaction of forms and colours. The shapes of objects and human
bodies appear to intersect and merge into each other, suggesting both a
dynamic, abstracted rhythmicality and a restructuring of antagonistic
entities.[1] The painting offers a hint of the complex synaesthetic
processes that took place at the Cabaret Voltaire from February to
April 1916, when Dada's radical modernist anti, its attempts to lay
bare what constitutes culture, and its brazen remapping of that culture
from the site of avant-gardist marginality were enacted primarily in
flawed, fleeting and continually modulated performative events. In the
early *soirées*, one encounters the wavering and emergent work in progress of a loosely delineated artistic community, before it had
acquired discursive status and before the term "dada" had been
coined. They fascinated with a degree of spontaneity, incoherence,
and aggression rarely duplicated beyond the summer of 1916. It was at
the point when the audience came to expect and to merely consume
the Dadaists' "services" that the Cabaret Voltaire faced its greatest
crisis, one from which it would not recover. By June, the group pro-
ceeded to relegate performance to a lesser status and began to fix its
art as objects and texts in exhibits and journals, thus entering a
different discursive economy of "art" and exchange. This programmatic shift resulted in Dada's geographical relocation to more
"controlled" venues, namely the grand guild houses on the west bank
of the river Limmat, where the composition of its audience changed
fundamentally. In the late summer of 1916, Tzara began to take
control of the group's daily operations and of its publications, after
Ball had retreated to the Ticino with Hennings to lead a religious life,
having made "a thinly disguised break" with his friends (Ball 1974:
73).
        Since no audio recordings and few photographs of the cabaret
exist, scholars have had to rely on scant source material in their efforts
to reconstruct the earliest Dada performances. Moreover, the writing
on this phase of Dada Zürich has proven resistant, constituting a

polyvalent web of texts that yields neither a definable Dada program nor a shared epistemology. The Dadaists recorded for posterity a mercurial spread of heterogeneous, unabashedly partisan and, in many cases, temporally distant accounts of their experiences in which alliances are shifted, positions reversed and charges levelled and recanted with dizzying frequency. While a few of these texts disparage the Dada Zürich project altogether as juvenile aberration and inconsequential nihilism, others reveal aesthetic and political repositionings that one might, in retrospect, consider essential to the Dadaists' cynical practice of ideological posturing and manifest discursive manipulation. Tzara's attempt in *Chronique Zurichoise 1915–1919* (1920) to situate Dada within an artistic avant-garde tradition is decisively rejected by Huelsenbeck in *En Avant Dada: Eine Geschichte des Dadaismus* (1920) where he seeks to free Dada from institutional and commercial suffocation – Tzara as a "racketeer" – and to anchor it in the sphere of radical politics.[2] While Kurt Schwitters, who was not on friendly terms with Huelsenbeck and the Berlin Dadaists, describes Tzara as the embodiment of aesthetic Dada in his memoir and manifesto *Merz* (1920), Ball derides Tzara as an overly ambitious finagler. To complicate matters further, the most-quoted text about early Dada, Ball's diary *Die Flucht aus der Zeit* (1927), was published after its author had undergone a substantial reorganisation of his belief system and with significant editorial changes implemented by Hennings. Resulting from this problematic situation concerning the documents and all their untidy contradictions, much of the scholarship has been marked by a tendency to circumnavigate Dada as a performative mode of expression in favour of more text- or object-oriented lines of inquiry.[3]

In two recent volumes edited by Stephen C. Foster, as part of the *Crisis and the Arts* series, important steps have been taken to broaden the scope of scholarship on Dada Zürich and to examine more specifically its places, practices, sounds, and language(s). Foster suggests that "there may be more to learn from the processes of their [the Dadaists'] coping than from the *products* of their coping". As responses to a deep social crisis and to the First World War, the Dada actions might be viewed more productively "as records of cultural transaction than as aesthetic objects", as negotiations of reality and its contingencies rather than as systematic attempts at ordering that reality (1996: 2). Informed by poststructuralist methodology, these read ings emphasise Dada's disruptiveness in performance and the radical separation of signifier and signified in its language as instances of a postmodernist debunking of the foundational discourses of modernity. By focusing on the elliptical, unfinished and fluid components of performance as clues to the vagaries of human action, the critique of performance inscribes spaces of significant critical import in the interstices of the open performative situation, exposing "the fissures, ruptures, and revisions that have settled into continuous reenactment" (Diamond 1996: 2), and, more generally, seeks to relate the material productions of culture, its institutional continuities, and its physical practices to signifying and symbolic systems.[4] Within such a discursive paradigm, performance can be read as the framed interplay of positioned utterances and situated in the historical moment configuring the specific interventions of the dominant power and its institutions.

Borrowing from cultural anthropology, recent scholarship has, furthermore, increasingly employed the category of "ritual" to complement the study of the performative genres and to formulate theories of cultural performances. In ritual studies, "performance" denotes the management of crisis on a symbolic plane through collective and dynamic action. As orchestrations of media in all available sensory codes, such performances are characterised by the simultaneous deployment of synchronic and diachronic rhythms and take place in privileged spaces and times, separate from the mundane domains of work, food, and sleep. In the course of ritual, a state of liminality, a middle space in which to mediate and explore for pleasure those interactions that are potentially most disruptive, takes the actors and participants to the threshold of culture's inside/outside and lets them experience a dramatic and paradoxical confrontation with the marginalised or repressed other. If, as Victor Turner has stated, social drama "contains the germs of aesthetic modes", then performance itself becomes a reflexive metacommentary on the lived, social roles of its participants and on the relations, codes, symbols, and ethics of a particular culture. In this context, the term "reflexivity" refers to the ability to think about one's own actions and the actions of others and is, itself, "highly contrived, artificial, of culture not nature, a deliberate work of art" (1984: 25). Such a reflexive performative domain requires a certain measure of violence to be inflicted on commonly held perceptions of society and of the self by splitting it into selves that gaze and act upon each "other" (Turner 1988: 24-25). Ritual, then, constitutes a type of critical juncture wherein opposing forces converge and that serves as "a paradigmatic means of socio-cultural integration, appropriation, or transformation" (Bell 1993: 16). The ritualised performance space, describable both as a structured and as a structuring environment, becomes the dynamic and liminal site of cultural contestation where the audience retains the freedom to make and transform meaning and where, potentially, the assumptions and embodiments of a culture can be undermined and resisted.

Mapping the ritualistic patterning of the Dada performance may indeed enable us to situate and assess more cogently the cultural transactions and social reconfigurations staged at the Cabaret Voltaire. In 1916, the soon-to-be Dadaists found themselves in a state of painful disillusionment and at a point of acute cultural crisis as the full destructive potential of modern warfare and the bankruptcy of the enlightenment project had become evident. They responded to an environment disembodied of social orientation and of cultural integrity with a ferocious attack on the social and symbolic structures of the hegemonic cultural forces. Most pressingly, they disavowed any form of national allegiance and aimed to expose and dismantle as cruel fictions discursive formations such as the "natural", "eternal", and "heroic", which were circulating with ever greater impetus among the belligerent nations. As a despairing renunciation of the communicability of language, Dada's metadiscourse on art and culture resisted representation and sought to escape recuperation by the compromised and affirmative circuits of textuality to the point of paradox. Its prime motivating force and, simultaneously, its most paradoxical goal was the disruption of meaning and the creation of a seductive practice. Dada refused to be interpreted in a discourse of artistic tradition, heritage, or teleology by appropriating and assembling disparate "life" materials and shards of an amputated past into a liminal frame and into explosive and contradictory acts of violent de-composition and visionary re-composition. The following reading of the early Dada *soirées* proceeds from a notion of cultural performance that hinges upon the materiality and historical density of the event within a ritualised frame encompassing residual forms, contemporary practices, and emergent structures. In contrast to common assumptions about Dada performance art as primarily a negating de-ritualisation of bourgeois art and about its purportedly apolitical, playful disregard for the

practical consequences of performance, I hope to outline more complex performative strategies than mere provocation and more differentiated receptive negotiations than mere shock. An important methodological caveat for such a critical undertaking results from the level
of linguistic overdetermination that occurs in ritualised performance,
in its polysemous "gymnastics" and its bodily articulations. Writing
about performance both simplifies and conceals the relations enacted
in it, as Pierre Bourdieu has cautioned in *Outline of a Theory of Practice*:

> By bringing to the level of discourse – as one must, if one wants
> to study it scientifically – a practice which owes a number of
> properties to the fact that it falls short of discourse (which does
> not mean that it is short on logic) one subjects it to nothing less
> than a change in ontological status the more serious in its theor-
> etical consequences because it has every chance of passing
> unnoticed. (1977: 120)

*

Some of the European artists who assembled in Zürich in 1916 came
to be near the artistic pulse of the times, some had been forced to
emigrate to neutral Switzerland for opposing German militarism,
while still others had experienced the horrors of trench warfare first-
hand and decided to wait out the war in Zürich, a city Hans Richter
characterises ambivalently as the "peaceful dead-centre of the war"
(1966: 12). Ball corroborates this sense of fragility and impending
doom, likening Switzerland to a "birdcage, surrounded by roaring
lions" (1974: 34). The *emigré*, by definition, assumes a highly precarious, dialogical and reflexive role, oscillating between involvement
and detachment, between interior and periphery. Brigitte Pichon has
argued that emigration can be regarded as a liminal state, as it forces a
group to address the unfamiliar and transitional circumstances of its
chosen or imposed marginality and that it may therefore crystallise
unknown possibilities to a point of clarity: "[E]migration is [...] seen
as a state of tension between realised and yet unrealised possibilities
inherent in its potential for response to its own dynamics" (1996: 5).
Significantly, Dada's first venue, the Holländische Meierei at Spiegelgasse 1, occupied a space within Zürich's urban topography that reflected its status on the margins of bourgeois respectability. The

Niederdorf quarter, a part of the city where, in angular and narrow alleyways and dark backrooms, variety shows, cabarets, and so-called "amusement bars" offered various spectacles and popular entertainments, was the kind of place municipal administrators and social hygienists considered a hotbed of alcoholism, crime, illicit sexuality, and political anarchy. For the newly arrived group of unknown, starving and enterprising artists, launching the Cabaret Voltaire represented a tremendous economic risk. Since the Dadaists aimed to provide a different kind of entertainment than their Niederdorf neighbours, they had to strike a delicate balance between challenging and attracting a paying audience. The initial press notice announcing the opening of the cabaret bears out this precarious strategy:

> Cabaret Voltaire. Under this name a group of young artists and writers has been formed whose aim is to create a center for artistic entertainment. The idea of the cabaret will be that guest artists will come and give musical performances and readings at the daily meetings. The young artists of Zürich, whatever their orientation, are invited to come along with suggestions and contributions of all kinds. (Ball 1974: 50)

The text carefully avoids setting any programmatic limitations and maps a space of creative exchange, an open forum for audience participation. Its insistence on youth and innovation implies a desired audience and hints at the kind of "artistic entertainment" one might expect to find at the Holländische Meierei. The cast at the cabaret consisted of a number of boisterous youngsters: in February 1916, Ball was 30, Huelsenbeck 23, Janco 20, and Tzara 19. In the beginning, the cabaret, which held about fifty, was usually sold out. Its audience was mostly male and comprised artists, drunken students, spies, deserters, transients, and a few errant burghers. Evoking a typically bohemian sentiment, the Dadaists' accounts construct a noisy, drunken, and homosocial space too orgiastic for female spectatorship: "There were almost no women in the cabaret, it was too wild, too smoky, too way out" (Huelsenbeck 1989: 10). Structured by sensual experience, chance and spontaneous interaction, and economic and creative pressure, the environment of the Cabaret Voltaire shapes and reflects back on the performances themselves. In an investigation of the different Dada venues, Debbie Lewer finds that "at no other

Dada event is the place so closely involved in the definition of the event itself" (1996: 47ff.).

In the dingy Cabaret Voltaire, the act of going out for an evening's entertainment, in itself a type of social performance marked by certain expectations and rules of conduct, clashes with a structuring environment that forcefully recasts the coordinates of the socially given and therefore affords the opportunity for negotiated integration or transformation on a number of levels. The Dadaists concerned themselves intensely with the dynamic of the space and its reciprocal effects, both detrimental and generative, on performance and audience, and happily exploited the resulting tensions. In these early days, the intensity of the cabaret's offerings derived above all from the artists' constant struggle to satisfy the audience through provocative stimulation. Ball points enthusiastically at a kind of day-to-day vanguardism that resembles the demanding work of popular entertainers: "Our attempt to entertain the audience with artistic things forces us in an exciting and instructive way to be incessantly lively, new, and naïve. It is a race with the expectations of the audience" (1974: 83).[5] As a result, the Dadaists freely improvised on the written texts and recited them in a liturgically earnest yet offbeat manner. By and large unskilled both as actors and as musicians, the Dada performers irked and challenged their audience with self-conscious dilettantism and through the ambiguous appropriation and spirited reinvention of movements, gestures, and sounds. Huelsenbeck recalls that he, along with Janco and Tzara, deceptively "bowed like a yodelling band about to celebrate lakes and forests", before a decidedly anti-pastoral and raucous recitation of the simultaneous poem "The admiral is searching for a house to rent" (1974: 44). Huelsenbeck riled the patrons with his "college-boy insolence", not as a gesture of solidarity but rather to heap scorn on the students, "who in Switzerland as elsewhere are the stupidest and most reactionary rabble" (1989: 24). By all accounts, this seemingly gratuitous and spontaneous ferociousness roused the baffled audiences into "frenzied involvement with what was going on", as Richter remarks (1966: 19), and caused tumultuous confrontations on and off the stage. Ball's diary entry of March 15 conveys the physical and mental strain the cabaret inflicted upon its performers: "The cabaret needs a rest. With all the tension the daily performances are not just exhausting, they are crippling" (1974: 57).

Before arriving in Zürich, the original members of the Cabaret Voltaire had already absorbed a variety of avant-garde techniques and programmes and were now eager to debate, modulate and put them into practice The anarchical discourse of Italian Futurism in particular had been reverberating loudly in artistic circles throughout Europe.[6] In their scandalous manifestos, the Futurists urged a *tabula rasa* in the arts, promising to erase all commonly held notions of "beauty" and to destroy the institutional temples of bourgeois art. Concerning both music and language, the futurists called for the assimilation of the material into the wider acoustical environment. In "The Art of Noises" (1913), Luigi Russolo proposes a radically materialist conception of music and its production and reception, postulating the bruitistic "noise-sound" as the definitive destroyer of all traditional harmonic, melodic and rhythmic strictures and forms. The spectrum of available tones would be infinitely expanded along an enharmonic continuum and replace the "pure" tonal unit with dynamic clusters of noises. Noise is to lead music back to its most material essence and to its utmost authenticity. Moreover, noise serves as the acoustic signifier of the cacophonous city and of the din of machinery and, as such, represents a more realistic sounding of modernity than the consonant and, in Futurist terms, "sentimental" tone of western tonality. Russolo envisages a transformation of listening affected by the objectively brutal dissonance of noise. In contrast to the "idiotic" religious rapture of the traditional act of listening, the brutalised and thus rejuvenated ear of the future would be endowed with "multiplied sensibilities". Russolo calls for the overthrow of the compositional traditions of European art music, manifest in the musical logocentrism of the score, and for their replacement by the Futurist orchestra's imaginative and "fantastic juxtaposition" of noises (1973: 85-87). According to F. T. Marinetti, Futurism's practice of bruitism finds its most pointed synaesthetic expression, its highest level of gestural brutality, and its greatest transformative potential in the variety theatre, a setting for which he confesses his highest admiration in one of the core essays of the movement. Speed, spontaneity, improvisation, and the simul-taneous deployment of various media can give shape to an art of electrifying action and astonishing effect, generating "the Futurist marvellous" (1973: 126). Marinetti suggests a number of ways to en-liven the experience of the avant-garde's performance and to promote audience "collaboration", among them spreading glue on the seats and selling a single seat to several patrons.

Back in Germany, Huelsenbeck grew ever more antagonistic toward the hypocrisy of Germany's militarist culture, which he held responsible for the senseless butchery in the trenches, and began searching for new, more provocative modes of artistic expression. His disenchantment translated increasingly into a vehement critique of Expressionism, Germany's then prevalent avant-garde movement, and its perceived espousal of a mythical, ecstatic inwardness. Huelsenbeck nevertheless organised an Expressionist *soirée* in commemoration of fallen literati at the Harmoniumsaal in Berlin in 1915, advertising himself and his co-organisers as "negationists". At this occasion, he presented some "Negro poems" that seem to have elicited a mocking chorus of "Umba! Umba!" cries from the audience as he departed from the stage. In wartime Berlin, his clown-like, primitivist self-fashioning constituted a decidedly political gesture. When he arrived in Zürich in February of 1916, he displayed this predilection for "primitive" noise with unwavering audacity, as Ball observes: "Huelsenbeck has arrived. He pleads for stronger rhythm (Negro rhythm). He would prefer to drum literature into the ground" (1974: 51). Stereotypical images of minstrel clowns and overtones of *Kulturpessimismus* echo in Huelsenbeck's blueprint for a regenerative transformation of socio-cultural consciousness, which he locates in the transition from music to *bruit*: "In modern Europe, the same initiative which in America made ragtime a national music, led to the convulsion of bruitism" (1989: 26). The odd analogy to American ragtime subsumes the musical genre's structure to the avant-garde's desire for a fusion of the popular and the high, taken to hold the promise of reinvigorating an encrusted and petrified culture.[7] Polydirectional, syncopated rhythms are taken to be reflective of modern fragmentation and alienation and inscribed as metaphors for (cross)cultural shifts and exchanges. Huelsenbeck's first reading at the Cabaret Voltaire on 9 March combined the apocalyptic vision of Expressionism with a Futurist-inspired drumfire that served grotesquely to dislodge signification from his fantastic word creations.

What Ball describes as "a burning search, more blatant every day, for the specific rhythm and the buried face of this age" (1974: 59), finds its practical application in the *concert bruitiste*, which is reconfigured from its Futurist variety into Dada. Discussing the original significance of bruitism, Huelsenbeck finds: "'Le bruit', noise with imitative effects [...] was intended as nothing more than a rather violent reminder of the colourfulness of life". In contrast to "abstract" and harmonious music, it represents a call to action, intonating "life itself, which attacks us, pursues us, and tears us to pieces" (1989: 25-26). Although Huelsenbeck welcomes Futurism's *bruits* as concrete, vigorous and jarring, he also postulates the opposite, demonstrating Dada's investment in paradox and self-cancellation:

> Bruitism is a kind of return to nature. It is the music produced by circuits of atoms: death ceases to be an escape from earthly misery and becomes a vomiting, screaming and choking. The Dadaists of the Cabaret Voltaire took over bruitism without sus-pecting its philosophy – basically they desired the opposite: calming of the soul, an endless lullaby, art, abstract art. The Dadaists of the Cabaret Voltaire actually had no idea what they wanted.[8] (1989: 25-26)

The passage lays out Dada's resistance to inserting itself in any kind of discourse of "style" or "aesthetics" and to the teleological impera-tive of synthetic reduction. Instead, Huelsenbeck's text sketches out a process of re-abstraction through which the *concert bruitiste* can be opened up and made to resonate with new and multiple possibilities of signification.

*

The simultaneous poem "The admiral is searching for a house to rent", performed by Huelsenbeck, Tzara, and Janco on 30 March, was the result of the Dadaists' reworking of Futurist and Expressionist influences.[9] It constitutes one of the premier examples of the Dadaists' attempts to explode prevalent cultural assumptions about the function and the production of art and to dissimulate the structures of social role-playing. The text, a nonsensical montage of semantic material, consists of news items, grotesque titbits, non-referential phonemes, and imagined primitivisms.[10] The use of such sound-words in the simultaneous poem marks the beginning of the Dadaists' search for an archaic, pre-logical language opposed to the mechanistic materialism of the age and capable of drawing the listener into a kind of mystical, associative participation beyond the parameters of institutionalised religion. It was primarily Huelsenbeck and Ball who later continued to explore these regions of cosmic religiosity, in which language transports to the threshold of mystery, and assumed the ancient role of the shamanistic bridge-builder between two worlds.[11] Ball seeks to reinvest the poetic process with the power to enchant:

> two-thirds of the wonderfully plaintive words that no human can resist come from ancient magical texts. The use of "gram-mologues", of magical floating words and resonant sound characterises the way we both write. Such word images, when they are successful, are irresistibly and hypnotically engraved on the memory [...] It has frequently happened that people who visited our evening performances without being prepared for them were so impressed by a single word or phrase that it stayed with them for weeks [...] We have loaded the word with strengths and energies that helped us to rediscover the evangelical concept of the "word" (logos) as a magical complex image. (1974: 66-68)[12]

Simultaneously, the text engages in a more violent and direct un-masking of the hated age and of human subjects as decentred by language and unconscious desire, invoking a fractured and "ragged" reality. Denouncing the powers invested in instituting rigid and exclusive discursive borders around national and cultural entities, the simultaneous poem resounds instead with a multiplicity of languages. By eliding a unified, authoritative voice ("I" or "we") the text prob-lematises its own position within these strained discursive formations maintaining the nations at war and their others. The German (Huelsenbeck) features primitivist visions of an "oriental" provenance and a scathing assault on the priesthood, whose hypocritical loins it exposes: "The high priest bawls in his sleeping bag and displays the full length of his thighs". In English, Janco sings the praise of raw desire, intoning a series of orgasmic screams, and unveils military obedience as masochistic desire for the officer/father while, at the same time, juxtaposing the alleged luridness of the ragtime milieu to Wilhelminian puritanism: "Every body is doing it doing it see that ragtime coupple [sic] over there [...] oh yes oh yes yes yes oh yes sir". Tzara's French lines weave through disparate images of nature and technology while interjecting the admiral's strange visions: "He will uncover his flesh when the wet frogs begin to burn I have put the horse in the serpent's soul [...] O my darling it's so difficult / The street runs away with my luggage". As a final insult, the three per-formers end in harmonic and rhythmic synchronicity with the text's only truly comprehensible statement, exclaiming laconically: "The admiral did not find anything". This anticlimactic coda mockingly affirms a tonic at the end of an utterly atonal work. Under the guise of granting the exhausted audience a moment of harmonic resolution, the admiral's daunting quest, which began with the simplest of assignments, is brought to a mundane conclusion, and the irreparable schism between the contesting parties reaffirmed. In an economy of performed aggression, the admiral serves as the sacrificial victim, yet the recitation also manifests the freedom from the tyranny of having to succeed as a claim in social as well as aesthetic terrains. The performance both acts out the violence of the prevailing order and offers an alternative to its (own) destructive logic. As a performance about performances, it orchestrates a polysemous interaction between the embodiment of the social roles of soldier and patriot and their subversion. By keeping the admiral and the audience in a migratory, *unheimlich* state, simultaneous and multiple trajectories of signification become available to reception and reflexivity.

Conceived for three voices, "The admiral is searching for a house to rent" is a kind of contrapuntal recitative and appears on the printed page as a musical score, complete with rhythmic and dynamic instructions. Spacings of varying length between the words seem to indicate measure-like units. A rhythmic intermezzo featuring screams of Dada's demonic laughter and other phonemes splits two segments of recitation. At the same time, Huelsenbeck banged away on his drum, Tzara shook the rattle, and Janco blew the whistle. This part of the performance culminated in a deafening *fortissimo*. Formally, the poem's compositional structure follows the tripartite aba-form and may be rendered roughly as voices-noise-voices. As the spectacle of music's representation, a musical performance fulfils both a social and a symbolic function. Whereas the traditional symphony orchestra enacts the rationalisation and specialisation of the prevailing economic order, the Dada trio collapses these parameters by integrating the roles of composer, instrumentalist, and vocalist, tipping its hat to popular modes of performance. The analysis of the parts notwithstanding, one might argue that the performed text may well have represented an alienating eruption of dissonances and a fundamentally unintelligible acoustical experience. The cabaret audience was put in a position of having to listen to three different languages musically – that is synchronously and diachronously – and probably caught no more than a

word here and there. The fact that Huelsenbeck, Janco, and Tzara engaged in improvised distortions of the linguistic material by lengthening or shortening syllables, shifting accents and varying loudness
and tempo was likely to further hinder access to the text. In performance, the semantic material was lifted out of its grammatical
radius and into a space marked by acoustical indeterminacy. To complement the performance with a kind of visual bruitism, the trio also
twisted in edgy step movements and bizarre gesturing. For Ball, the
spontaneous and inherently unique combination of these performative
techniques in the avant-garde's construction of sound and of auditory
space constitutes a qualitative broadening of the written text and
encompasses claims to both high art and popular entertainment:
"Reciting aloud has become the touchstone of the quality of a poem
for me" (1974: 54). About the *soirée* of 30 March, Ball notes in his
diary:

> All the styles of the last twenty years came together yesterday [...]
> The "simultaneous poem" has to do with the value of the voice.
> The human organ represents the soul, the individuality in its
> wanderings with its demonic companions. The noises represent
> the background – the inarticulate, the disastrous, the decisive. The
> poem tries to elucidate the fact that man is swallowed up in the
> mechanistic process. In a typically compressed way it shows the
> conflict of the *vox humana* with a world that threatens, ensnares,
> and destroys it, a world whose rhythm and noise are ineluctable.[13]
> (1974: 57)

Like philosophers equipped with drumsticks, the Dadaists pound and
play out their cultural critique. Again, discourse encapsulates the
multilayered simultaneity of performance and the indescribable spaces
of speechlessness in binaries, dividing the continuum into fore-
ground/background, individuality/world, and voice/noise. The precar-
iousness of experience, communicable only in the flow of performance and in the interlocking of inchoate voices and noises, can at
best be approximated in the vagueness of the phrase "in a typically
compressed way". In contrast to the Futurists' bruitist and imitative
celebration of technology, Ball's text hints at the reclamation of a
contingent humanity.

Many of the memoirs and texts the Dadaists have written
invoke the symbolic significance of the drum for bruitist performance
and its privileged position in the ritualised space of the cabaret. Dated

some months before the founding of the Cabaret Voltaire, Ball's diary contains the description of a journey to Basel, the city of "grave-diggers" and "anomalies". Upon arriving, a sensation of impending doom befalls the traveller, while rain is pounding on the roofs. Ball goes on to sketch a carnivalesque scene, recording his impressions of a bizarre and terrifying drumming ritual celebrated annually in Basel. Irrespective of rank or social standing, the citizens of Basel convene for a "veritable orgy of rattling" that would send all sinners "into the gloomiest Orcus". The text distances itself from the drum as a conjurer of dead spirits and awakener of all apocalyptic traumata recorded by history and locates it in the below of the body: "It is the belly of the age, emitting rumbling noises" (1974: 39-40). After the initial, frightening experience, Ball appears to have recognised the explosive potential of *la grande caisse* for the cabaret and its place as an instrument for shocking unsuspecting audiences. This recognition was accelerated with the arrival of Huelsenbeck who became associated famously with the drum.

In the performance of "The admiral is searching for a house to rent" and many others before and after it, the Dadaists use the drum to tap into multiple strata of symbolic association, connecting horizontally with the carnage on Europe's battlefields and vertically with various archetypal regions. Rhythmic drum beats call up visions of the disciplined drill of goose-stepping military formations and of the formidable battle calls of nationalist lore, such as the Hessian units of the American Revolutionary War. In the hands of the Dada performers, these associations are mobilised to ridicule the military.[14] Ball apes the gruff quality of order-shouting and drowns out the military's hardware with his own superior, guttural drumrolls and a *double entendre* on the term "drumfire": "I will drrrrrrrrrum extremely well. Drrrrrrrum outstandingly. I will burst their ear drrrrrrrrrrums. I will drrrrrrrum more loudly than their drrrrrrrreadful drrrrrrrrrrumfires" (Ball and Hennings 1978: 102).[15] In addition, the Dadaists imagine the drum beats as an echo of the bestial sounds of the jungle and, consequently, as an antidote to bourgeois sentimentality and complacency. The sound's concreteness and ugliness is deployed to rattle the audience out of its torpor, while its low-frequency thuds were to break open channels of retrogression into infantile dream worlds and into realms of primal brutality. Among the other instruments used during the performances, the Dadaists favoured children's toys and noisemakers such as sirens, gongs, bells, rattles, keys, tin cans, and wood blocks. As the dominant ritual symbol in Dada performance and as the smallest instrument of the transformation and integration effected in ritual, the drum represents a nodal point joining classificatory planes to one another and condensing disparate significations. More importantly, it serves as a dynamic entity that acquires valences of meaning dependent on its positioning in a relational context composed of other symbols and events of the social process. This multivocality of the drum in the Cabaret Voltaire provides an open space for the audience's cultural agency. By imbuing the ideological trajectory of their use of the drum with strong sensory stimulation, the Dadaists attempted to control the contention involved in the appropriation of the symbol.

Dada's noise stands in relation to the omnipresent noise of its age. The din of the performances inserts itself acoustically into the power struggle in which the proprietors of hegemonic culture denounce all new and emergent cultural forms as "noise" and fetishise their own as "music". The mad Dada drummer reclaims the right to sonic violence. In a genealogical study of the relationship between various ordering systems of sounds, Jacques Attali has explored pre-enlightenment networks of musical production and reception and found that to make noise is to kill: *"Noise is a weapon and music, primordially, is the formation, domestication, and ritualisation of that weapon as a simulacrum of ritual murder"*. Music, consequently, represents nothing more than "an impoverished memory of its ritual nature" (1985: 24). Tonality, the harmonic structure of Western art music, subsumes dissonances into an ideological scheme in which they serve formally to project "the music harmonically forward towards cadence", and subjectively to establish "a dialectic of desires and expectations which are subsequently gratified in pleasures of resolution" (Durant 1984: 75), thus affirming organicity, a central fetish of early twentieth century bourgeois culture. Ball remarks caustically: "Harmony is the Germans' Messiah; it will come to deliver its people from the multiplicity of resounding contradiction" (1974: 37). By 1916, dissonance and noise were associated not only with freedom from musical strictures and aesthetic valuations but also regarded as reflections of social relations and as tools for the provocation of audiences schooled in tonality and composed of subjects maimed by rationalisation and commodification. Adorno has written extensively on the bourgeois's abhorrence of atonal "noise" music: "The dissonances which horrify them testify to their own conditions; for that reason alone do they find them unbearable" (1973: 9). Noise, irrevocably inscribed in power relations, temporarily cleans the slate by establishing disorder, the absence of all meaning. At the same time, it provides the perceptual and somatic conditions for previously un- heard signals.

In text, the Dadaists consistently write performance by em- ploying grand metaphors of violence and evoking a whole litany of crimes. They define violence loosely as a form of absolute scepticism, a provocative condemnation, and as a source of energy. Promises to "burn all libraries", to murder the bourgeois, to sign the "death warrant" for false morality, and to prepare "the great spectacle of disaster, fire, decomposition" reverberate through these retrospectives. The Dada performance is likened to "fantastic destruction", to a "gladiator's gesture", to weaponry, and to avalanche. Huelsenbeck asserts that he wants "to make literature with a gun in hand [...] to something like a robber baron of the pen" and to beat time with a coffin lid (1989: 28). The Dadaists' body language on stage both em- bodied and dissimulated the familiar gestures and symbols of the authoritarian types. Aside from madly beating the drum, Huelsenbeck wore a monocle, cracked a whip over the audience's heads and delivered blows to any object within reach. Tzara punctuated his performances with screams and sobs. The Dadaists profess to desire nothing less than to effect a transformation of consciousness. With typical hyperbole, Tzara evokes the necessity of chaos in order to break open a violent passage into the fluid realm of the audience's subconscious: "Every night we thrust the triton of the grotesque of the god of the beautiful into each and every spectator, and the wind was not gentle – the consciousness of so many was shaken – tumult and solar avalanche – vitality and the silent corner close to wisdom and folly – who can define its frontiers?" (1989: 236). Beyond the creation of "art", which would merely deflect from the surface and enter the circuits of capitalist exchange as nihilistic polemic against the "dir- ectors of public cretinisation" (Arp 1948: 45), the Dadaists are con- cerned with a more complex unleashing of violence against the self. This deliberate de- or ex-personalisation, a typical manifestation of neuroses, is to activate a memory of instinct/nature and to destroy the cultural fabrication of the "ego". Citing Cesare Lombroso's *Genius and Madness*, Ball inserts himself into the contemporary discursive equation of creativity and insanity and celebrates the lunatic's crossing into uncharted psychic territory: "A world with its own laws and its own form; it poses new problems and new tasks, just like a newly discovered continent" (1974: 75).[16]

*

At the site of the fragmentary and violated self, or, as Ball recalls, through the suffering "from the dissonances to the point of self-disintegration" (1974: 66), one encounters traces of the (e)migratory, liminal figures of the madman/fool and the shaman. In the medieval imagination, the fool provides the impetus for laughter and irony in the omnipresence of death. As Michel Foucault has asserted, the fool travels ceaselessly through discourses that imprison him in an in-between existence, most pointedly in the literary metaphor of the ship of fools:

> The madman's voyage is at once a rigorous division and an Absolute Passage [...] his exclusion must enclose him; if he cannot and must not have another *prison* than the *threshold* itself, he is kept at the point of passage. He is put in the interior of the exterior, and inversely [...] He has his truth and his homeland only in that fruitless expanse between two countries that cannot belong to him.[17] (1965: 11)

The shaman, on the other hand, plays out a broader range of roles, acting as artist, performer, healer, psychotic, priest, and entertainer. He is, above all, the wounded healer whose body and movements bear the imprints of history's calamities and of the rigours of the liminal experience. He transgresses cultural thresholds both painfully and cathartically and facilitates such tormenting crossings for the participants, whom he brings under the sway of variable drum rhythms. Ball, who, along with Huelsenbeck, suffered from exhaustion and nervous breakdowns, registers both the pain and the rapture of transgressive commonality in the ritualised environment of the Cabaret Voltaire: "In the middle of the crowds I start to tremble all over" (1974: 57). One witnesses in the early Dada performances the soundings of an idiosyncratic, mediated spirituality that would later reach higher levels of crystallisation. In June of 1916, Ball delivered a solo performance of his sound poem "Gadji beri bimba" donning a "witch doctor's hat" and a cardboard costume that did not allow him to move onto or about the stage. His diary entry conveys a heightened awareness of the entranced, liminal state in which a disembodied, other-worldly voice flows from the immovable shell of his vestment: "My voice had no choice but to take on the ancient cadence of priestly lamentation [...] Bathed in sweat, I was carried down off the stage like a magical bishop" (1974: 71). Having achieved a violent derangement of the senses, the Dada performer assumes the identity of an unorthodox, quasi-religious visionary and transformer of souls. The Dadaists' daily rewriting of life through performance becomes an experimental project of re-enchantment and re-mystification: "What we are celebrating is both buffoonery and a requiem mass" (1974: 56). [18]

In the words of Peter Sloterdijk, Dada's initial task was to act as a "garbage disposal in the depraved European superstructure of ideas" and to break down the cynical separation between reality and its aesthetic and idealist (mis)representations by entering the fray and by applying "the most advanced destructive procedures into the arts" (1987: 394ff.). During the first few weeks of their Zürich experiment, the Dadaists discovered that their performances transformed the Cabaret Voltaire into a timeless, liminal space of suspended subjectivities: "Everyone has been seized by an indefinable intoxication. The little cabaret is about to come apart at the seams" (Ball 1974: 51-52). Their provocations seemed to stretch the audience's perceptual capabilities and to lead to previously unknown realms of experience. Whether the avant-garde's attempt to reintegrate art into social praxis or even to intervene in that reality through the openness of the aesthetic fragment was effectual has been at the centre of a long-lived debate among cultural theorists. Peter Bürger, whose work has had a lasting impact on the critical discourse on Dada, situates Dada's anti-institutional art historically as the apogee of vanguard self-criticism, but simultaneously couches his analysis in a devolutionary and teleological narrative of "failure", joining a chorus of multiple announcements of the "death" of the avant-garde in the 1960s and 1970s. [19] More specifically, Bürger criticises the "shock" engendered by Dada art as a merely consumptive and therefore inconsequential mode of reception: "The public's reactions to Dada manifestations are typical of the nonspecificity of the reaction. It responds to the provocation of the Dadaists with blind fury. And changes in the life praxis of the public probably did not result" (1984: 80). In light of the valuable work of historicising that Bürger does accomplish, much of his analysis of Dada remains oddly ahistorical and vague. The conceptual reductionism of the terms "shock" and "life praxis" forces the different venues, phases, forms of expression, and audiences of Dada into an overarching dialectical totality. In outlining the avant-garde's success in directing the recipients' attention to non-organic art's principle of construction and less toward content, Bürger concentrates on Dada's printed texts and *objets trouvés* and wholly elides performance as a category of inquiry, falling short of pursuing the complex processes of mediation and negotiation further.[20]

Closer in time to the Dada events, Walter Benjamin also explored the question whether the atrophied modern subject's shrinkage of experience, which manifests itself in either failed contact (*Erlebnis*) or violent encounter (*Chock*) with the object-world, might not contain a pathway to a future form of magical experience (*Erfahrung*). He locates the potential for cognitive and authentic experience in ecstatic community rather than in the transcendental subject:

> The ancients' intercourse with the cosmos had been different: the ecstatic trance. For it is in this experience (*Erfahrung*) alone that we gain certain knowledge of what is nearest to us and what is remotest to us, and never of one without the other. This means, however, that man can be in ecstatic contact with the cosmos only communally. It is the dangerous error of modern men to regard this experience as unimportant and avoidable, and to consign it to the individual as the poetic rapture of starry nights. (1979: 103)

In "Surrealism: The Last Snapshot of the European Intelligentsia", Benjamin offers a further differentiated conceptualisation of experience in capitalist societies and of the possibility of turning such lived experience into awareness. He sees dream and intoxication as vehicles for freeing subjects abruptly from their mutual separation from objects: "In the world's structure dream loosens individuality like a bad tooth. This loosening of the self by intoxication is, at the same time, precisely the fruitful, living experience that allowed these people to step outside the domain of intoxication". The ecstatic states, which may be either drug-induced or religious, can be heightened and creatively overcome through "a *profane illumination* [*Erleuchtung*], a materialistic, anthropological inspiration, to which hashish, opium, or whatever else can give an introductory lesson" (1979: 227). Correspondingly, one might argue that, initially, the violent encounter of the subject with an indefinable exterior force in the Dada performance represents a moment of disharmonious exchange that overwhelms the subject's shock defences, accessing his/her unprepared subconscious. The structure of ritualised performance may subsequently facilitate the transfiguration of experience, *Erleuchtung*, as a passage to a middle domain, tapping into the collective, sonorous and living unconsciousness of the past and its revolutionary energies.[21] Benjamin's essay can be read as a vision of praxis that invests vanguard artistic activity with the potential for leading subjective memory to disrupt the hegemonic structures that affect a degradation of experience. This recuperative moment becomes possible through the paradoxical interplay of a redemptive pessimism, the principle of constructive destruction, and an art-as-experience that integrates the social.

Dada's ritualised cultural performances, which held their provocative intensity for but a few months, broke down conventional dichotomies of sacred and secular, oral and written, primitive and modern, high and low, and constantly integrated, differentiated, and subverted the field of social relations. Assuming the facilitating role of shamans, the Dada performers acted as heterogeneous agents whose feverish, contorted bodies and whose self-effacing madness reframed the threatening perimeters of culture and modelled a crossing into the subjunctive structure of an alternative commonality. They sought to make dazzlingly present the conditions for authentic, cultic experience and to restore a numinous quality to art through marvellous violence. Yet the ambiguity of all ritual lies in the possibility of its participants recognising culture as an arbitrary construct. As meta-commentary and action, ritualised performance may both manifest reflexivity in the somatic matrix of the performance space and, at times, produce reflexivity. Whether rituals can generate conditions not only for reflexivity but also for reflexive action, a condition that is approximately rendered by the anthropological term "efficacy", is at the heart of Critical Theory's desideratum and its palpable disillusionment with the waning of a particular political conjuncture. On this account, the Dadaists' texts are replete with statements of self-doubt and recoil from making overwrought claims. Predicting their own exorcism, they acknowledge that today's transgressions may fall short and seem trite and harmless tomorrow:

> I do not know if we will go beyond Wilde and Baudelaire in spite
> of all our efforts; or if we will not just remain romantics. There
> are probably other ways of achieving the miracle and other ways
> of opposition too – asceticism, for example, the church. But are
> these ways not completely blocked? There is a danger that only
> our mistakes are new.[22] (Ball, 1974: 66)

The writing of Dada performance confines its subject either within
linear time or cyclical recurrence and is incapable of articulating the
traceless, expansive moment. The result is a profound defeatism anchored in the realisation that Dada's creative practice is entirely
implicated in the ideology and the false ethics of hegemonic cultural
discourse. Unable to get over the paradoxical experience or to formulate in retrospect its epistemological foundation, the Dadaists were
later drawn again and again to the Cabaret Voltaire, attempting to
dislodge it from its historicised site in what Greil Marcus has called an
urgent "reach for the gnostic myth" (1989: 197). The Dadaists' self-
critical comments reveal the unresolved conflict within the avant-
garde between the desire both to tear away the boundaries between
life and art and to retain a liminal site for art outside of the mundane, a
place from which critical transactions can be launched. The ritualised,
conspicuously artificial performance of early Dada Zürich constituted
a spirited negotiation of these pressing challenges for modern art and
may be characterised, with caution, as a disruptive situation whose
participants operated in the in-between of language, structure, and
time, and as a spectacular blind spot in the order of things.

Notes

[1] See reproduction in Scheunemann 2000: 124. Although Arp playfully critiques
Cabaret Voltaire as "zigzag naturalism" (1948: 45), it might be more accurately
placed within a cubo-futurist aesthetic.
[2] In the 1960s, Janco proclaimed: "Do not trust anything that calls itself 'Dada history'", before proceeding to pen his own (1971: 35-38).
[3] Most of the scholarly work on Dada's performance art has taken the shape of the
broadly conceived anthology (Senelick, Segel) or the descriptive history (Goldberg,
Gordon, Melzer) and has not examined individual performances in depth or formulated a theory of Dada performance.
[4] In my reading, this conceptual framework finds a correlative in recent musicological
approaches to musical performance, which have directed their analytical focus to
relationality and positionality, "supplying music with socially specific frameworks of
intelligibility" (Durant 1984: 13), and expanded the study of music from purely

formal concerns to its position within various discursive networks of empowerment. For a good general introduction to performance as a critical vantage point, see Diamond.

[5] Remembering their days in Munich, where they frequented Kathi Kobus's cabaret *Simplizissimus*, Ball and Huelsenbeck explicitly connect the new venture in Zürich to the vaudeville/variety tradition. Typical of both performance genres is their non-narrative, compartmented structure of a series of self-contained and hermetic performed units, framed in time and space. Dada's particular brand of vaudeville-like performances is regarded as one of the precursors to what subsequently came to be known as performance art or happening. See especially Sandford.

[6] For a detailed account of the contacts between Futurists and Dadaists, see Sheppard.

[7] The Dadaists were probably not aware that ragtime is characterized by a syncopated melodic line with an accompaniment in regular rhythm and was, unlike improvised jazz, composed (with printable scores).

[8] Falsely translated here as "lullaby", the German term "Wogalaweia" refers specifically to Richard Wagner's onomatopoetic creations for the Rhine Maidens in *Das Rheingold*. Huelsenbeck scolds Wagner's music for showing "all the hypocrisy inherent in a pathetic faculty for abstraction" (1974: 25).

[9] This text is reprinted in its original form in Tzara, *Œuvres Complètes* (1975: 492-493). In a footnote "pour le bourgeois", Tzara cites the works of Delaunay, Apollinaire, and Cendrars as models for his Dada poetry. For an analysis of French simultaneism, see Shattuck.

[10] Although Dada performance dramatised culture on the margins, it did so only in the confines of white European culture. By inserting itself in a modernist discourse of essentialising the racial other, it fixed rather than made fluent the imposition of marginality upon an imagined, timeless, exotic and primitive world.

[11] An immense body of work has been contributed to the study of shamanism since Mircea Eliade's classic *Shamanism. Archaic Techniques of Ecstasy* (1964). Recently, Grimes has introduced the term "parashamanism" to denote the emergent religiosities and ritual activities of countercultural movements that occur on the margins of institutions in large-scale industrial societies. Parashamanism is characterised by an "ad hoc and eclectic" use of ritual, one which freely samples and borrows in order to create a "fictive religiosity" (1995: 253-268). For a broad study of shamanism in art, see Tucker.

[12] According to Walter Benjamin, the historical avant-garde's "passionate phonetic and graphical transformation games" must be understood as "magical experiments with words" (1979: 232).

[13] For a more detailed analysis of the Dadaists' configuration of time, see Kieruj (1995: 57ff).

[14] Huelsenbeck's insolent stage persona may have reminded connoisseurs of German theatre of the brutish drum major of Georg Büchner's dramatic fragment *Woyzeck*.

[15] My translation. The German text reads:
"Ich werde ganz vorzüglich trrrrrrrrrommeln. Hervorragend trrrrrrrrrommeln. Ich werde die Trrrrrrrrrommelfelle zerplatzen. Ich werde trrrrrrrrrommeln, daß die Trrrrrrrrrommelfeuer ein Trrrrrrrrreck dagegen sind".

[16] To describe the effect these performances had on a contemporaneous audience remains a highly speculative task. Little is known about the receptive habits of those

who attended the Cabaret Voltaire except that they appear to have been deeply affected. Peter A. J. Froehlich has undertaken a reception study and identified a succession of psychic states elicited during a performance of Kurt Schwitters's *Ursonate*. In Froehlich's schema, the audience suffered an initial attack of utter confusion and then made a concentrated effort to exercise self-control in order to remain at its best social behavior. Soon, however, the provocative thrust of the performance would gradually lead to a complete loss of control manifesting itself in a variety of ways among which anger and revolt were the most common responses. By the end of the performance, silence often settled in. It must be remembered that the *Ursonate* is a meticulously structured text and was recited in a more concert-like manner than the texts that were performed at the Cabaret Voltaire. For a further exploration of the complex relationship between audience/reader and performance/text, see Halley. Froehlich's account is the same as referenced by Rudolf Kuenzli, cited by Wall and Jones in the following essay, "The Body of the Voice: corporeal poetics in Dada".

[17] On the connection between Dada, madness, and infantilism, see Bergius.

[18] Ball's statement suggests that the Dadaists reflected on the purposeful deployment and proportioning of playfulness and solemnity in their performances. The ludic aspect of ritual is thought to signal the non-pragmatic and useless and represents a turn against the dominant work ethic and its cultural symbols. On the other hand, the stated seriousness of these performances reinserts them in an economy of efficiency and affect. Peter Sloterdijk has described Dada's strategy as "a provisional philosophy of Yes" in search of "the miracle of an eternal, fleeting present", referring to the type of spirituality I have outlined above as the "kynical aspects of religion" (1987: 395).

[19] In a trenchant critique of these theoretical *coups de grâce*, Paul Mann has argued that "the death of the avant-garde is the n-state of the recuperation of its critical potential by a narrative of failure [...] In the obituary the avant-garde is completely historicised [...] The triumph of death-theory occurs when it can trace the aetiology of the avant-garde's fatality back to the very fact of its origin, when it can write the whole history of the avant-garde as a death" (1991: 40).

[20] Cf. Jochen Schulte-Sasse's introductory essay to the English edition of Bürger's classic text.

[21] See also Cohen 186ff.

[22] The language of retrospection sometimes suggests that the Dadaists were indeed on a neo-romantic retreat from the world and from politics: "In Zürich in 1915, losing interest in the slaughterhouses of the world war, we turned to the Fine Arts. While the thunder of the batteries rumbled in the distance, we pasted, we recited, we versified, we sang with all our soul. We searched for an elementary art that would, we thought, save mankind from the furious folly of these times" (Arp 1948: 39).

References

Adorno, Theodor
>   1973   *Philosophy of New Music*. Anne G. Mitchell and Wesley V.
>   Blomster (eds). New York: Seabury Press.

Arp, Hans
>   1948   *On My Way: Poetry and Essays 1912–1947*. New York:
>   Wittenborn, Schultz.

Attali, Jacques
>   1985   *Noise. The Political Economy of Music* (tr. Brian Massumi).
>   Minneapolis: University of Minnesota Press.

Ball, Hugo
>   1974   *Flight out of Time: A Dada Diary* (ed. John Elderfield, tr. Ann
>   Raimes). New York: Viking Press.

Ball, Hugo, and Emmy Hennings
>   1978   *Damals in Zürich. Briefe aus den Jahren 1915–1917*. Zürich:
>   Arche.

Bell, Catherine
>   1992   *Ritual Theory. Ritual Practice*. New York: Oxford University
>   Press.

Benjamin, Walter
>   1979   *One-Way Street and Other Writings* (trs Edmund Jephcott and
>   Kingsley Shorter). London: New Left Books.

Bergius, Hanne
>   1981   "Dada als 'Buffonade und Totenmesse zugleich'". In Stephanie
>   Poley (ed.) *Unter der Maske des Narren*. Stuttgart: Gerd Hatje:
>   208-220.

Bourdieu, Pierre
>   1977   *Outline of a Theory of Practice*. (tr. Richard Nice). Cambridge:
>   Cambridge University Press.

Bürger, Peter
>   1984   *Theory of the Avant-Garde* (tr. Michael Shaw). Minneapolis:
>   University of Minnesota Press.

Cohen, Margaret
>   1993   *Profane Illumination. Walter Benjamin and the Paris Surrealist
>   Revolution*. Berkeley: University of California Press.

62   *Cornelius Partsch*

Diamond, Elin (ed.)
    1996   *Performance and Cultural Politics*. New York: Routledge.

Durant, Alan
    1984   *Conditions of Music*. Albany: State University of New York
            Press.

Foster, Stephen C.
    1996   "Disaster and the Habits of Culture". In Stephen C. Foster (ed.)
            Dada. The Coordinates of Cultural Politics. New York: G.K.
            Hall: 1-6.

    1988   *"Event" Arts and Art Events*. Ann Arbor: UMI Research Press.

Foucault, Michel
    1965   *Madness and Civilisation. A History of Insanity in the Age of
            Reason* (tr. Richard Howard). New York: Random House.

Froehlich, Peter A. J.
    1982   "Reaktionen des Publikums auf Vorführungen nach abstrakten
            Vorlagen". In Wolfgang Paulsen and Helmut G. Herrmann (eds)
            Sinn aus Unsinn: Dada International (Zwölftes Amherster
            Kolloquium zur deutschen Literatur). Bern: Francke: 15-28.

Goldberg, RoseLee
    1988   *Performance Art: From Futurism to the Present*. New York:
            H. N. Abrams.

Gordon, Mel
    1987   *Dada Performance*. New York: PAJ Publications.

Grimes, Ronald L.
    1995   *Beginnings in Ritual Studies*. Columbia: University of South
            Carolina Press.

Halley, Jeffrey A.
    1989   "Bakhtin and the Sociology of Culture: Polyphony and the
            Interaction of Object and Audience". In *Critical Studies* 1(2):
            163-179.

Huelsenbeck, Richard
    1974   *Memoirs of a Dada Drummer* (ed. Hans Kleinschmidt, tr. Joachim
            Neugroschel). Berkeley: University of California Press.

    1989   "En Avant Dada: A History of Dadaism". In Robert Motherwell
            (ed.) and Ralph Manheim (tr.) *The Dada Painters and Poets: An
            Anthology*. Cambridge: Belknap Press: 21-47.

Janco, Marcel
    1971   "Creative Dada". In Lucy R. Lippard (ed.) *Dadas on Art*.
                Englewood Cliffs, NJ: Prentice-Hall: 35-38.

Kieruj, Mariusz
    1995   *Zeitbewußtsein, Erinnern und die Wiederkehr des Kultischen:*
                Kontinuität und Bruch in der deutschen Avantgarde 1910–1930.
                Frankfurt: Peter Lang.

Lewer, Debbie
    1996   "From the Cabaret Voltaire to the Kaufleutensaal: 'Mapping'
                Zurich Dada". In Stephen C. Foster, Brigitte Pichon and Karl Riha
                (eds) *Dada Zurich: A Clown's Game from Nothing*. New York:
                G.K. Hall: 45-59.

Mann, Paul
    1991   *The Theory-Death of the Avant-Garde*. Bloomington: Indiana
                University Press.

Marcus, Greil
    1989   *Lipstick Traces. A Secret History of the Twentieth Century*.
                Cambridge: Harvard University Press.

Marinetti, F. T.
    1973   "The Variety Theatre 1913". In Umbro Apollonio (ed.) and R. W.
                Flint (tr.) *Futurist Manifestos*. New York: Viking Press: 126-131.

Melzer, Annabelle
    1980   *Latest Rage the Big Drum: Dada and Surrealist Performance*.
                Ann Arbor: UMI Research Press.

Pichon, Brigitte
    1996   "Revisiting Spie(ge)lgasse: Mirror(s) and Prism(s), Cultural and
                Political Stagings of Emigration and Liminality". In Stephen C.
                Foster, Brigitte Pichon and Karl Riha (eds) *Dada Zurich: A
                Clown's Game from Nothing*. New York: G.K. Hall: 1-35.

Richter, Hans
    1966   *Dada: Art and Antiart*. London: Thames and Hudson.

Russolo, Luigi
    1973   "The Art of Noises". In Umbro Apollonio (ed.) and Caroline
                Tisdall (tr.) *Futurist Manifestos*. New York: Viking Press: 74-88.

Sandford, Mariellen R. (ed.)
    1995   *Happenings and Other Acts*. New York: Routledge.

Scheunemann, Dietrich (ed.)
2000   *European Avant-Garde: New Perspectives*, Avant Garde Critical Studies 15. Amsterdam and Atlanta: Rodopi.

Schulte-Sasse, Jochen
1984   "Foreword: Theory of Modernism versus Theory of the Avant-Garde". In Peter Bürger, *Theory of the Avant-Garde*. Michael Shaw (tr.). Minneapolis: University of Minnesota Press: ix-xlvii.

Segel, Harold B.
1987   *Turn-of-the-Century Cabaret*. New York: Columbia University Press.

Senelick, Laurence
1989   *Cabaret Performance: Sketches, Songs, Monologues, Memoirs*. New York: PAJ Publications.

Shattuck, Robert
1968   *The Banquet Years. The Origins of the Avantgarde in France 1885 to World War I*. New York: Vintage Books.

Sheppard, Richard
1982   "Dada und Futurismus". In Wolfgang Paulsen and Helmut G. Herrmann (eds) *Sinn aus Unsinn. Dada International* (Zwölftes Amherster Kolloquium zur deutschen Literatur). Bern: Francke: 29-70.

Sloterdijk, Peter
1987   *Critique of Cynical Reason* (tr. Michael Eldred). Minneapolis: University of Minnesota Press.

Tucker, Michael
1992   *The Shamanic Spirit in Twentieth-Century Art and Culture*. San Francisco: Aquarian/Harper.

Turner, Victor
1984   "Liminality and the Performative Genres". In John J. MacAloon (ed.) *Rite, Drama, Festival, Spectacle. Rehearsals toward a Theory of Cultural Performance*. Philadelphia: Institute for the Study of Human Issues: 19-41.

1988   *The Anthropology of Performance*. New York: PAJ Publications.

Tzara, Tristan
1975   *Œuvres Complètes*. Vol. 1 (1912–1924) (ed. Henri Béhar). Paris: Flammarion.

1989   "Zurich Chronicle (1915–1919)". In Robert Motherwell (ed.) and Ralph Manheim (tr.) *The Dada Painters and Poets: An Anthology.* Cambridge: Belknap Press: 235-242.

The Body of the Voice: corporeal poetics in Dada

John Wall and Dafydd Jones

Abstract: This essay begins with a brief history of the problem of the body in philosophy showing how various philosophers have approached the problem and linked it to theory of language. The essay then offers a critique of structuralist/ poststructuralist insistence that there is nothing outside the text, and that the only way the body appears in it is as a representation or trace. Kristeva says of modernist poetry that it tries to write in a language that manifests the points of the irruption of the body into language; semiosis, the bodily aspect of the generation of such symbolic systems as language. The aim is to work towards a dialectical theory of body and language – beginning with Tristan Tzara's early manifesto soundings – although the term "dialectic" functions here as a metaphor for interaction. Thus aspects of Dada poetry can be looked at in terms of the corporeal dimensions of rhythms (as opposed to the purely linguistic understanding of formal rhythms such as meter), the importance of contradiction, paradox and nonsense, delirium, body image, and the performativity of the body – body as sign, such as is seen in the move from a purely verbal drama where the body is of secondary importance, to the kind of drama where the body is a significant part of the repertoire of gestures (including language) that make up dramatic performance, of whatever kind. What is centrally addressed is the relation between body and language, and the essay identifies the tension between a radically systemic and disembodied construal of language and the poetic practice of bringing into play an elemental dynamic. Language and the elemental body are equally constitutive of symbolic representation and are fused in what the phenomenology of Merleau-Ponty terms "incarnate logic". This incarnate logic, or voice, is expressed both in the movement of bodies across the dreamlike geography of the narrative, and the paradoxical figures which sustain narrative momentum; thus, space is neither purely mental nor objective (the observer is in the observation).

"Thought is made in the mouth" – Tristan Tzara

1. The corporeality of language

In his *Critique of Cynical Reason*, Peter Sloterdijk argues that the Enlightenment has bequeathed to contemporary western society a seriously distorted form of thought, one that constitutes itself as the negation of the materialism of the body. Thus knowledge has come to be understood purely in terms of the categories of the understanding and the logical intricacies of moral reasoning. Whether one is an empiricist or a rationalist, idealist or realist, the epistemological orientation to the world neglects the fact that the act of knowing is bound up not only with logic, but also the world of sensation, of sedimented bodily knowledge. For Sloterdijk, such disembodied knowledge is a form of evil insofar as knowledge of the other comes to be based on the paradigm of objectivity (Sloterdijk 1988: xxxi). In his opinion, the corrective involves what he terms a physiognomic philosophy, one that bases itself on knowledge of the body. He goes on to develop a kynical philosophy based on thinkers and writers in the past who posited the body as the revolutionary moment in history. According to Sloterdijk, the study of the body would offer society an inverse representation of itself, one that nonetheless would be eminently recognisable, if contrary to social *mores*. Even if Sloterdijk speaks of trying to find what it is that lies beneath knowledge systems, he does not envisage a being-in-itself, a realm of brute reality overlaid by social symbolic systems. What he does envisage is a philosophy wherein language and knowledge systems retain the dialectical relation with the body that constitutes a dynamic and not passive component in any symbolic system. In the following lines he states what, for example, the inclusion of the arse would mean for any future philosophy:

> The arse seems doomed to spend its life in the dark, as the beggar among body parts. It is the real idiot of the family. However, it would be a wonder if this black sheep of the body did not have its own opinion about everything that takes place in higher regions. [...] Dying and shitting are the only things one must do. [...] The arse is thus, of all bodily organs, the one closest to the dialectical relation of freedom and necessity. [...] To understand the arse

would be therefore the best preparatory study for philosophy, the
somatic propaedeutic. (Sloterdijk 1988: 147-149)

Our reasons for citing these lines are analytical as well as rhetorical.
Reading them, one is aware of the contradictory nature of Kant's
struggle to establish beauty and the sublime as foundational experiences conditioning the moral and epistemological understanding, a
struggle that was at least partially corrected by the somatic nature of
the Schopenhauerean will. In fact one could claim, ironically, that
what Kant sought in the experience of the sublime and the beautiful
was never just around the corner of some torturous deduction but, in
fact, always behind him, like a faithful shadow; or, as Leopold Bloom
would surely insist, in the daily rhythms of the body and its fusion
with social discourse, the Dublin City reservoir, and perhaps the
cosmos. The aim of this essay is not to conduct an analysis of the role
of any particular organ in generating knowledge, and neither is it to
record the scatological intuitions secreted in the interstices of literary
language. Rather, we aim to show that the avant-garde preoccupation
with the formal qualities of art and their performative destruction may
be construed as an attempt to make explicit the corporeal nature of
linguistic and symbolic form. Of particular interest is the specifically
Dada and generally avant-garde claim that art and literature are less
concerned with particular representations than with their form, materiality and the corporeality of semantic and ideological functions.

    Tristan Tzara posits what may be construed as a direct onto-
logical link between the radical artist, representation and the material
of production: "The new artist protests: he no longer paints (symbolic
and illusionistic reproduction) but creates directly in stone, wood,
iron, tin, rocks, or locomotive structures capable of being spun in all
directions by the limpid wind of the momentary sensation" (1992: 7).
For Tzara, the dynamic of representation, and not the representation
itself, is addressed in the (highly questionable) convergence of sensation and materiality. This direct ontology, however reminiscent of
Mallarméan symbolism, may be offset by Tzara's scatological immersion in flesh – "the three essential laws ... eating, making love and
shitting" (1992: 34) – which suggests the centrality of the corporeal
principle in his work: "The finger bores into all sorts of flesh till it
gets to the innermost part that shrieks and vibrates, where it becomes a
flower, and laughs" (1992 61). Moreover, the dynamic of the body in
Tzara takes on an ontological significance. Whereas a thinker like the

sceptical Descartes, for example, sees "fire" and "wind" as secondary and derivative metaphors of an insubstantial soul that is unable to serve as the basis of a rationally conceived identity (Descartes 1968: 104), Tzara sees them as fundamental to artistic productivity, quipping that the poet "is a fart in a steam engine" (1992: 33). The seemingly happy convergence of sensation and the material of representation is in fact nonidentical with itself due to the wind and fire of the body, which must be accorded the status of corporeal *difference,* and not just solid, inarticulate meat. In the same way, writers like Marcel Proust with his notion of the sensuous memory, and James Joyce (happily coincidentally resident in Zürich when the Cabaret Voltaire opened in 1916) with his linguistic sonority, were already in the early twentieth century experimenting with the limits of representational form in an attempt to bring into relief the corporeal dimension of mental and linguistic experience. In a similar vein, by the late 1920s, Samuel Beckett had begun a series of meditations on the comedy of Descartes's corporeal paradoxes that would take him from youthful anxiety about the role of the body in an artistic world that demanded a high level of sublimation, through the swamps of flesh of his middle period, and onto the lyricism of old bones that characterised the later work.[1] Indeed, Julia Kristeva has argued more recently that the defining feature of literary modernism is the attempt by poets and writers, since Mallarmé and Lautréamont, to infuse poetic and narrative language with the dynamism of psycho-physiological drives (Kristeva 1984: 186).

For Tzara, the principles of negativity and *difference* are seldom expressed as abstractions and have a direct critical and excremental bearing. Returning to Sloterdijk's ideal kynic – the arse – we might note a particular resonance to this body part (among others) in our engagement with Dada as a culturally oppositional and hostile formation, which found its oppositional status continually compromised, always by default remaining "within the framework of European weaknesses, it's still shit, but from now on we want to shit in different colours" (Tzara 1992: 1). Tzara, whose contradictory appeal to anarchic revolution made its back door entry through the constant disruption of meaning as it is enshrined in social and linguistic norms, here makes a characteristic appeal to the lower bodily stratum. In practice, deliberately "talking through his arse" (clever, yes, but precisely the wrong step: following through on the invocation of the talking, or better *speaking*, arse is to transform the site of Tzara's true subjectivity, consequently to subjectivise the arse, and ultimately to resign to the logic of bourgeois subjectivity – not, it should be stressed, the desired trajectory of the present essay) allowed Tzara to expose and implicitly to denounce all conditions laid down by society, precisely to allow the functioning of such conditions to be thought, the impetus being, as Kristeva makes clear, to "break out of our interpersonal and intersocial experience if we are to gain access to what is repressed in the social mechanism: the generating of signifiance" (1984: 13).

8. Tristan Tzara, Calligramme, *1920*

Language in Tzara's writings is considered as a material entity specifically of the body, although it too in his pronouncements possesses a high level of ethereality: "the trajectory of a word, a cry, thrown into the air like an acoustic disc" (1992: 13). Being of the body, although not exclusively so, language exists in Tzara's artistic configuration on an equal footing with "stone, wood, iron, tin, rocks … [and] sensation", while it possesses the "spiritual" force of the "fart in a steam engine". Tzara was not inclined to derive his speculative meditations on language from linguistic theories of the time. Rather, language was conceived of in terms of a poetics of dynamic rhythmic movement, much as was found in the poetic practice of writers like Joyce in *Ulysses* and *Finnegan's Wake*, Surrealism's language of the unconscious, and the floating lines of Kandinsky.[2] According to Tzara, the primary feature of language lies in the fact that it "is the gait of the intonations we hear" (1992: 77).

In poetic and dramatic practice the rhythms of language were expressed through a poetry of the voice, the dislocation of syntax and the dissociation of word and lexigraphical meaning. The simultaneous poetry of the Cabaret Voltaire performances brought into relief the materiality of the vocal dimension of poetic language. Furthermore, the vocalisation of language always extends beyond individual subjectivity, beyond the catharsis of shouting random and invented words. "Noises", Hugo Ball notes, "are existentially more powerful than the human voice" (Richter 1966: 30), but in this seeming cacophony, of which the voice is a part, the voice is constantly under threat of extinction, not through the sheer volume of the former, but through its properties of organisation into the mechanistic process, and its absorption of the voice therein. It must be noted however that part of the dynamic process that resists absorption of the voice into the systematising functions of language is inherent in the body. Tzara's response to the systemic dynamic of language was deconstructive and interruptive with his boombooms and page-long "howls" (1992: 8, 48), and the simultaneous poems. In the performance piece, "The First Celestial Adventure of Mr. Antipyrine, Fire Extinguisher", the interjection of "meaningless" sounds into verse forms based otherwise on free association augments the vocalic-performative dimension of the poem, enacting the poem as a corporeal emission, albeit of linguistic structure:

> zdranga zdranga zdranga zdranga
> di di di di di di di di
> zoumbye zoumbye zoumbye zoumbye
> dzi dzi dzi dzi dzi dzi dzi dzi (Tzara 1916a)

For Hugo Ball, the performance of such chaotic linguistic material proved intolerable and, in an epiphanic moment, rejecting Tzara's poetics of noise, he introduced to his performances the organisational principle of religious liturgy (Richter 1966: 31). While it is not necessary to endorse the religious aspect of this conclusion, Ball's insight is nonetheless profound in its recognition that the repetition of vocal sound series without lexigraphical meaning reveals a sonorous and ritualistic dimension of language, a temporal and corporeal dimension through which semiotic systems are generated and sustained. The syllable itself is an eructation from the body carrying with it the contortions of the lungs, throat, tongue, mouth and even arms – "they have lost their arms / mouncangama / they have lost their arms / managara / they have lost their arms" (Tzara 1916a) – required for linguistic articulation. The word in the context of a semiotic system is a sign that derives its meaning in part from the fact that it is differentiated through the physiology of those who utter it, and thus, while it congeals into a hypostatic system expunging the body from its semantic functions, the body remains as an elemental trace carried on the rhythms of breathing and phonetic differentiation.

2. The senselessness of the text

The resistance to lexigraphical sense was strategically developed elsewhere in dadaland, of course; Raoul Hausmann, we know, wilfully abandoned communication in his optophonetic poetry. Kurt Schwitters subsequently performed his own strategic manipulation of Hausmann's innovation – specifically, Schwitters's *Ursonate* or primal sonata, his long phonetic poem developed from Hausmann's optophonetic "fmsbw" ("tözäupggiv"),[3] expanded with the addition of vowels and the resonance of inner sound:

> Fümms bö wö tää zää Uu,
>   pögiff,
>   kwïï Ee (Schwitters 1973: 214)

What Schwitters did (and what Hausmann deliberately did not) was positively to engage his audience in its responding to the *Ursonate* at a collective level of cognition – not because the word-like configurations functioned in any sense as stable signifiers, but because of Schwitters's use of the rhythmic structure of the classical sonata.[4] By so doing, he restored a signifying structure to a phonetic composition, which, during its public performance, successfully engaged the audience for the full twenty-eight minute duration. From the initial confusion as its expectations were offended, the audience reassumed self-control as any hope of finding a conventional meaning was abandoned. But,

> [t]he suppressed feeling of uneasiness gives way to an increased tension, which leads to a loss of control, to a collective laughter of the audience. The laughter, which broke the resistance to the

work, is followed by a period of silence by the listeners. They enjoy the rhythms, patterns, and become aware that their pre-conceptions were wrong, that perhaps all phenomena are mean-ingless patterns. (Kuenzli)[5]

Where this summary ends, the audience's horizons begin to change as, by a process of defamiliarisation, there occurs an "artistic decon-struction of the pseudoreality of everyday life", and the confounding of codes forces their constant revision.

There is a charged political import to this social perception of changing horizons, characterised at one level by spontaneous "schizo-phrenic laughter or revolutionary joy ... not the anguish of petty narcissism", but joy at the freedom grasped when thought is put "into contact with the exterior ... [giving] birth to Dionysian laughter" (Deleuze 1985: 147). Laughter functioned – and functions – as a means to intensify states of experience that, for Gilles Deleuze at least, must resist codification and conversely must be seen as a dy-namic flux that intensifies the distancing movement as we are carried to our horizons, and beyond them:

> It is a continuous flux and the disruption of flux, and each pulsional intensity necessarily bears a relation to another intensity, a point of contact and transmission. *This* is what underlies all codes, what escapes all codes, and it is what the codes themselves seek to translate, convert, and mint anew. In his own pulsional form of writing, Nietzsche tells us not to barter away intensity for mere representations. Intensity refers neither to the signifier (the represented word) nor to the signified (the represented thing). (Deleuze 1985: 146)

Such intensity then resides outside of code, outside of our ability to conceptualise it as the agent *and* object of decodification. It is pre-cisely in these terms that Deleuze identifies Nietzsche's originality in producing a form of aphoristic writing that not only resists but defies codification: rather than signify meanings, Nietzsche's aphorisms transmit forces (1985: 146).

Quite evidently, Deleuze's intention is to discard any inter-pretive pretence in the reading of texts, and is rather to experiment and to promote change on political grounds, made explicit in his obser-vation that "[i]n a book, there is nothing to understand, but much to make use of. Nothing to interpret or signify, but much to experiment with" (Deleuze and Guattari 1981: 67-68). The processes of codifi-

cation in all their socially manifest forms are what he sees as constituting the very being of politics, and to the extent that reading is a
political act, the imperative for Deleuze is to move out not only of the
text but also of the context. Noting in contrast Derrida's "*Il n'y a pas
de hors-texte*", whose meaning in a later attempt to salvage it from
misinterpretation has been suggested as "there is nothing outside
context" (Derrida 1988: 136), Alan Schrift suggests that "the task is
not to remain within the textual network but to execute lines of escape
into extra-textual practice (not to interpret the world, Marx would say,
but to change it!)" (Schrift 1995: 256). So on this level, Deleuze specifies Nietzsche's use of aphorism, and its relation to the exterior as a
field where forces meet head on, where "new forces come from without, that traverse and cut across the Nietzschean text within the framework of … the aphorism as a phenomenon … that waits for new
forces to come and 'subdue' it, or to make it work, or even to make it
explode" (Deleuze 1985: 146). The text *works* as a tool, as a machine
part in the extra-textual practice, and its functional use as such is
precisely what prolongs the text. Thus literary texts do not function in
purely descriptive and representational terms, and literary language
revolutionises itself by drawing on its corporeal provenance.

3. The incarnate logic of paradox

In *Revolution in Poetic Language*, Julia Kristeva famously presents
her description of the text as a practice directly comparable to political
revolution ("the one brings about in the subject what the other introduces into society"; 1984: 17). According to Kristeva, this revolutionary moment occurs in "modifications of the function of negation or in
syntactic and lexical modifications" (1984: 124). In modernist poetry,
the excess of negativity destroys the preeminence of the mutually
exclusive opposition, and in its place introduces a process of infinite
differentiation. Tzara is adamant in his rejection of a form of thought
wherein the truth of a situation or proposition is based purely on the
power of logical negation or the exclusion of the counter claim. Such
thought, for Tzara, goes against what he takes to be the principle of
life: "the roar of contorted pains, the interweaving of contraries and of
all contradictions, freaks and irrelevancies" (1992: 13). What is more,
Tzara speculates that insofar as logic has any validity outside of its

semantic function, it is as an "organic disease" (1992: 9), suggesting not only the poet's rejection of the demand to follow the rule of the syllogism, but also the notion that contradiction, paradox and *impasse*, and other such figures of rational limit, point to the body as both the other of reason and an integral component of it.

Here we might instructively consider Schopenhauer's critique of Kantian and Cartesian philosophy. For Schopenhauer, the world can only ever be known to us as it is mediated through formal systems of language and knowledge (Schopenhauer 1969: 3). However, this means that knowledge of the body is always ontologically equivalent to that of objects in the world. If the world is a representation – a claim to which Schopenhauer is committed – then the body is always only known as a representational object. Yet, in fact, the body conditions representation in the first place; therefore, the body is part of the subjective structure of knowledge (Schopenhauer 1969: 19-20), an insight that is impermissible in the Kantian and Cartesian frames of reference. Schopenhauer then proceeds to argue that there is such a thing as immediate knowledge of the body, only it does not possess an epistemological form. It is rather a kind of power, or *kraft,* a corporeal idea that he termed *will* (Schopenhauer 1969: 103-110). Art, especially music, is the symbolic form of this kind of knowledge. This being said, however, art or literature can never attain to such direct knowledge of will, insofar as that which exceeds representation can only ever be known through representational form (Schopenhauer 1969: 184-186). Art thus contains at its centre a logical and existential paradox, a constant deferral of symbolic certainty. As such, artistic activity serves as the nonhypostatic dynamic of linguistic and symbolic systems. Art, for Schopenhauer, eschews the abstract transcendence of the Kantian system, embracing instead the temporality of the body for which the only certainty is the fluctuating movement of living and dying, and, of course, as Sloterdijk (and Tzara) would insist, shitting.

The very uncertainty of this temporal, if not temporary, body loosens its conceptual stability and corporeality, unhinging it from "the depraved European superstructure of ideas" that previously rigidly held it in place (Sloterdijk 1988: 397); necessarily therefore to loosen everything that claims security, transforming fixity into mobility, precisely to the extent that "to be a Dadaist means to let oneself be thrown by things, to oppose all sedimentation; to sit in a chair for a

single moment is to risk one's life" (Huelsenbeck 1989: 246).
Sloterdijk poses this as the affirmative, invigorating cultural potential
of dada as intellectual movement that is constant in its resistance to
the formation of sediment by the rejection of all notions of style. The
Letzte Lockerung manifest, written by a complex figure in relation to
Zürich Dada – disgraced Viennese doctor Walter Serner – was a text
"composed of cultural critique and cyanide" (Sloterdijk 1988: 397)
rousing into "a violent and simultaneously playful bursting of all cultural semantics, of positing meaning, philosophies, and exercises in
art" (Serner 1995: 160). For Serner himself, preempting the Deleuzean
trajectory to put thought into contact with the exterior, "one must
bellow the utterly indescribable, the totally inexpressible, so unbear-
ably close up that no dog would wish to continue leading its life so
smartly – but rather far more stupidly! So that everyone loses their
wits and gets their heads back again!" (1995: 160).

Serner's declamatory tone carries the political charge and
urgency of the manifesto, an urgency imparted upon its public to
move towards a new sensibility whose "feeling of well-being is as
great as the mere feeling of woosiness they had experienced until then.
One must. One simply must. *Teremtete!*" (1995: 160). There are here,
of course, consequences in terms of the body that are not unproblematic, to the extent that certain of the manifesto's logical conclusions
might quite literally be very difficult to live with. Serner's intellectual
disgust at the constitution of the subject within western society makes
no concession for his own desperate subjectivity, his rejection of
which as being devoid of any value is consistent with his manifesto
logic in a broader sense: "before falling asleep imagine with the
greatest clarity the terminal mental state of a suicide who at last
wishes to plumb the depths of self-awareness with a bullet" (1995:
159). The act of suicide makes known its uncomfortable presence in
the form of the ultimate emancipation, as Serner would have it, a
moment of intensity that fuses together the self and its consciousness;
it is the Dadaist's unbiased and equal treatment of all meaning and all
generation of meaning with the same contempt. His cynical intro-
spection sees nothing but disconnected "word mixtures" and he
reverses the projection from inside to outside:

> [T]o clap a redeeming heaven over this chaos of filth and enigma!
> To perfume and order this pile of human excrement! Thanks a lot!
> [...] THAT's the reason ... why philosophies and novels are

sweated out of people's pores, pictures are daubed, sculptures
hewn, symphonies groaned out and religions founded. What ap-
palling ambition, especially because of these vain asinine games
… have come to a complete nought. (Serner 1995: 156-157)

Even under state coercion into a system and a structure, the dis-
connectedness of the world, and representation in the world, remains
such.

9. Walter Serner and Tristan Tzara, Zürich 1919

There are metaphysical assumptions in Serner's claims that
warrant critical treatment, assumptions that he himself through the
despair of his declamations seeks to overcome, not through transcendence or utopian renewal, but through direct kynical engagement.
Beneath the clinical and orderly world of language and thought, which
Serner abhors, there lies a substratum of "chaos of filth", split off from
but underpinning the social symbolic order in the classic dualistic
form of mind and matter. This point may be illustrated by reference to
structuralist linguistics, where signification is seen as a purely systemic affair. Structuralism removed the paradoxical relation between
the body and the system of language by privileging the linguistic
system over the act of speaking. It is understandable that theorists
want to show that the field of signification does not necessarily arise
from subjective intentionality, but rather from systemic dynamics and

differentials. However, the consequence of this is that the body is removed from the field of meaning only to return as a *tabula rasa* upon which society would inscribe its imperatives. To be sure, it is the case that our bodies are shaped by the systems in which we are inculturated, but it is also the case that such systems exist in a dialectical, if paradoxical, relation with the body, as Schopenhauer and much post-structuralist thinking has claimed. Thus, it is necessary to show that while the signifier and the signified are indeed bound by convention, there is also at play a crucial corporeal dynamic – Dada may be seen to be engaged in an exploration of the complex corporeality of language, that is of the social symbolic system. This is not to suggest that the body takes over where enlightenment subjectivity left off. On the contrary, the embodied voice may be intentional in a phenomenological sense, but it does not determine meaning; rather, it is a point of intervention, an elemental differential that drives the linguistic system.

Merleau-Ponty characterises the logic that binds the linguistic act with the linguistic system as an "incarnate logic", and the particular form that this logic takes is what he terms the chiasm, a circular logic where opposites, such as *maxima* and *minima*, become one another. Such a theory of language is based on a particular analysis of the structure of sentience, where the relation between the perceiver and the perceived is characterised not by the ability to absorb and reconstitute or to recognise and decipher, but by "reversibility". Between bodies and within bodies there is a fundamental split into the sentient and the sensible, the one that actively feels, and the one that is felt. The reversibility of the relation is "a sort of dehiscence [that] opens my body in two" (Merleau-Ponty 1968: 123). One does not bring about the identity of an external object through an act of negation. The distance between the object perceived and the perception is the distance of "flesh". It is the "thickness of being", as Merleau-Ponty terms it. Such distance is simultaneously proximity, insofar as it is what connects the individual body with the world:

> The flesh is not matter, is not mind, is not substance. To designate it, we should need the old term "element", in the sense it was used to speak of water, air, earth, and fire, that is, in the sense of a *general thing*, midway between the spatio-temporal individual and the idea, a sort of incarnate principle that brings a style of being wherever there is a fragment of being. (Merleau-Ponty 1968: 139)

Flesh is a carnal principle of divergence without coincidence, the "hiatus" between the sentient and the sensible that allows both of these elements to take on a certain function and bring about the dynamic of perception. There is no causal relation between language and Serner's "filth of chaos", nor does language involve a superimposition: "the meaning is not on the phrase like the butter on the bread" (Merleau-Ponty 1968: 155). What Merleau-Ponty does speak of is a nascent logos of the world, an architectonic of the body which is also that of language, and accordingly, quoting Valéry, language is "the voice of no one" (1968: 155). It is impersonal and it speaks through us. Yet it is human beings who speak, who are moved by music, who converse, tell jokes and use language creatively in conversation, literature, science and philosophy. It is not necessary, insists Merleau-Ponty, to discover some synthetic rule that would bind the two contradictory elements of the impersonal *langue* with the speech act (*parole*). Rather, they are two aspects of the reversibility thesis: "speech prolongs into the invisible, extends unto the semantic operations, the belongingness of the body to being and the corporeal relevance of every being" (1968: 118). It is precisely at the point where a synthesis would be sought to resolve the relationship between language and world, word and body, that Merleau-Ponty locates the term "flesh".

Elements in Tzara's poetry construct the work as anatomy. The phonetic eructations spoken of above are words that reveal their formative processes as a relation between the body and the social symbolic, the act of speaking, breathing, the pulse of the organism and the impersonality of the linguistic systems. The poetics of flesh reside here not exclusively on one side or the other, and thereby resist the analytical pull of dualistic reductionism. If an utterance may be considered a breath, it is also one that carries with it from the start its metamorphosis into language, where the latter is based on elemental difference. The opening lines of Tzara's *Vingt-cinq poèmes* – "le sel se groupe en constellation / d'oiseaux sur la tumeur do ouate / dans ses poumons les astéries et / les punaises se balancent / les microbes" – describes a cosmos wherein the crystallisation of saline particles, a tumour on the lungs, galaxies, insects, the microscopic world, phonetic emissions from the mouth, and, by extension, the existence of a poem, function in the contexts of complex forces of configuration and dissolution. The poem itself is a nontotalisable world of body parts and other spatially located objects in a temporal flux. There is no narrative subject that might embody the poetic voice in a unified and living physiology. Instead, the fragmented voice is this world of objects in a state of species specific movement. Here one may not speak of the body as a metaphor for the voice, or the voice as an expression of the body. There is no metaphoric structure to speak of, a fact guaranteed by the fragmentary nature of the voice.

A similar phenomenon exists in "The First Celestial Adventure of Mr. Antipyrine", where Mr. Shriekshriek's sexual organ takes on the dimensions of a volcano:

> masks and rotting snows circus
> pskow
> i push factory in the circus pskow
> the sexual organ is square is iron is
> bigger
> than the volcano and flies off
> above mgabati
> offspring of distant mountain
> crevasses (Tzara 1916a)

The poem sets up a comparison of the sexual organ and the volcano, yet the sexual organ also inhabits the same world as "offspring of distant mountain", and further on in the verse the poem links all elements in a kind of gigantic virgin birth (parthenogenesis). Here again, there is no notion of metaphor; or rather, metaphor is a power of linguistic semiosis, or the corporeal generation of abstract symbolic systems. Deleuze and Guattari state that the metaphor is not *like* something; it *is* that something; Freud's Wolfman does not represent himself as a wolf, but fears the process of becoming a wolf, if not being one (Deleuze and Guattari 1988: 32). Thus metaphor is not so much a matter of similarity, but of becoming, a concrete and dynamic ontology; the sexual organ and the mountain become, through the dynamic of elemental differentiation (flesh), the body of the signifier, and concomitantly it is through this process that the social symbolic is sustained in a process of becoming.

4. Agency, avant-garde and the body

"Dada is working with all its might towards the universal installation of the idiot", said Tzara (1992: 42). The social correlative of the desubjectivised, fragmented voice of the Dadaist poem is the idiot, a social actor who refuses the certainty of the relation between signifier and signified that society offers. The "universal installation of the idiot" is strongly resonant of Sloterdijk's ideal philosopher, the kynic Diogenes, whose refusal to live according to social-symbolic convention earned him the nickname "dog", but who, in insisting on autonomy, "negates not only the desire for power, but the power of desire as such" (Sloterdijk 1988: 161); that is, subjective desire assumed to emanate from, and to serve the needs of, the ego. It is important not to mistake Diogenes's indifference for apathy, just as Tzara's idiot is not a person who has been crushed by society. In both of these figures, as in the fragmented, unplaced voice of flesh in Tzara, desire flows through pathways that far exceed those of the individual subject, with its miserable ego. Thus, a corporeal dynamic, shaped by and shaping the forces of our inculturation, draws into its gathering pace a re-inscribed notion of agency and, inevitably, a not-easily dismissible aspect of autonomy (as it might be embodied in Serner's disengaged identity, for instance).

The always implied freedom in claims for autonomy tends towards generating a sense of social independence for the individual in metaphysical terms, but crucially it does not exclude views of the individual as shaped by the social environment. However, maintaining that same notion, the language of autonomy will reproduce the conditions that hide the shaping process from view, and mask the way an individual is constituted by language and culture as they are continually renewed in the social environment. What constitutes the social is as irreducible to an aggregation of individuals as is its relation with each individual to causal interaction. The social is also constitutive of the individual, as self-defining interpretations are drawn from the interchange by which the social proceeds. The distinction in place is between ourselves as organisms and ourselves as human beings: the former are separable from the social, but for human beings such separation is unthinkable. Taken outside of the social, the human being would no longer *be*, and the notion of human agency becomes inconceivable: predictably, even the autonomous agent is only conceivable

within social limits, and autonomy consequently appears as an illusion. What does not necessarily follow, however, is passive compliance with the culturally constructed notion of transparency, which
is always the assumed premise for the use of words in language as a
means to marshal ideas. The danger in this assumption is that it
perpetuates the belief that ideas are assembled to match the real, when
what occurs in fact is compliance with the continuing construction of
ideas, and the words that ought to function as instruments gain in the
ascendant: using words, then, we are controlled instead of controlling.

To reach the point at which language functions efficiently as
the infamous mobile army of metaphors requires maintenance of the
illusion of the total transparency of language as a theoretical instrument of control, assembling ideas into thought. What transparency
does is secure the meanings of words to nothing more than the ideas
they designate, and this connection gives each word its definitive
meaning. But, in the absence of any attentiveness to or stress on definition and consistency in the use of words, the collective lie gains
momentum, and

> the alternative is to lose control, to slip into a kind of slavery;
> where it is no longer I who make my lexicon, by definitional fiat,
> but rather it takes shape independently and in doing this shapes
> my thought. It is an alienation of my freedom as well as the great
> source of illusion [...]. (Taylor 1985: 226)

This alienation anticipates capture and arrest by the army of metaphors, not least because the structuralist critiques generated out of
theoretical observation on language claim to have accounted fully for
purely designative views; and further, the expansion of Frege's
original emphasis on the sentence as the crucial unit of meaning (as
opposed to the word) leads to the poststructuralist assertion of the text
as an indissoluble whole. But it is to this concern with meaning that
the above alienation most directly refers and alerts us, in terms of the
deployment of segments of language to say something through the
symbolic constructions they constitute. The residence of meaning
therein as significant by virtue of the individual's aspiration rests on
what we can break down in the symbolic object (the word or the sign)
to its initial dimension as designative, as being meaningful by what it
can be used to refer to or talk about in the world; out of the
designative then emerges the expressive dimension where feelings are

made manifest in a way that cannot be contrasted with a non-expressive (that is the empiricist designative) mode of presentation: "what expression manifests can *only* be manifested in expression" (Taylor 1985: 219). The combined functioning of the designative and the expressive therefore positions the symbolic construction as meaningful in terms of relating both to the objects it is about and to the feeling or thought it expresses.

Where, then, does this leave the arse ... and specifically the speaking arse? Its inclusion in any future physiognomic philosophy would necessarily posit the somatic propaedeutic as an "organ without a body" (OwB), an object that we would not argue as being subject-less, but rather "the correlate of the 'pure' subject prior to subject-ivisation" (Žižek 2004: 174). This priority is the condition that allows the kynic to speak as a subject that has not yet been subjectivised and, as Slavoj Žižek reasons following Deleuze, "the subject emerges out of the person as the product of the violent reduction of the person's body to a partial object" – in our instance, the arse (2004: 175). The expressive theory of language can potentially yield far more than the descriptive designative theory, opening up a dimension wherein we might not only achieve a new descriptive awareness of things, but moreover new feelings and responses to things as being constitutive of more than the expression of already existing feelings.[6] By a logical progression, the suggestion is that if our expression of thoughts results in our having new thoughts, then our expression of feelings can engender in us transformed feelings that are in some way heightened and more self-aware. This is to signal in us a reflective awareness, clearly so, but a reflective awareness that is always deployed within the structure. Importantly, it is not only the potential use of language that is transformed and extended by the expressive theory, but equally the conception of the *subject* of language. When we admit to the primacy of language as an activity, as what the process of speech constantly creates and recreates, then the conversant constituency generating speech becomes relevant in terms of the functioning of the social system reshaping language as a speech community. To this extent, language shaping, effect and reshaping here becomes reminiscent of the description of the process of signification, but resists the subsequent closures at which a negative reading of structuralist conclusions is prone to arrive. Through an expressive theory, language can be shown to take its place within a range of activities encompassing the spectrum of symbolic expressive capacities, allowing us in turn to realise a certain way of being in the world.

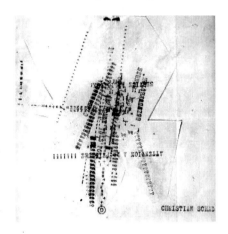

10. Christian Schad, Portrait of Walter Serner, *1920*

The impetus inevitably is to move language away from its function as a multi-purpose tool of thought, and towards a conception of it as an activity constituting a specific way of *being*. But, increasingly, what is at stake is not simply the nature of expression, but also the question of *who* or *what* expresses when metaphor and the theory of the lie operative within the language community activates agency. There is no conflict, of course, according to the designative view, which upholds that my lexicon is always under my control; but in its application, my speech is only ever effective beyond solitary existence for as long as I remain an interlocutor in a speech community, whose currency is formed through intersubjective agreement and an acknowledged need to communicate. The choice emerges, then, in terms of the expression that makes us human as being *either* a romantic self-expression *or* some kind of response to the communal reality in which we exist, a reality in which we are included, but which nonetheless is not reducible to the experience of it expressed by us. It is all too easy to recognise the unquestioned assumptions that western society makes in terms of a thinly disguised romanticism, which holds that what we are expressing in artistic creation is the *self*. The structuralist departure from such an assumption, however, maintains that our most expressive creations are in fact not *self*-expressions. Rather, their expressive power results from their manifestation of our own expressive capacity and its relation to the world: instead of romantically exteriorising our feelings, in this kind of expression we respond to the way things are. This is indeed radical in its departure towards a notion of expressivism that is anti-subjectivist – or pre-subjectivist, as Žižek suggests – taking up Nietzsche's original observations on the illusion of truth in language, and moving towards what Heidegger has described in connection with the human assumption of mastery over language, when in fact the opposite is the case:

> for in the proper sense of these terms, it is language which speaks. Man speaks insofar as he replies to language by listening to what it says to him. Language makes us a sign and it is language which first and last conducts us in this way towards the being of a thing. (Heidegger 1975: 239)

In the sense that we function as signs, we recognise (painfully, at the loss in prospect of our own, metaphysical angst) that what we are attempting to express is primarily something other than our selves – something that comes *before* our selves as subjects. Far from forcing the abandonment of the metaphysical position, what now concerns us is a *different* application of objective accounts of the form the body assumes linguistically and symbolically in western culture.

Notes

[1] This trajectory of Beckett's work begins with his first published novel, *Murphy* (1938), is deepened in the trilogy of novels (1950, 1951, 1952 respectively) and the "quagmire" *How It Is* (1964), becoming less intense but more pervasive in *Worstward Ho* (1983).

[2] Kandinsky speculated that words, as well as designating objects, experiences and concepts, were inner sounds and as such possessed emotionally poignant qualities like rhythm, colour, and light. Wassily Kandinsky, "On the Spiritual in Art". In *Kandinsky: Complete Writings on Art*. 1994. Kenneth Lindsay and Peter Vergo (eds). New York: Da Capo Press: 147-148.

[3] Illustrated in Anna Schaffner, "Assaulting the Order of Signs", page 122 in the present volume.

[4] Hausmann criticised Schwitters: "I reproached him for having transformed my innovation ... into a 'classical' sonata. That seemed to me a blasphemy, a contradiction of the phonetic function of the letters which I had chosen." "Kurt Schwitters wird Merz", in *Am Anfang war Dada*, p.68.

---

[5] This summary is provided by Kuenzli of a contemporary account of Schwitters's first reading of the *Ursonate* to an audience consisting mainly of military officers in 1925, in "Communication and the Avant-Garde", with reference to A. J. Peter Froehlich, "Reaktionen des Publikums auf Vorführungen nach abstrakten Vorlagen", in Wolfgang Paulsen (ed.), 1982, *Sinn aus Unsinn: Dada International*, Bern: Francke: pp. 15-28. See also Richter's account in *Dada: Art and Antiart*: p.142-143.

[6] Taylor cites Condillac's theory of the invention of language in the expressive cry, a theory that itself relies on certain presuppositions, i.e. that there already exists an understanding of what it is for a word to stand for something (Taylor 1985: 227).

References

Deleuze, Gilles
    1985   "Nomad Thought". In David B. Allison (ed.). *The New Nietzsche: Contemporary Styles of Interpretation*. Cambridge: MIT Press.

Deleuze, Gilles and Guattari, Félix
    1981   "Rhizome" (trs Paul Foss and Paul Patton). In *I&C* 8 (Spring).

    1988   *A Thousand Plateaus: Capitalism and Schizophrenia* (tr. Brian Massumi). London: Athlone.

Derrida, Jacques
    1988   *Limited Inc* (tr. Samuel Weber). Evanston: Northwestern University Press.

Descartes, René
    1968   *Discourse on Method and the Meditations* (tr. F.E. Sutcliffe). Harmondsworth: Penguin.

Hausmann, Raoul
    1980   "Kurt Schwitters wird Merz". In *Am Anfang War Dada*. Karl Riha and Günter Kämpf (eds). Giessen: Anabas-Verlag.

Heidegger, Martin
    1975   *Poetry, Language, Thought* (tr. A. Hofstadter). New York and London: Harper Colophon.

Huelsenbeck, Richard
    1989   "Collective Dada Manifesto" (1920). In Robert Motherwell (ed.) and Ralph Manheim (tr.). *The Dada Painters and Poets: An Anthology*. Cambridge: Belknap Press: 242-246.

Kristeva, Julia
    1984   *Revolution in Poetic Language* (tr. Margaret Waller). New York: Columbia University Press.

Kuenzli, Rudolf
    Forthcoming   "Communication and the Avant-Garde". The University of Iowa.

Merleau-Ponty, Maurice
    1968   *The Visible and the Invisible* (tr. A. Lingis). Evanston: Northwestern University Press.

Richter, Hans
    1966   *Dada: Art and Antiart*. London: Thames and Hudson.

Schopenhauer, Arthur
    1969   *The World as Will and Representation* (tr. E.F.J. Payne). New York: Dover.

Schrift, Alan D.
    1995   "Putting Nietzsche to Work: The Case of Gilles Deleuze". In Peter R. Sedgwick (ed.) *Nietzsche: A Critical Reader*. Oxford and Cambridge: Blackwell.

Schwitters, Kurt
    1973   *Das literarische Werk*. F. Lach (ed.). Cologne: DuMont.

Serner, Walter
    1995   "Last Loosening Manifesto". Malcolm Green (tr.). In *Blago Bung Blago Bung Bosso Fataka!* London: Atlas.

Sloterdijk, Peter
    1988   *Critique of Cynical Reason*. Michael Eldred (tr.). London: Verso.

Taylor, Charles
    1985   *Human Agency and Language: Philosophical Papers 1*. New York: Cambridge University Press.

Tzara, Tristan
    1916a   *La Première aventure céleste de Mr. Antipyrine*. Zürich: Collection Dada. Translation by Ruth Wilson, "The First Celestial Adventure of Mr Antipyrine, Fire Extinguisher", available at: http://www.cis.vt.edu/modernworld/d/tzara.html

    1916b   *Vingt-cinq poèmes. H. Arp, dix gravures sur bois*. Zürich: J. Heuberger.

    1992   *Seven Manifestos and Lampisteries*. Barbara Wright (tr.). London: Calder.

Žižek, Slavoj
    2004   *Organs Without Bodies: On Deleuze and Consequences*. New York and London: Routledge.

II. Dada and Language

The Language of "Expatriation"

T. J. Demos

Abstract: "The Language of 'Expatriation'" places the language games of Marcel Duchamp in relation to the artist's exile during the years of the First World War. The essay argues that Duchamp's self-professed "spirit of expatriation", through which he conceptualised his decontextualisation from dominant systems of conventional identity (including the pervasive culture of nationalism), was negotiated at the level of artistic form. Pieces including *The*, *Erratum Musical*, and *With Hidden Noise* released upon language the force of "becoming" – articulated by Duchamp, related to Bergsonian philosophy, and resonating with Deleuzean theoretical insights – which intertwined identity and difference in a mutually transformative and infinite cycle. The resulting internal mobility that was established within Duchamp's artistic practice expatriated language from its basis in repetition, thereby opening up a new modelling of indeterminate existence beyond the rule of equivalence, habit, and tradition.

"I had left France basically for lack of militarism. For lack of patriotism, if you wish. I had fallen into American patriotism, which certainly was worse." – Marcel Duchamp

"In particularly unfavourable social conditions, such a separation between the person and the ideological environment that feeds him can lead to a total decomposition of consciousness, to madness or dementia." – Mikhail Bakhtin

In 1915, Duchamp arrived in New York, escaping from the unfavourable social conditions of French patriotism. One of the first artworks he created in that new context was a peculiar piece entitled *The*. On a simple piece of paper he handwrote a series of sentences in English. Each word is recognisable and the elements of each sentence agree grammatically, yet the meaning of each phrase only leads to nonsense. "If you come into * linen, your time is thirsty because * ink saw some wood intelligent enough to get giddiness from a sister." Further disfiguring these sentences is the seemingly random invasion of a number of stars, or asterisks, into the text. At first this is baffling, but we soon discover directions at the bottom of the page: "remplacer chaque * par le mot: the". This is easily enough done, but the stars still interfere with the text, and even with the appropriate substitutions it continues to make no sense. One reason is that various codes inexplicably intersect. Decomposing, language verges into a visual materiality beyond its symbolic functions, while the graphic contours of the text come to life and grow into a pictorial landscape. We are simultaneously made sensitive to both the morphological elements of writing and the signifying potential of abstract signs. The piece madly juggles these categories and thus confuses its own assignment in terms of medium. Is it a poem or a drawing? It wants to be both. *The* straddles the terrain between the linguistic and the visual, producing taxonomic indeterminacy and general disorientation – a madness that is key to Duchamp's project during this time.[1]

This radical uprooting of language has no clear precedent with regards to either artistic practice newly investigating hybrid constructions of text and image, or avant-garde poetry that had recently begun to explore the plastic capacities of writing. While Cubist collage around 1912 had recontextualised the pages of French newspapers, relieving words of their symbolic functions as mechanically reproduced text entered the terrain of drawing, the resulting still lifes retain a handmade preciousness and the mark of extraordinary creative invention.[2] This commitment to artisanal skill and the display of virtuosity is completely absent in *The*. And in the realm of poetry, while certain authors had recently experimented with the expressive possibilities of the visual properties of writing, exemplified in the Italian Futurist context and specifically in the compositions of Marinetti (who benefited from the earlier advances of Mallarmé, particularly his famous poem *Un Coup de dès jamais n'abolira le hasard*), the aim was to direct the symbolic power of typography and print layout to redouble the referential force of words. Marinetti desired that his terms explode like bombs on the page – an ominous goal in the context of the author's pro-fascist militarism. This political aggressivity and bombast couldn't be further from Duchamp's pacifist convictions at this time.

The is completely casual, committed to arbitrariness, resolutely asymbolic and anti-expressionist. Yet while certainly modest, it was not without its own power: *The* forces language to create its own originary and constituent condition, inviting unconventional invention and spontaneous construction, allowing the viewer/reader to figure out his or her own interpretive approach to the piece.

11. Marcel Duchamp, The, *1915*

The signals a flight from visual and linguistic conventions, manifesting a wilful rejection of the structuring conditions of traditional identity, especially its orientation within language. Through it, Duchamp negotiated his numerous flights during the war years. It was Duchamp's spirit of expatriation and life in exile that gave rise to this radically alternative aesthetic, as he, and other participants in what would later be called Dada, focused specifically on the experimental possibilities of language, seeking ways to channel it toward endless decodings and recodings beyond the conventions of tradition.[3] Duchamp, in fact, was himself like that star within *The*, positioned precariously within shifting geographical fields, continually casting himself into ever new environments, or fleeing old ones, discovering

room for play within a field constricted by the pressures of nationalism through an embrace of indeterminacy and the wilful confusion of
categories. His artistic practice gestures toward the resulting fluid
identity, which we might say was the goal of his travels: to discover a
flexible relationality that would adapt to any new location, that would
define the self through foreignness. *The* is exemplary. Rather than
merely undertaking a systematic application of substitution, which
would itself suggest a logic of equivalence in the repetition of the
same (* = the), the exchanges in *The* lead to the continual production
of singular iterations, to the differential rather than the similar. Each
star appears unique – even if subtly so – according to its ever-shifting
location and the specificities of its hand-written inscription. Thus
Duchamp's use of the star does not simplify language, render it hiero-
glyphic, or reduce it to an eventual homogeneity or universal system.
Instead, it makes the meaning of language uncertain, blocking its supposed transparency or assumed neutrality, and thereby opens a zone of
indeterminacy within language. "Perhaps I had the spirit of expatriation, if that's a word", Duchamp later explained, pointing toward a
provocative way in which we might reconsider his practice (cited in
Gough-Cooper and Caumont 1993: 6 January, 1961). It is this "spirit
of expatriation" that infuses *The*.

*

Duchamp's "spirit of expatriation", according to one possible interpretive approach, represented an oppositional force directed against nationalism, which was reaching its apogee during these early years of
the twentieth century. While this definition of his expatriation may not
fully determine Duchamp's work during this period – it is precisely
the flight from totalisation, I would argue, that marks his exodus – it
does extend the reach of his practice and render it a new level of intelligibility unappreciated in past scholarship. Of course, wartime European nationalism was multifaceted, culturally and historically specific,
and Duchamp's practice contests certain aspects of it more than others
– particularly its effects on language and its construction of subjectivity and social relations. Analysed by various commentators after the
First World War, nationalism has been understood as both cause and
effect of the formation of a group subject according to which individual volition was outweighed by participation within what Benedict

Anderson would later call an "imagined community" that suppressed regional divisions and ethnic particularities to give rise to national consciousness (Anderson 1983). This "imagined community" – a useful term because it stresses the fictional basis of such a collective – no doubt responded to and was constituted by several factors. These include: the growth of new social bodies following the demographic shifts toward urbanisation; political pressures to define a mode of collective unity that would counter the splintering effects of capitalist economic inequality and the uneasy integration into the shocking reality of industrial production; and the development of new systems of cultural imagination produced through advertising and propaganda, facilitated by emerging technologies of reproduction and mass distribution. Present within all of these complex modern formations, far from an exhaustive list, was the homogenising pressure placed on language – from within print media, radio, and the visual arts – which encouraged the binding of group members through a shared medium of commonality (Hobsbawm 1990; Silver 1989).

As an engine of fusion, nationalism would unite difference into "identity", tending toward a culture of enforced sameness that activates the etymological foundation of the latter term (*idem* in Latin, meaning "the same"). For Freud, who analysed it in 1921 after the brutal catastrophe it brought about, nationalism represented a massive "picture of regression" characterised by the desire of the subject to return to an earlier psychological state of Oedipal attachment through social fusion, which drowns out capacities for independent thinking and critical distance (Freud 1959). Its psychology betrays a fundamentally destructive relation to the other, as observed by Lacan slightly later during its ominous repeat in the 1930s. Yearning to recapture a sense of psychic integration by seeking out an imaginary lost state of oneness, the nationalist, according to Lacan, remains haunted by repressed anxieties of fragmentation, which he sadistically projects outward, potentially engendering a genocidal moment of destruction (Lacan 1977). Lacan's analysis proved an accurate forecast of things to come. Meanwhile, for Bakhtin, writing within the Soviet context, the destructive workings of nationalism were exposed in the Stalinist pressures of ideological regimentation exerted in the realm of language, where one encountered "forces that unite and centralise verbal-ideological thought, creating ... the firm, stable linguistic nucleus of an officially recognised ... language" (Bakhtin

1992: 270-271).[4] In other words, nationalism's structure of social-isation aims at the achievment of collective fusion through a unified language purified of differentiation. While these views represent ad-mittedly only a brief précis of the many insightful analyses of nation-alism during the inter-war period, they are sufficient to define its gen-eral system from the critical perspective of its opponents.

Duchamp's term "expatriation" similarly opposed the unify-ing and centralising tendencies of nationalism: "From a psychological standpoint I find the spectacle of war very impressive", he announced while in the States in 1915. "The instinct which sends men marching out to cut down other men is an instinct worthy of careful scrutiny. What an absurd thing such a conception of patriotism is!" (cited in Tomkins 1996: 152-53). Yet beyond a simple anti-nationalist political position, Duchamp's expatriation expanded to the generalised rejec-tion of the various and broadly defined institutions that regulate language and its subject, unfolding to a tripartite negation of paternal filiation (*ex-père*), national loyalty (*ex-patrie*), and fidelity to the contract and hierarchies of labor (*ex-patron*). This was performced in Duchamp's various abandonments – of France, of paternal ties to the ruling systems of reproduction (dramatised especially in his creation of the feminine alter-ego Rrose Sélavy, but incipient in his voluntary exile), and of traditional forms of manual craft and expertise that still defined artistic labor in the early twentieth century. As he explained, his "spirit of expatriation ... was part of a possibility of my going out in the traditional sense of the word: that is to say from my birth, my childhood, from my habits, my totally French fabrication. The fact that you have been transplanted into something completely new, from the point of view of environment, there is a chance of you blossoming differently, which is what happened to me" (cited in Gough-Cooper and Caumont 1993: 6 January, 1961). According to this expansive definition of the term expatriation, extending it beyond a simply pol-itical critique of nationalism, Duchamp represented the perfect *anti-Oedipus*, tracing an independent existence outside the state of "gener-alised Oedipalism," meaning the overlapping and mutually reinforcing familial, social, and political hierarchies through which the forces of modernity have constituted identity and tamed its desires, according to the complex but strikingly relevant analysis presented by Deleuze and Guattari (1993).[5]

What is left in the wake of the abandonment of these conventional institutions? Perhaps it is best here to return once again to *The*. The piece projects language outside of any unitary or normative system, opening it up to a polyphony of discourses, from jumbled verses of hybrid textual fragments to visual codes of abstract inscription. For Duchamp, it was a "kind of amusement" (Schwarz 1997: 638). He was only at the time beginning to learn English, and the recourse to his own geographical dislocation suggests a conceptual entrance to the stakes of *The*. His language was neither simply a humorously failed attempt at the practice of a foreign tongue, nor a wry exposition of the embarrassing mistakes of the non-native or hapless immigrant. Rather, the encounter with a different language posed an opportunity for Duchamp to dwell with pleasure in language as pure material otherness, to actively dislodge it from its normal instrumentalised or expressive functions. "The meaning in these sentences was a thing I had to avoid", he later explained. "The construction was very painful in a way, because the minute I *did* think of a verb to add to the subject, I would very often see a meaning and immediately ... I would cross out the verb and change it." The goal was to create a text "without any echo of the physical world" (Schwarz 1997: 638). This game entailed not so much the avoidance of physicality *per se*, but instead the will to avoid that form of repetition that would merely re-present the world as it already exists, including past artistic strategies and linguistic conventions. The resulting space was one of splintered meanings, shifting forms, opening a passage to becoming – in other words, the uncertain and radically undetermined space of expatriation, as defined by Duchamp.

Expatriation embraces the force of dispersion – breaking from father, boss, and country – also similarly discovered in its family of like terms. This includes "exile", from the Greek *ex* ("away") + *al* ("to wander"; cf. *alasthai*, "I wander"); and "diaspora", from the Greek *dia* ("apart" or "through") + *speirein* ("to scatter"). Unlike the unifying energy of nationalism, expatriation reveals fissures within official institutions and dominant ideological configurations, opening up areas of indeterminacy within language which is, one might say, inherently driven toward multiplicity. "Language – like the living concrete environment in which the consciousness of the verbal artist lives – is never unitary", Bakhtin notes. "It is unitary only as an abstract grammatical system of normative forms, taken in isolation from the

concrete, ideological conceptualisations that fill it, and in isolation
from the uninterrupted process of historical becoming that is a
characteristic of all living language" (Bakhtin 1992: 288). Writing in
exile in Kazakhstan during the mid-thirties, Bakhtin theorised what he
termed "heteroglossia", and named the process by which language
shatters in multiple discursive directions, its centripetal energy placed
in a constitutive relationality with other speakers, codes, forms of
speech, all of which shift over time. The heteroglot would naturally
resist the monolingual reductions of nationalist forces, and thus offers
one way to theorise the aesthetics of expatriation.

   If the rupture from the dominant ideological environment and
from its system of unified language resulted in a kind of "madness",
as observed by Bakhtin, then that term describes the circumstances
according to which language no longer makes sense in any traditional
way. No doubt the diagnosis of madness, however, owes to the
illegibility of the break from convention *from a conventional perspective*, for the new language – as in *The* – exceeds its categories and
flees its modes of comprehension. Yet projects like *The* engender not
so much a state of decomposed consciousness and dementia in a
clinical sense, but rather what Todorov calls a "mad polyphony",
occurring when the codes of language are unexpectedly cross-wired
and creatively modified. *The* materialises a pure state of linguistic
possibility, one not yet constituted or institutionalised, but suggestive
of different possible paths of development. That this notion of mad
polyphony intimates a space of multiple languages is not surprising; in
the case of Duchamp, it relates back to the thematics of geographical
travel (Todorov 1992).

*

The origin of Duchamp's spirit of expatriation might be traced to
1912, when he witnessed the staging of *Impressions d'Afrique*, a play
adapted from Raymond Roussel's eponymous novel (Gough-Cooper
and Caumont 1993: June 12, 1912). It is a quirky story of a group of
European passengers on board a ship bound for Buenos Aires that is
blown off course and runs aground off the coast of West Africa. The
extravagant King Talou VII takes the survivors captive, and during
their hostage they set themselves to making a series of bizarre inven-
tions and performing outrageous feats for Talou's coronation cere-

mony – the one-legged Breton, Lelgoualch, plays melodies on a flute made from his own tibia; La Billaudière-Maisonnial invents a fantastic fencing apparatus; Balbet, a marksman, shoots the shell off an egg at a distance without breaking the inner membrane; and Louise creates a painting machine out of a combination of photographic camera parts and mechanised paint brushes, which duplicates on canvas any landscape before it with all of the perfect subtleties of its natural colour. The book is a story of European modernity confronting its primitive fantasies, where travel to distant lands inspires fascination and reveals new sources of creativity through winding tales of humorous intercultural translations.

For Duchamp, the exposure to *Impression d'Afrique* was critical, and he later claimed that Roussel, beyond all other influences, "showed him the way" toward subsequent artistic developments:

> It was fundamentally Roussel who was responsible for my glass, *The Bride Stripped Bare by Her Bachelors, Even.* From his *Impression d'Afrique* I got the general approach. This play of his which I saw with Apollinaire helped me greatly on one side of my expression. I saw at once I could use Roussel as an influence. I felt that as a painter it was much better to be influenced by a writer than by another painter. And Roussel showed me the way. (Sanouillet 1973: 126)

What had he seen in the play? One thing is certain: Roussel deployed a thematics of displacement, wherein the geographic decontextualisation of subjects was matched by the cultural transposition of objects, and this greatly appealed to Duchamp. In Roussel's play, everyday things were projected outside their normal context and forced to function in unexpected ways. This opened up creative options beyond the stultifying routines of daily life.

Later that year, Duchamp took this to heart and was off to Munich, casting himself into a foreign environment where he knew virtually no one, later claiming it was the "occasion for my complete liberation" (cited in De Duve 1991: 104). It was there that he entered a radically different cultural context and became sensitive to the relativity of artistic practice, evident in German artistic approaches utterly foreign to the priorities of his local group of painters back in Puteaux. It was there, argues Thierry de Duve, that Duchamp inaugurated his so-called nominalist aesthetic, according to which artistic practice, namely painting, was severed from any substantial form or foundational activity, cut off from any essential materiality, medium, or style, and instead understood to be fully conventional, relative, and dependent upon the shifting regulatory mechanisms of cultural, linguistic, and socio-political institutions. It was according to this system that a readymade could be considered a painting, as Duchamp reasoned: "Since the tubes of paint used by the artist are manufactured and ready made products we must conclude that all the paintings in the world are 'readymades aided' and also works of assemblage" (Sanouillet 1973: 142).

This transformation was obviously prompted by Roussel, whose aesthetic strategies were taken up within Duchamp's own practice. As several commentators have observed, and as Duchamp himself has confirmed, Roussel's zany machines clearly resemble the bio-mechanical hybrids that populate the *Large Glass* (Krauss 1977; Joselit 1992). Composed in lead and dust on glass, its medium, which he began to conceptualise in Munich, lies completely outside French artistic traditions. The placement of a chocolate grinder within an elaborately imagined mechanical apparatus that schematised the psycho-sexual drama of a bride and several bachelors was surely inspired by *Impression d'Afrique*. It is also easy to see in Roussel's aesthetic model a point of departure for Duchamp's invention of the readymade. The projection of an object into a completely foreign environment, as in the example of a snow shovel placed in an art gallery, enabled its function to be re-imagined, and this proposes a clear artistic analogue to Roussel's testimony to the creative promise of dislocation. This procedure of decontextualisation for Duchamp would overturn traditional artistic protocols of artisanal production and formalist modes of reception, as well as the definitions of artistic medium and the functions of the art institution. The following year, in 1913, Duchamp would inaugurate this project with a bicycle fork and wheel turned upside down and mounted on a stool, presented in his Paris studio – an unusual hybrid of repurposed everyday things, which created a foreign space of indeterminacy that comes straight out of a Rousselian grammar.

One function of Roussel's conventionalisation of aesthetic form was his mechanistic method for building narrative development. *Impression d'Afrique* was written through an extraordinary system in which the author generated outlandish narratives by playing with near-identical phrases that served as bookends to his stories. He explained the logic behind what he called his "method" in *How I wrote Certain of my Books*, published posthumously in 1935: he would choose identical terms, or homonymic words, yet draw on their different meanings in order to wrap identity and difference into uncanny association,[6] the famous example being: "Les lettres du blanc sur les bandes du vieux billard" [The white letters on the cushions of the old billiard table], which he transformed into: "Les lettres du blanc sur les bandes du vieux pillard" [The white man's letters on the hordes of the old plunderer] (Roussel 1995: 3-4). In each instance, the contextual placement of individual words (though always remaining ambiguous) defines the meaning of the entire sentence. As in the case above, what matters is whether *billard* or *pillard* ends the phrase, and, in addition, where the line is placed contextually within the larger diegetic structure of the book.

Due to this profound relationality, the desubstantialisation of language was total: words lose any sense of an essential or natural value. Rather, they become homeless. Like readymades, they are completely context-dependent, contingent, and precarious, ever adapting to new locales that redefine them in turn. As Foucault writes in his study of Roussel, which could be easily extended to Duchamp's language games with minor alterations: "Words from anywhere, words with neither home nor hearth, shreds of sentences, the old collages of the ready-made language, recent couplings – an entire language whose only meaning is to submit to being raffled off and ordered according to its own fate is blindly given over to the grandiose decoration of the process" (Foucault 1986: 38). In other words, rather than returning to the recycling of the same, Roussel's repetition was directed toward the ongoing production of singularities, whereby homonyms would simultaneously generate identity (resemblance between like terms), yet produce endless differentiations in form and meaning. This provokes the continual eradication of equivalence. In its course, identity would be given over to difference, as the thematics of travel join up with the expatriation of language.

*

Duchamp soon came up with his own Rousselian compositions, as described in one of his notes from the teens, later included in the *Green Box*:

> Take a Larousse dictionary and copy all the so-called "abstract"
> words, i.e. those which have no concrete reference. Compose a
> schematic sign designating each of these words (this sign can be
> composed with the standard stops). These signs must be thought
> of as the letters of a new alphabet. (Sanuoillet 1973: 126)

To some degree, the note describes *The*, where the "schematic sign"
of the star signifies an "abstract word" and comes to designate a new
grammatical modulation within language, suggesting "a new alphabet" released from "concrete reference". That Duchamp employed this
mechanistic process and followed its instructions fairly robotically
suggests a bureaucratic procedure, which would denude the myths of
creative inspiration and claims of originality to posit artistic practice
fully within the grips of capitalist administration, itself a remarkable
artistic innovation at this time. Beginning with a dictionary, Duchamp
paradoxically found the resource for creative newness within the
already made. Yet clearly, the motivation was not limited to a parodic
mimicry of administrative order and its deadening repeated behav-
iours.

Why create a new alphabet? Several of Duchamp's notes written during the teens offer a clue. In them he describes the desire to
release the force of "becoming" on things defined by repetition –
which suggests another articulation of expatriation. In one note, titled
"shadows cast by Readymades," Duchamp conjures

> a figure formed by an equal [length] (for example) taken in each
> Readymade and becoming by the projection a part of the cast
> shadow … Take these "having become" and from them make a
> tracing without of course changing their position in relation to
> each other in the original projection. (Duchamp 1960: n.p.)[7]

In slightly simpler terms, the note describes the transformation of
readymades – objects fabricated within the system of industrial mass
production – into "having become." In other words, readymades
would be freed from the rule of repetition and pushed into the materialisation of difference. As such, they answered a proposition that
Duchamp posed in another note: "To lose the possibility of identify-
ing/recognising 2 similar objects – 2 colours, 2 laces, 2 hats, 2 forms
whatsoever to reach the Impossibility of sufficient <u>visual</u> memory"
(Duchamp 1960: n.p.).

To unleash the force of becoming from within the very site of repetition so that the very perception of similarity was lost – this was at the heart of Duchamp's practice. Duchamp was thus not solely interested in exposing the repetition that had come to dominate modern life, which the readymade nevertheless did reveal:

> Another aspect of the "Readymade" is its lack of uniqueness ... the replica of a "Readymade" delivering the same message; in fact nearly every one of the "Readymades" existing today is not an original in the conventional sense," as Duchamp noted in "Apropos of Readymades". (Sanouillet 1973: 142)

Going further, Duchamp wished to create room for play within that very system, such that perception and visual memory would no longer be obligated by repetition, even if his creations critically acknowledged its rule. The readymade would also materialise difference within repetition, enacting a form of expatriation from dominant epistemologies. By designating a mass-produced object as a readymade, Duchamp would thereby recontextualise it – both spatially, conceptually, and linguistically – brooking new possibilities of contextual redefinition, creating "a new thought for that object".[8] The figure of repetition was thus thrown into uncertainty, unleashing a self-differing identity from within the homogeneous sphere of sameness. Moreover, by developing this source of "becoming" in relation to language, by *speaking* it, Duchamp channelled that force of difference so that it flowed through the body. The force of becoming would materialise on the tongue, causing the viewer to break free from his or her habitual forms of reading and articulation. This would initiate a new and unexpected relation to the world gained through a flight from it, exemplifying how Duchamp would continue to "blossom differently".

*

After seeing Roussel's play, Duchamp experimented with other methods for expatriating language, as evidenced in *Erratum Musical* (Musical Misprint), created with his two sisters Yvonne and Magdeleine during a trip home to Rouen in January 1913. It consists of a score for three voices, each of which would sing the same line adopted from the banal dictionary definition of "imprimer" (to print): "Faire une empreinte; marquer des traits; une figure sur une surface; imprimer un scau sur cire" (To make an imprint; to mark with lines; a figure on a surface; to impress a seal in wax). While its Latin title makes a nod to traditional sacred music, familiar in France's Catholic rituals, its content acknowledges his family's involvement in the printing industry, forming two references the song then proceeds to scandalise by mixing categories into an aural clash. Like Roussel, Duchamp began his compositional method with multiple instances of the same sentence – the dictionary definition sung by each voice. Then the three musical melodies were thrown into chaos by an aleatory procedure: musical notes (from F below middle C to high F) were written down on individual pieces of paper to be picked out randomly from a hat. "Each one of us drew as many notes out of a hat as there were syllables in the dictionary definition of the word *imprimer*, picked by chance" (cited in Schwarz 1997: 572). Their order was re-corded in three sequences, which provided the vocal compositions. In these atonal lines, notes alternate arbitrarily between treble and bass clefs, and the relation from one note to the next was always un-expected and utterly dissonant, no doubt presenting challenges to singers trained in traditional melody. No performance instructions were given: the voices could be sung sequentially or simultaneously.[9]

For Duchamp, this was certainly one of his first attempts at what he would soon term "canned chance," entailing the domesti-cation of the arbitrary through its systematic, predetermined deploy-ment.[10] In so doing, he humorously juxtaposed the standardisation of printing technique, evidenced in its dictionary definition, and the arbi-trariness of chance-based procedures, furthered by hand-printing the score. Seemingly modest, *Erratum Musical* is a signal development in Duchamp's practice. It first broached the dialectic of standard measure and chance variation, thereby generating a relay between identity and difference, which would carry tremendous significance for his later practice, as well as for future developments in minimalist and con-ceptual art and music. Not only do the two categories intertwine in the course of the composition of *Erratum Musical*, producing three very singular musical articulations of the same sentence (which, when sung together, would be free from the contrapuntal requirements of trad-itional musical harmonies), but also each new performance would yield a unique iteration – one performance would never be the same twice. Repetition was thereby joined to multiplicity, rather than de-fined by identity. This was no structure of theme and variation familiar in traditional music – there was no theme to begin with. A similar logic was employed in the more famous but equally enigmatic *Three Standard Stoppages* later that year, in which three lines of thread, each a meter long, were dropped from a distance of a metre to the ground.[11] Here too Duchamp threw identity and difference into a mutually disruptive relay. The self-difference that resulted owed to the failure of the dropped thread to equal its abstract measurement, or to ever exactly repeat the forms of its counterparts, despite all being of the same measure. For Duchamp, this was "a joke about the metre", made by flouting the claims of abstract measure.[12]

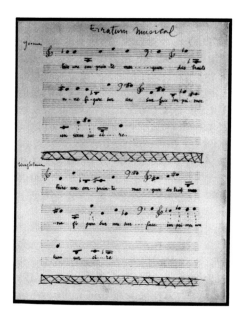

12. Marcel Duchamp, Erratum Musical, *1913*

Yet unlike *Three Standard Stoppages, Erratum Musical* stands out for its collaborative creation and performance. Composed and sung originally by three siblings, it projects difference into the family structure – the supposedly primordial unit of the community and fundamental template of the nation (etymologically from the Greek *natio*, or "born from"), often understood variously as the home-land, mother- or fatherland. While collaborative, the piece opposes harmony and unity – unless it means the unity of difference. This is also true in terms of the single voice, which would be no unified structure. Duchamp's expatriation initiated a profound sense of self-division, which he playfully called "a little game between 'I' and 'me'". "My intention was always to get away from myself, though I knew perfectly well that I was using myself" (Kuh 1962: 90). In other words, Duchamp replaces the "group subject" of nationalism, founded upon social fusion and collective unity, with the "subject-group" of expatriation (to use a term of Deleuze and Guattari's), meaning the fundamental and inexorable multiplicity of the self (divided between "I" and "me") and positioned in the relay of identity and difference. The piece proposes a collective sharing around forms of hetero-geneity, which was true to Duchamp's lifelong goal to avoid his own subsumption by, or within, a group. This was not simply about splin-tering language into irretrievable parts; rather, division would be the basis upon which the social could be re-constituted, which would propose an intriguing and humble alternative to nationalism. This ex-perimental sociability would prefigure Duchamp's later experimental exhibition projects, which would create spaces of collective belonging built upon differentiation, prohibiting the formation of social unities or fused communities.[13] As such, *Musical Erratum* is a perfect instanti-ation of mad polyphony, mad because it resists the unity of identity, its continuity, and selfsame structure, giving rise to a polyphony that divides the self and prohibits regressive social union.

The bilingualism of *Erratum Musical* – split between its Latin title and French verse – was further advanced as a source of expatriate destabilisation in Duchamp's *With Hidden Noise*, created slightly later in 1915. Composed of a ball of twine, the sculptural work contains an object supplied by Walter Arensberg and unknown to Duchamp. The ball is enclosed between two brass plates connected at their corners by four large screws. Inscribed on each surface are three rows of un-related, fragmented words in English and French, whose letters are intermittently omitted and replaced with periods. To complete the terms – banal words like "leg", "lorsque", "however", and "carré" – letters must be borrowed from words in the lines above or below, like an alternative form of a crossword puzzle. Duchamp called it "an ex-ercise in comparative orthography (English–French)" (Schwarz 1997: 644). As in *The*, substitution comes into play, but now it becomes variable – the periods, like the fragments of so many ellipses, stand in for a variety of letters, which can be further determined based on their contextual location. The dot becomes a site where, as Joselit observes, material inscription and virtual meaning interact in multiple ways (Joselit 1998: 79-83). But *solving* the puzzle and completing the words so that they become identifiable is not exactly the point. As Duchamp explained, "French and English are mixed and make no 'sense'". Nor do these terms propose any connection – whether symbolic or otherwise – to each other or to the materials on which they are inscribed. This senselessness also issues from the noise made by shaking the piece, which parallels the meaninglessness of the text that follows language's reduction to pure sensation and pure material possibility. *With Hidden Noise* possesses a centre that remains hidden, thus thwarting the verification of identity. Yet the hiding of an object is only the most obvious sign of this negation; the language itself opposes the notion of identity, as it is formed through the intertwinement of repetition and difference. The point is to experience the slide of language into a non-symbolising materiality and the opening up of materiality to a multiplicity of meanings – allowing, as in *The*, both language and material to "become".

13. Marcel Duchamp, With Hidden Noise, *1916*

This relay between identity and difference also extends to the bilingual character of *With Hidden Noise*. By dividing itself between two systems – French and English – the purity of any one language is abandoned. The piece stresses the relation *between* two languages, rather than privileging or naturalising either. Because one can never fully replace the other, or adequately translate it, each is made to face its own limits, which is further stressed by the fragmentary and precarious quality of the words. Such a strategy of self-hybridisation, for others, became a weapon: The German-Jewish Adorno remembered the effects of his own use of foreign words in everyday speech at the same time: The careful deployment of "foreign words constituted little cells of resistance to the nationalism of the First World War", which delivered a rending violence to the nationalisation of language, such that "with our esoteric foreign words we were shooting arrows at our indispensable patriots" (Adorno 1991: 186). The power of these arrows owed to the fact that they demonstrated the incompleteness of any one language, thus dramatising language's ultimate inability to exhaustively represent the world or to totalise its own system to the degree that translation is unnecessary. Similarly, to employ a foreign language, for Duchamp, did not entail turning to another tongue out of convenience, as if pragmatically making use of its own parallel set of conventions and vocabulary appropriate to this or that geographical or cultural context. Instead, the point was to create a hybrid of polylingual terms and diverse materials that mixed codes and functions – such that translation became endless and unavoidable, indeed representing the very possibility of *any* meaning. Duchamp drew on this expatriation as a source of disruption that revealed the partiality and the internal discursive multiplicity of *all* languages. This was an extraordinary gesture at a time when nationalism was at its height of ideological functioning, which entailed, among other things, the purification and homogenisation of language as if it were organically rooted in the territory and its community. Duchamp's gesture may have lacked the overt political motivations of Adorno's use of foreign words; yet it remains a striking example of the resistant force of his "spirit of expatriation".

The following year, Duchamp created *Rendez-Vous du Dimanche 6 Février 1916*, which continues this trajectory. The piece is constructed from four postcards that are taped together and addressed to his American patrons, the Arensbergs, with whom he was then staying in New York. On its verso, a nonsensical text typed in French runs over the four cards, its logic similar to *The*. "There would be a verb, a subject, a complement, adverbs, and everything perfectly correct, as such, as words, but meaning in these sentences was a thing I had to avoid," Duchamp explained. "The verb was meant to be an abstract word acting on a subject that is a material object, in this way the verb would make the sentence look abstract" (Schwarz 1997: 642). In this Rousselian gambit, *Rendez-vous* empties out language through systematic contextual confusion. The text retains syntactic structure but sacrifices semantic sense, dispersing the coherence of sentences by atomising their meaning. Individual words and syntax make sense, but they fail to add up to any commonsensical significance. Moreover, the frequent hyphenation of terms at the edges of each postcard casts them further into estrangement and makes the text recede into de-signifying graphic matter. The visual repetition occasioned by the frequent devolution of letters to horizontal dashes at the ends of the cards suggests an all-over composition, which further undermines the referential functions of language and the text's narrative cohesion. *Rendez-vous* privileges its purely visual organisation and makes language travel, as much as the postcards were meant to, implying a radical linguistic-geographical migration. It was only appropriate that in exile, Duchamp threw his mother-tongue into flight.[14]

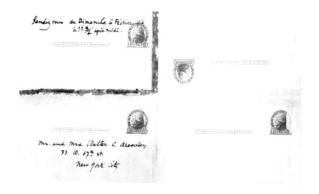

14a. Marcel Duchamp, Rendez-vous du Dimanche 6 Février 1916, *1916*

This suggestion of an artwork that travels reveals further lines of flight from institutional control. The errant spatial positioning of the artwork – projected outside of the museum/gallery and into the mail (though it was never actually sent) – parallels its linguistic deracination from the traditional centres of language. Duchamp was clearly looking for ways to break out of the established circuits of artistic display, just as he was personally committed to his own expatriate dislocation. It is precisely this radical decontextualisation – to be dispersed, blown off course, placed in a relation to incongruous

circumstances, whether from language, land, or traditional institutional structures – that defines Duchamp's spirit of expatriation.

14b. Marcel Duchamp, Rendez-vous du Dimanche 6 Février 1916, *1916*

*

Duchamp's expatriation throws repetition into a relay with difference,
which is succinctly articulated by Deleuze: "what repeats, repeats the
unrepeatable" (Deleuze 1993: 1). Rather than viewing the identical
under the sign of the similar, which works to produce generality,
Deleuze redefined repetition along Bergsonian lines, such that variation does not obscure repetition, but serves as its very condition.
Consequently, "that which becomes" overwhelms the repetition of the
"same," which contests longstanding Platonic reason and its subordination of difference to the power of the One. Returning is precisely
the becoming-identical of becoming itself, and within this cycle identity is constituted over space and time in the repetitive movements of
change, spiralling off into perpetual revolution.

    Ultimately, Duchamp was not after a radically different iden-
tity that would replace traditional forms yet retain its own rigid in-

ability to change. Neither was he chasing an impossible form of pure difference outside of the continuity that serves as the minimal requirement of identity, for otherwise change would be unintelligible. He was instead attempting to approach a position of mutability driven by the continuous force of becoming, a repetition within difference that would itself be the meaning of his self and the object of his artistic practice. The result would be artworks open to endless transmutation, given over to ceaseless forms of relationality, but maintaining a minimal degree of continuity. This would entail an exodus not from, but within identity.

15. Marcel Duchamp, Tonsure
(Duchamp with haircut by George de Zayas, Paris, photo by Man Ray), 1921

In 1919 Duchamp had the shape of a star cut into the hair on the back of his head (*Tonsure*). Here, the articulations of his artistic practice – as in *The* – intersected with his bodily appearance, as language's flight crossed over Duchamp's own physical decontextualisation. Duchamp threw himself into the flux of expatriation, rewriting his own appearance, and giving life to his own inscriptions. The star, or comet, would be a sign of his own becoming, a kind of ephemeral tattoo, impermanent, open to its own eventual erasure or cut. It was a conventional symbol, readymade: Duchamp was of course aware that no sublime state of pure becoming could ever exist; rather, one could only move between institutional structures and readymade forms in a perpetual counterpoint of capture and escape. In this sense, the star prefigured the coming transformations of Duchamp's identity, such as the invention of Rrose Sélavy a few years later, which wrapped him in a new clothing of signs whose referents mixed altered genders and the language of capitalist marketing. There, in the midst of the social, political, and economic reproductions of the self, Duchamp would find his own sources of identity and difference. While Duchamp was never so naïve as to believe he could live perpetually in a pure state of possibility, he never agreed to exist simply within the repetitions of everyday life.

Notes

[1] Duchamp first published *The* in the October 1916 issue of *The Rogue* (New York).

[2] The *reading* of the text of Picasso's collages is a contentious issue, divided between the position of Krauss (1989) and that of Leighten (1990).

[3] See my "Zürich Dada: The Aesthetics of Exile".

[4] As Stalin himself wrote in *Marxism and the National and Colonial Question* (1912): "A nation is an historically evolved, stable community of language, territory, economic life and psychological make-up manifested in a community of culture" (cited in Hobsbawm 1990: 5).

[5] For further analysis of Duchamp's work in relation to Deleuze and Guattari's *Anti-Oedipus*, see Joselit (1992).

[6] Of course, the Surrealists loved Roussel, and during his lifetime formed his most dedicated audience.

[7] This note relates to Duchamp's photograph *Shadows of Readymades*, 1918, which I treat at length in "Sculptures for Traveling", in *The Exile of Marcel Duchamp*. My analysis here develops out of that chapter.

[8] In "The Richard Mutt Case" (1917), Duchamp writes: "Whether Mr Mutt with his own hands made the fountain or not has no importance. He CHOSE it. He took an ordinary article of life, placed it so that its useful significance disappeared under the new title and point of view – created a new thought for that object" (reprinted in Harrison and Wood 2003: 252).

[9] When the S.E.M. Ensemble performed the piece at the Paula Cooper Gallery in New York, 17 December 1991, they sang each voice in order, then all simultaneously. Sung all together, the piece provides a precedent to the simultaneous poem, developed by Tristan Tzara in the context of the Cabaret Voltaire in 1916.

[10] In one note from the *Green Box*, Duchamp wrote: "3 Standard Stops = canned chance – 1914" (Sanouillet 1973: 33).

[11] Illustrated in David Cunningham, "Making an Example of Duchamp", page 248 in the present volume.

[12] Duchamp describes the piece in a questionnaire from the Museum of Modern Art as "a joke about the metre – a humorous application of Riemann's post Euclidean geometry which was devoid of straight lines" (cited in Henderson 1998: 61). See Joselit, who develops a reading that focuses on the "infinite regress" between abstract

systems of measurement and material flux in Duchamp's work during the teens, in "Between Reification and Regression: Readymade and Words" (Joselit 1998: 31).
[13] For further analysis of these projects, see my *The Exile of Marcel Duchamp*.
[14] While Joselit articulates the relation between this artwork and the force of deterritorialisation, his reading remains at a somewhat ethereal theoretical level. The question of how Duchamp's practice animated this disruptive force within the conflicts around identity and community as they were caught within the nationalist pressures of the First World War remains (Joselit 2005).

References

Adorno, Theodor
      1991   "Words from Abroad" in Tiedemann, Rolf (ed.) *Notes to
                Literature. Volume 1 (tr. Shierry Weber Nicholsen). New York:
                Columbia University Press: 185-199.

Anderson, Benedict
      1983   *Imagined Communities*. New York: Verso.

Bakhtin, M. M.
      1992   "Discourse in the Novel" (1934–35), in *The Dialogic Imagination*
                (tr. Caryl Emerson and Michael Holquist). Austin: University of
                Texas Press.

Deleuze, Gilles
      1993   *Difference and Repetition* (tr. Paul Patton). New York: Columbia
                University Press.

Deleuze, Gilles and Guattari, Félix
      1983   *Anti-Oedipus: Capitalism and Schizophrenia* (tr. Robert Jurley,
                Mark Seem, and Helen R. Lane). Minneapolis: University of
                Minnesota Press.

Demos, T. J.
      2005   "The Aesthetics of Exile" in *The Dada Seminars* (ed. Leah
                Dickerman). Washington: National Gallery of Art: 7-31.

      Forthcoming   *The Exile of Marcel Duchamp*. Cambridge: MIT Press.

Duchamp, Marcel
      1960   *The Bride Stripped Bare by her Bachelors, Even* (tr. George
                Heard Hamilton). London: Edition Hansjörg Mayer.

De Duve, Thierry
      1991   *Pictorial Nominalism* (tr. Dana Polan with the author).
                Minneapolis: University of Minnesota Press.

Foucault, Michel
      1986   *Death and the Labyrinth: The World of Raymond Roussel* (tr.
                Charles Ruas). Garden City: Doubleday.

Freud, Sigmund
      1959   *Group Psychology and the Analysis of the Ego* (tr. James
                Strachey). New York: Norton.

Gough-Cooper, Jennifer and Caumont, Jacques
    1993   "Ephemerides on and about Marcel Duchamp and Rrose Sélavy,"
    in Pontus Hulten (ed.) *Marcel Duchamp: Work and Life.*
    Cambridge: MIT Press: n.p.

Harrison, Charles and Wood, Paul (eds)
    2003   *Art in Theory: 1900–2000.* London: Blackwell.

Henderson, Linda Dalrymple
    1998   *Duchamp in Context.* Princeton: Princeton University Press.

Hobsbawm, E. J.
    1990   *Nations and Nationalism since 1780.* New York: Cambridge
    University Press.

Joselit, David
    1992   "Duchamp's Monte Carlo Bond Machine" in *October* (59): 9-26.

    1998   *Infinite Regress: Marcel Duchamp, 1910–1941.* Cambridge: MIT
    Press.

    2005   "Dada's Diagrams" in *The Dada Seminars* (ed. Leah Dickerman).
    Washington: National Gallery of Art: 221-240.

Krauss, Rosalind
    1977   "Forms of Readymades: Duchamp and Brancusi" in *Passages in
    Modern Sculpture.* New York: Thames and Hudson: 69-104.

    1989   "The Motivation of the Sign" in *Picasso and Braque: A
    Symposium* (eds Lynn Zelevansky and William Rubin). New
    York: Museum of Modern Art: 261-286.

Kuh, Katherine
    1962   "Marcel Duchamp" in *The Artist's Voice: Talks with Seventeen
    Artists.* New York: Harper & Row.

Lacan, Jacques
    1977   "The Mirror Stage as Formative of the Function of the I" in *Écrits*
    (tr. Alan Sheridan). New York: Norton: 1-7.

    1977   "Aggressivity In Psychoanalysis" in *Écrits* (tr. Alan Sheridan).
    New York: Norton: 8-29.

Leighten, Patricia
    1990   *Re-ordering the Universe: Picasso and Anarchism, 1897–1914.*
    Princeton: Princeton University Press.

Roussel, Raymond
    1995   *How I Wrote Certain of My Books* (ed. Trevor Winkfield, tr. John
            Ashbery et al). Boston: Exact Change.

Sanouillet, Michel and Peterson, Elmer (eds)
    1973   *The Writings of Marcel Duchamp*. New York: Da Capo.

Schwarz, Arturo
    1997   *The Complete Works of Marcel Duchamp*. London: Thames and
            Hudson.

Silver, Kenneth
    1989   *Esprit de Corps: The Art of the Parisian Avant-Garde and the
            First World War, 1914–1925*. Princeton: Princeton University
            Press.

Todorov, Tzvetan
    1992   "Bilingualism, Dialogism and Schizophrenia" in *New Formations*
            (17): 16-25.

Tomkins, Calvin
    1996   *Marcel Duchamp: A Biography*. New York: Holt.

Assaulting the Order of Signs

Anna Katharina Schaffner

Abstract: "Even signs must burn", Jean Baudrillard programmatically proclaimed in 1972. More than fifty years earlier, the Dadaists in Zürich and Berlin both poetically effectuated and theoretically anticipated Baudrillard's call for the assault upon the order of signs as a strategy of cultural intervention. The Dadaists shattered the order of discourse, dissected language on different levels of linguistic organisation and waged a cultural war at the level of signs by means of giving priority to the signifiers at the cost of the signifieds. They withdrew the most fundamental prerequisite of cultural consensus: the adherence to given linguistic laws. The points of convergence of Baudrillard's notion of the radical implications of attacking the order of the dominant code and the Dadaists' poetic practice, theoretical incentives and revolutionary intentions, are striking indeed and entangled in a complex web of anticipation, practical realisation and theoretical radicalisation. But is the assault on the order of signs doomed to remain a merely symbolic gesture of protest, or is there more to it?

1. Dada and Baudrillard: points of convergence

"Even signs must burn", Jean Baudrillard programmatically proclaimed in 1972 (1981: 163). More than fifty years earlier, the Dadaists in Zürich and Berlin both poetically effectuated and theoretically anticipated Baudrillard's call for the assault upon the order of signs as a strategy of cultural intervention. The Dadaists shattered the order of discourse, dissected language on different levels of linguistic organisation and waged a cultural war at the level of signs by means of giving priority to the signifiers at the cost of the signifieds. They withdrew the most fundamental prerequisite of cultural consensus: the adherence to given linguistic laws. The points of convergence of Baudrillard's notion of the radical implications of attacking the order of the dominant code and the Dadaists' poetic practice, theoretical in-

centives and revolutionary intentions, are striking indeed and entangled in a complex web of anticipation, practical realisation and
theoretical radicalisation.[1] But is the assault on the order of signs
doomed to remain a merely symbolic gesture of protest, or is there
more to it?

*

At the beginning of the twentieth century, times were tumultuous and
convictions in all fields of human knowledge disintegrated: technological changes impacted visibly upon the sphere of everyday-life,
epistemological, ethical and scientific certainties began to crumble
and the cruelties of the First World War crudely crushed humanist
hopes for a progressive and positive development of western societies.
"We are experiencing the most outrageous revolution of all areas of
human organisation today", writes Raoul Hausmann, protagonist of
Berlin Dada, in 1919. "Not only capitalist economy, but all truth,
order, law, morality, and all things masculine and feminine are dis-
integrating" (Hausmann 1982a: 50).

Art for the Dadaists was never art for art's sake, but in fact a
vehicle for the transportation of a profound and all-encompassing cultural criticism: "[t]he members of Club Dada were [initially] not concerned with art, but with materially new forms of expression of new
contents", Hausmann writes: "Dadaism [was] a kind of cultural criticism" (1982: 130). The Zürich Dadaist Hugo Ball voices a similar attitude:

> It can probably be said that for us art is not an end in itself –
> more pure *naïveté* is necessary for that – but it is an opportunity
> for true perception and criticism of the times we live in, both of
> which are essential for an unstriking but characteristic style.
> (1974: 58)

The Dadaists' disenchantment with the cultural and political status
quo was so fundamental and deep-seated that they felt they could no
longer express it within the boundaries of existing artistic and communicative conventions. "The most strident pamphlets did not manage
to pour enough contempt and scorn on the universally prevalent
hypocrisy", writes Ball (1974: 67), touching upon the very essence of
the problem: a critique so essential, radical and profound as required

by these circumstances, one which penetrates into and questions the very foundations of culture, cannot be delivered with the existing means of communication. In fact *all* orders – social, artistic and especially linguistic ones – could no longer be accepted as given, but had to be challenged.

"Dada is the deliberate decomposition of the bourgeois world of concepts/conceptual range [*Begriffswelt*]", reads a poster at the Berlin Dada fair in 1920 (Dachy 1989: 104). This statement is significant in two ways. Firstly, it very literally refers to one of the key techniques of the Dadaist poets: language dissection, the act of taking language apart on different levels of linguistic organisation. But beyond this, it alludes to the very reason why this technique was and still is so revolutionary and far-reaching in its implications in the first place. It is not just language which is dismembered, but in fact the bourgeois *Begriffswelt* and all that comes with it: convention, agreement and social consensus, hierarchies and power structures, the "Weltbild in der Sprache" ("conception of the world within language") and the possibility of stable meaning.

*

More than fifty years later, Baudrillard proclaims that signs and the code by which they are governed always already contain and perpetuate the logic and ideologies of the dominant order: "[a]ll the repressive and reductive strategies of power systems are already present in the internal logic of the sign" (1981: 163). The code itself, Baudrillard maintains, reproduces and enforces social order and has infiltrated and now dominates every aspect of it – and consequently, only an attack upon the code, upon the internal structure and organisation of the sign system of usage, can bring about change.

The era of the *simulacra*, Baudrillard writes in *Symbolic Exchange and Death*, is characterised above all by the fact that the classical dialectic of exchange- and use-value, as well as that of the signifier and signified, is in shreds: signs have gained complete autonomy from their referents, they float about autonomously, referring only to each other and no longer to any external values. Referential value is annihilated, and all that remains is the structural play of signifiers, instituted upon the death of reference. Just as exchange value is now completely detached from use value, existing independently from real needs and desires, the semiotic system operates autonomously from reality. Reality itself becomes *hyperreal*, Baudrillard argues: "[t]oday everyday, political, social, historical, economic, etc., reality has already incorporated the hyperrealist dimension of simulation so that we are now living entirely within the 'aesthetic' hallucination of reality" (1993: 74).

This new order of autonomous signs is dominated by the law of the code, which is "the purest, most illegible form of social domination, like surplus value". It is not class-bound, and is operative everywhere, beyond dialectics of industry and class, "a symbolic violence inscribed everywhere in signs, even in the signs of the revolution" (1993: 10). In Baudrillard's theoretical framework, it is the code that now effectively dominates everything.[2]

But does this notion imply that all protest becomes futile by definition, that the reign of the code is absolute and impenetrable? Or is there "a theory or a practice which is subversive because it is more aleatory than the system itself", asks Baudrillard, "an indeterminate subversion which would be to the order of the code what the revolution was to the order of political economy?" (1993: 4). There is in fact one and only one revolutionary strategy left in the age of the *simulacra*, Baudrillard argues: to attack the code itself. The war for social change has to be waged on a meta-semiotic level; the assault upon the order of signs now presents the equivalent to social revolution. The code has to be outwitted on its own territory and beaten with its own weapons, its own logic must be turned against itself, its own non-referentiality exceeded: "[t]hings must be pushed to the limit, where quite naturally they collapse and are inverted" (1993: 4).

2. Empty signifiers: zero-message in graffiti and sound poetry

"Western thought", Baudrillard claims, "cannot bear, and has at bottom never been able to bear, a void of signification, a non-place and a non-value" (1993: 234). In a spate of graffiti swamping New York in the spring of 1972, a flood of graphics consisting solely of names and numbers, sprayed or scribbled onto walls, subways and monuments, Baudrillard detects such a void of signification and potentially subversive zero-messages. Both the graffitists and the muralists, who acted upon the same political and social impulses but painted walls with explicit political and often aesthetically appealing images, Baud-rillard argues, emerged as a result of the repression of the great urban riots of 1966-70, and devised a "new type of intervention in the city" (1993: 76). However, graffiti operates on a completely different level than the figurative paintings of the muralists, and is much more sub-versive and radical in its implications: "graffiti is more offensive and more radical", Baudrillard argues, because it is "trans-ideological, trans-artistic ... graffiti, composed of nothing but names, effectively avoids every reference and every origin. It alone is savage, in that its message is zero" (1993: 83).[3] So graffiti has no content and no mes-sage, and it is precisely this emptiness that gives it strength: the recession in terms of content is the result of "revolutionary intuition", Baudrillard maintains, namely the suspicion "that deep ideology no longer functions at the level of political signifieds, but at the level of the signifier, and that this is where the system is vulnerable and must be dismantled" (1993: 80).

Explicit political protest, according to Baudrillard, is futile because it leaves the order of signs intact and thus just helps to repro-duce and perpetuate the existing system (1993: 80). Any transform-ation of the system can only be brought about by difference: the networks of codes must be exposed, and the code attacked by means "of an uncodeable absolute difference, over which the system will stumble and disintegrate". Only by exceeding the system's own es-sential non-referentiality, by producing something which is even more non-referential than all the signifiers which only refer to other signi-fiers, can the system be damaged and change instituted.

> [The graffitists] are seeking [...] to turn indeterminacy against the system, to turn *indeterminacy* into *extermination*. Retaliation, reversion of the code according to its own logic, on its own ter-rain, gaining victory over it because it exceeds semiocracy's own non-referentiality ... [The graffitists' terms] resist every inter-pretation and every connotation, no longer denoting anyone or anything. In this way, with neither connotation nor denotation, they escape the principle of signification and, as *empty signifiers*, erupt into the sphere of the *full* signs of the city, dissolving it on contact. (1993: 78-79)

*

Raoul Hausmann's "optophonetic" poetry is similarly or perhaps even more radically devoid of semantic content and essentially self-referential: in his poster poems "OFFEAH" and "fmsbw" from 1918, letters do not refer to any external reality but only to themselves. They do not fuse into words, but form a string of isolated monadic units, due to the fact that the typesetter commissioned with printing allegedly chose them at random, as Hausmann claims: "[i]t was the first literary 'readymade', carried out according to the laws of chance" (1970: 156). The role of chance in the generation of these poems is significant: chance presents yet another weapon against the prerogatives of rationality and usefulness, coherence and conventions. It effectively devalues cause and effect and thus subverts and eclipses bourgeois logic. Roberto Simanowski rightly points out "that aleatoric procedures aim at a creativity beyond familiar patterns of construction and that, at the same time, chance liberates from a subjectivity which is perceived as arbitrary" (2002: 71).

fmshwtözäu
pggiv-.?mü

16. Raoul Hausmann, fmsbw, *poster poem, 1918*

In "OFFEAH" and "fmsbw", the linguistic signs have abandoned their task to point to something other than themselves and have gained aesthetic autonomy. The chain of signification is interrupted; signifiers become their own referents and signify only themselves. Language is dissected into its smallest independent units, phonemes and graphemes. They do not represent an absent object any more, they do not fill an empty presence acting as *Stellvertreter* (deputies) for the real thing, but refer only to their own material essence, to their visual and their acoustic qualities.

The focus on the material dimension of language, on its physically perceptible features, is highlighted by the fact that the poems are designated as poster-poems: Hausmann exchanged the conventional medium of poetry for a medium affiliated with the sphere of fine arts, one which is public rather than private and the purpose of which is functional rather than literary. He was among the first to dispense with the traditional haven of the page, and paved the way for poetry to leave its designated realm and climb the walls of galleries and invade public space. Ironically, Hausmann radically subverted the poster's very function, namely to communicate concrete functional messages: his poems are characterised particularly by the absence of any message. As Enno Stahl has pointed out, Hausmann's choice of an information-medium poignantly mocks the very lack of information (1997: 336-337).

Although Ball's sound poems are not as radically abstract and self-referential as Hausmann's, they are modules of the same process and motivation: here too language is dissected and the order of signs is taken apart. On June 23, 1916, Ball recited "Karawane" and five other poems of the cycle "gadji beri bimba", the "Verse ohne Worte" ("verses without words"), in the Cabaret Voltaire, claiming in his diary: "I have invented a new genre of poems, 'Verse ohne Worte' [poems without words] or Lautgedichte [sound poems]" (1974: 70).[4]

17. *"Karawane" (1916),* Dada Almanach, *Berlin, 1920*

On paper, "Karawane" is set in eighteen different typefaces, each line, including the title, in a different one, some bold, some in italics, thus emphasising the importance of the visual aspect of the sign, the graphical, perceivable dimension of language.[5] The title of the poem is the only signifier that unambiguously denotes a phenomenon of the external world, and thus decidedly channels and directs the interpretation of the following seventeen verses. In the title already, an important structural principle is introduced: the repetition of vowels, of slow, long ones in particular. The vowels *a*, *o* and *u*, all of them lengthy and rather dark in tone, dominate. The overall impression is that of euphony, a pleasant smoothness of sound, due to the domination of the languidly drawling back-vowels and of voiceless, lateral and nasal consonants. Harsher consonants, like plosives and fricatives, are in the minority. Sounds are clearly the motifs, the themes of the poem, dominating and structuring the verses by means of alliteration, interior rhyme and repetition. Subtle variations of sounds weave through the entire poem. All words seem to drawl lazily, due to the lengthening vowels, as one would expect elephants to move. The words pass slowly, like a cumbersome caravan.

"Karawane", however, in contrast to Hausmann's poster poems, is not entirely self-referential, but marked by a juxtaposition of fragments from a *potpourri* of existing languages, for instance "jolifanto", alluding to the French for baby elephant, and the "men" of "goramen" to English, onomatopoeias such as "ba-umf" and "bung", and abstract sound clusters like "ssubudu". But "Karawane" is nevertheless a prime example for the exploration of the material, the "Prüfung der Mittel" ("scrutiny of the means"): the acoustic dimension of the linguistic sign is emphasised at the cost of the unequivocal referential quality, the relatively free play of signifying material is given priority over the signifieds: "[w]e have now driven the plasticity of the word to the point where it can scarcely be equalled", writes Ball.

> We achieved this at the expense of the rational, logically constructed sentence, and also by abandoning documentary work (which is possible only by means of a time-consuming grouping of sentences in logically ordered syntax). (1974: 67)

Additionally, the visual shape of language and the impacts of typography are explored in the written version. Sound as evocative aesthetic material and means of coherence is the self-sufficient subject matter of the poem, just as lines, colours and forms have become autonomous in painting. The attention is drawn to texture, formation and plasticity of language. Sound in all its facets, sound as carrier of meaning, sound as imitation of nature, sound as harmonious composition and sound as stimulus for associations, is explored.

3. The poet as revolutionary

The programmatic focus on the material dimension of language at the cost both of unequivocal signifieds and the communication of concrete messages in Hausmann's and Ball's poems is strikingly similar to the non-referential "zero-message" of graffiti which resists every interpretation and connotation.[6] The Dadaist poets too operate with empty signifiers, which escape the principle of signification – a manoeuvre that Baudrillard hails as the ultimate attack upon the code and, by implication, the order of society itself. And the Dadaists did indeed consider their poetry as manifestations of protest. "We want to deprive the sleepy security-brain of the bourgeois of everything", Hausmann proclaims (1982: 70), and that includes above all semantic compatibility and logical coherence, discursive, communicative and semantic values and the abandonment of the message-orientated deployment of language in favour of the exposure of the code itself. This is what makes the Dadaists' cultural critique so evasive and hard to get a hold of: "[t]he fact that they cannot put us against the wall makes us solemn" (1970: 79). The audience of the Dada *soirées*, as Hausmann recalls, seems to have grasped this radical assault upon their values intuitively:

> the most important manifestations were of course those during which thousands of people, raging with fury against us, were ready to kill us – because they had understood that DADA threatened their highest possessions and holiest ideals. (Riha and Schaefer 1977: 9)

At the heart of Ball's motivation for language dissection lies the notion that language too is a stained ritual of a deeply despised society: language had been abused and defiled, and was inextricably intertwined and part of a culture of which nothing could any longer be accepted as given and unproblematic, not even language. Referential value is dispensed with because it is considered tainted and corrupted, infected by the times and the people who have abused it.

> In these phonetic poems we totally renounce the language that journalism has abused and corrupted. We must return to the innermost alchemy of the word, we must even give up the word too, to keep for poetry its last and holiest refuge. (Ball 1974: 71)

The withdrawal into the innermost alchemy of the word and the exploration of the material qualities of language presented an opportunity to avoid the deployment of existing language:

> A verse presents the opportunity to do more or less without words and language. This accursed language, to which dirt adheres as if from brokers' hands, which wear out the coins. (Riha 1994: 34)

Language and signs are not neutral carriers of meaning, but are themselves acutely infected by, and are in fact integral components of, the intricate network of value structures, ideologies, conventions and traditions that constitute culture. Ball intuitively understood and anticipated what was to be formulated theoretically only much later: that signification itself is always a part of, and often involuntarily helps to perpetuate and enforce, the dominant power structures. It is within language itself that the process of cultural decontamination must be initiated, Ball maintains: "[i]t is with language that purification must begin, the imagination must be purified" (1974: 76). Referring to fine arts, but talking about a modality of the same process, he writes: "It is perhaps not a question of art but of the uncorrupt image" (1974: 115). This statement poignantly illustrates the main objective for Ball's abandonment of the signified and exploration of the material properties of the signifier: this operation is not aesthetically motivated, but primarily an attempt to break free from the all-encompassing cultural corruption which has even ventured forth and permeated and infected the sign systems themselves, both in art and in literature.

Language as a social practice is what is at stake in Ball's poems, and thus it is not just language which is shattered, but that which comes with it as well: "Language as social organ can be destroyed without the creative process having to suffer. In fact, it seems that the creative powers even benefit from it" (1974: 76). It is only by means of breaching predefined restrictions and limitations, be they artistic or linguistic in nature, that Ball feels he can express his criticism of the times. It is the transgression and displacement of boundaries that is important here, those of socially established signifying practices, of linguistic and literary conventions, of that which is speakable and thus thinkable, and ultimately of the individual and society.

Hausmann, by referring to the rift between conflicting factions in Berlin Dada, clearly differentiates between concrete political criticism conveyed on the content level and the art of "semiological warfare", as John Picchione (1996: 106) puts it – which is reminiscent of the difference between the strategies of the graffitists and muralists.

> Above all, Dada should have been an anti-cultural operation. Anti-art withdraws the use-value of things and materials, as well as their concrete and social meaning; it overturns classical values and makes them semi-abstract. But this process has only been understood partly and only by a few DADAists, who did not want to forsake their political objectives. This is where the whole guilt of the DADAists can be found, caused by their irresponsibility. (Riha and Schaefer 1977: 10-11)

Moreover, Hausmann draws explicit parallels between social revolution and the artistic assault upon established orders and conventions, drawing attention to the fact that the Dadaists did not just depict or try to come to terms with a changing world order, but actively demanded transformations of existing structures themselves. Their art is not just a mirror, but in fact a cultural tool. Hausmann writes:

> one dissolved established pictorial units just as one attempted to dissolve old legal forms or types of state. These attempts correspond to a spiritual form of life, a demanded truth rather than a mere acknowledgement of given reality [...]. (1982: 10)

In *The Mirror of Production*, Baudrillard lifts the analogy between artistically assaulting the order of signs and social revolution to yet another level: for him, the avant-garde poet is the only one who immediately realises and effectuates revolution by means of embracing direct linguistic action rather than endlessly deferring it in the political dimension. Poetry and social revolution have a radical "presentness" in common, Baudrillard argues, and are both marked by the "actualisation of desire no longer relegated to a future liberation, but demanded here, immediately" (1975: 165):

> The cursed poet, non-official art, and utopian writings in general, by giving a current and immediate content to man's liberation, should be the very speech of communism, its direct prophecy.

They are only its bad conscience precisely because in them
something of man is *immediately* realised, because they object
without pity to the "political" dimension of the revolution, which
is merely the dimension of its final postponement. They are the
equivalent, at the level of discourse, of the savage social movements that were born in a symbolic situation of rupture (symbolic
– which means non-universalised, non-dialectical, non-rational-
ised in the mirror of an imaginary objective history). (1975: 164)

4. Effectuation, symbolic gesture and breaking open ideology

Paradoxically, Dadaist poetry is marked by two seemingly conflicting
characteristics: on the one hand it does indeed represent an immediate
effectuation and realisation of both aesthetic and more wide-ranging
assumptions about literature, language and society. In contrast to the
language sceptics at the turn of the last century, the Dadaists did not
just talk about their dissatisfaction with language, but acted on that
impulse, directly intervening in and dismantling the very structures
they objected to. Dadaist poetry can thus be considered as direct linguistic action, as revolutionary transformation of existing configurations put into practice within language.

On the other hand, assaulting signs is also a symbolic act, a
demonstrative gesture: by attacking signs, one attacks the deputies
rather than the real things.[7] Language in Dadaist poetry epitomises
cultural and socio-political structures and rituals as well as social
consensus in general, and the avant-garde poets do to language what
they would like to do to society as a whole: to uncover and lay bare its
hidden structures and to thoroughly transform them. In this sense, the
revolution in poetic language can be considered a *Modellversuch*:
language acts as model and surrogate for ungraspable, unchangeable
and much more complex structures; it is *Ersatz* for the real thing.
Language is burned in effigy.

However, there is a third dimension to the problem: Baudrillard considers the abandonment of reference as a direct assault upon
the code which governs the arbitrary self-referential play of signifiers:
by exceeding, exaggerating and reversing the system's own non-
referentiality, the system, he hopes, will begin to disintegrate and
crumble as a result. The Dadaists, in contrast, seem to be more realistic in the assessment of the utopian possibilities inherent in their
poetry. While their agenda is similar to Baudrillard's, their specific

target differs: rather than aiming at the grand scheme, an all-encompassing and abstract system, they try to trigger and stimulate change within the individual, hoping that they could get the audience at their *soirées* or the readers of their publications to rethink their positions, to make them confront habitual thinking structures, to question their attitudes towards literature, convention and perhaps even social order.

Though the focus of the Dadaists is upon frustrating categorical ways of thinking and impeding automatised strategies of perception of the individual recipient, it entails a strong concern with social structures nevertheless: as Julia Kristeva has pointed out in *Revolution in Poetic Language*, the shattering of discourse in modernist and avant-garde poetry is not only about linguistic transgressions, but goes much deeper. What is at stake in such a signifying practice, according to Kristeva, is not just language: the explosion of phonetic, lexical and syntactic laws implies the bursting open of epistemological, psychological and ideological limitations of the subject and, by implication, society. Every social construct is questioned and under attack in these texts: "Such a practice does not address itself at all; it sweeps along everything that belongs to the same space of practice: human 'units' in process/on trial" (1984: 102).

Social change is inseparable from psychological and linguistic change, Kristeva writes: "the text is a practice that could be compared to political revolution: the one brings about in the subject what the other introduces into society" (1984: 17). Political revolution and the shattering of discourse are two modalities of the same process which differ only in their field of application: while political revolutionary action aims at transforming social structures and initially leaves linguistic structures intact, it does produce a landslide which will change and affect linguistic structures as well. Linguistic revolution functions the other way round: the social function of texts in which the semiotic order is assaulted is "the production of a different kind of subject, one capable of bringing about new social relations, and thus joining in the process of capitalism's subversion:

> Imperialism produces its true gravedigger in the non-subjected man, the man-process who sets ablaze and transforms all laws, including – and perhaps especially – those of signifying structures. The productive process of the text thus belongs not to this

established society, but to the social change that is inseparable
from instinctual and linguistic change. (1984: 105)

Language dissection in Dadaist poetry can hence be considered to be
operative on three levels simultaneously: firstly, it is a direct imple-
mentation and realisation of poetic and more wide-ranging political
beliefs within language. Secondly, it is a symbolic gesture of protest:
the order of signs is taken to represent the order of society as a whole,
it is perceived as a stained ritual, which is dismantled in lieu of the
real thing. Lastly, by bursting open language, the Dadaists try to burst
open and transform the social preconceptions and the ideological
boundaries of the recipient and, by implication, society. By means of
programmatically withdrawing sense and violating the expectations of
the recipients, they hope to open up ways of thinking outside the
tangible and to stimulate a change in attitude and behaviour which
would, ideally, have repercussions upon social structures as well.

Notes

[1] For this essay, only Baudrillard's thoughts on the subject in *For a Critique of the
Political Economy of the Sign, Symbolic Exchange and Death* and *The Mirror of Production* have been taken into consideration. Earlier versions or later revisions of his
models will not be discussed, and neither will more general problems that come with
his theoretical positions be addressed, simply due to space limitation. For a critical
assessment of Baudrillard's works see for example Douglas Kellner (ed.), *Baudrillard: A Critical Reader*. Oxford: Blackwell, 1994.
[2] This is the point where Baudrillard's theory gets particularly hairy: signs are not
autonomous sentient beings with a will of their own, but they are social constructs
created, orchestrated and manipulated by humans. They do not operate autonomously,
even if they do refer only to themselves, but are controlled and deployed for particular
purposes. "The code" is not an independent entity controlling the order of the world,
but on the contrary, it is a tool used, shaped and organised by men. As Steven Best
has rightly pointed out: "Baudrillard's radical rejection of referentiality is premised
upon a one-dimensional, No-Exit world of self-referring simulacra. But, however
reified and self-referential postmodern semiotics is, signs do not simply move in their
own signifying orbit. They are historically produced and circulated and while they
may not translucently refer to some originating world, they nonetheless can be socio-
historically contextualised, interpreted, and critiqued." Steven Best, "The commodification of reality and the reality of commodification: Baudrillard, Debord, and postmodern theory" in *Baudrillard: A Critical Reader*, p. 57.
[3] It is here that a minor logical problem in Baudrillard's example becomes apparent:
names are not really empty signifiers but do refer to something in the external world.
In the case of graffiti, they refer to their creator, the person who painted them onto the

wall, and could be considered to transport a message such as: I exist and I was here. Baudrillard counters this objection by maintaining that the names are not proper names but in fact pseudonyms derived from comics: "This would still be an identitarian revolt however, combating anonymity by demanding a proper name and a reality. The graffitists went further in that they opposed pseudonyms rather than names to anonymity. [...] SUPERBEE SPIX COLA 139 KOOL GUY CRAZY CROSS 136 means nothing, it is not even a proper name, but a symbolic matriculation number whose function it is to derail the common system of designations" (Baudrillard 1993: 78). Nevertheless, it seems as if the Dada sound poems, particularly Hausmann's, are actually more radically abstract and thus more convincing examples for empty signifiers.

[4] Ball was by no means the first to deploy non- or only partly-referential sounds in poetry, as Michael Lentz has pointed out. The first sound poem was Paul Scheerbart's "Kikakdu! Eloralops!" written in 1897, followed by Christian Morgenstern's "Der Grosse Lalula". Gertrude Stein's "Tender Buttons" was written as early as 1914, and Ball must also have been familiar with the "bruitist" experiments of the Italian Futurists, and their "parole in libertà" with partly non-referential onomatopoeia, since he published some of these works in the *Cabaret Voltaire* anthology. Moreover, he could also have learned about the *zaum*-explorations of the Russian Cubo-Futurists by way of Wassily Kandinsky. Cf Michael Lentz, *Lautpoesie/musik nach 1945. Eine kritisch-dokumentarische Bestandsaufnahme*. Vienna: Edition Selene, 2000, vol.1, p. 98.

[5] Christian Scholz points out that the typographically enhanced version of "Karawane" has never been authorised by Ball: "The different written versions of this sound poem have been authorised by the author only in the case of the typewritten version which is included in the 'Gesammelten Gedichten', a collection based on Ball's manuscripts edited by Annemarie Ball-Hennings. No authorisation existed for the two typographically enhanced versions for the DADA-Almanach, which was intended to appear in the Kurt Wolff Verlag, and for the 'DADA ALMANACH' edited by Richard Huelsenbeck, published by the Erich Reiss Verlag in 1920." Christian Scholz, "Bezüge zwischen 'Lautpoesie' und 'visueller Poesie'. Vom 'optophonetischen Gedicht' zum 'Multimedia-Text' – ein historischer Abriss" In: *VISUELLE POESIE. TEXT + KRITIK. Zeitschrift für Literatur. SONDERBAND*. Edited by Heinz Ludwig Arnold. Munich: edition text+kritik, 1997, p. 117f.

[6] Of course there is also an aesthetic as well as a poetic dimension to the Dadaist poems, particularly to Ball's, which graffiti arguably lacks.

[7] In Baudrillard's framework, however, signs have actually replaced and to a certain degree even *become* the real thing – they are all that is left. Attacking the order of signs is hence much more than attacking a surrogate system; according to Baudrillard's logic, it is equivalent to changing and interfering in actual structures since signs and their interrelationships are all there is.

References

Ball, Hugo
  1974   *Flight Out of Time: A Dada Diary* (ed. John Elderfield, tr. Ann Raimes). New York: Viking Press.

Baudrillard, Jean
  1975   *The Mirror of Production.* St Louis: Telos Press.

  1981   *For a Critique of the Political Economy of the Sign.* St Louis: Telos Press.

  1993   *Symbolic Exchange and Death.* London: Sage Publications.

Dachy, Marc (ed.)
  1989   *Journal du Mouvement Dada 1915–1923.* Geneva: Albert Skira.

Hausmann, Raoul
  1970   *Am Anfang War Dada.* Karl Riha and Günter Kämpf (eds). Giessen: Anabas Verlag.

  1982a   *Sieg, Triumph, Tabak mit Bohnen. Texte bis 1933.* Michael Erlhoff (ed.). Munich: Edition Text und Kritik, vol. 1.

  1982b   *Bilanz der Feierlichkeiten. Texte bis 1933.* Michael Erlhoff (ed.). Munich: Edition Text und Kritik, vol. 2.

Kristeva, Julia
  1984   *Revolution in Poetic Language.* Margaret Waller (tr.). New York: Columbia University Press.

Picchione, John
  1996   "Poetry in Revolt: Italian Avant-Garde Movements in the Sixties". In *Experimental – Visual – Concrete: Avant-Garde Poetry since the 1960s.* K. David Jackson, Eric Vos and Johanna Drucker (eds). Amsterdam: Rodopi Verlag.

Riha, Klaus (ed.)
  1994   *DADA total. Manifeste, Aktionen, Texte, Bilder.* Stuttgart: Phillip Reclam Junior.

Riha, Klaus and Schaefer, Joergen (eds)
  1977   *Dada Berlin. Texte, Manifeste, Aktionen.* Stuttgart: Phillip Reclam Junior.

Simanowski, Roberto
  2002   *Interfictions. Vom Schreiben im Netz*. Frankfurt am Main:
          Suhrkamp.

Stahl, Enno
  1997   *Anti-Kunst und Abstraktion in der literarischen Moderne (1909–
          1933). Vom italienischen Futurismus bis zum französischen
          Surrealismus*. Frankfurt am Main and New York: Lang.

III. Dada Siegt!

The Prosthetic Body in Early Modernism:
Dada's anti-humanist humanism

Martin Ignatius Gaughan

Abstract: This essay examines an interface between technological modernisation and visual culture in early modernism, briefly that of the prosthetic as an imaginary extension of the human body, as in Futurism, and the prosthetic as an image deployed to critique the anti-humanism of the capitalist system, as in Dada. Amongst the ideas referenced are those of the scientific work method of Taylor, Ford's mass production process, Marinetti's technological romanticism and the leftist critique of Dada.

In what might be seen as a kind of census of contemporary body types, Terry Eagleton has identified some of the categories:

> There will soon be more bodies in contemporary criticism than on the fields of Waterloo. Mangled members, tormented torsos, bodies emblazoned or incarcerated, disciplined or desirous: it is becoming harder, given this fashionable turn to the somatic, to distinguish the literary theory section of the local bookshop from the soft-porn shelves [...].

But amongst this plethora of bodies he notes particular absences:

> For the new somatics, not any old body will do. If the libidinal body is in, the labouring body is out. There are mutilated bodies galore, but few malnourished ones, belonging as they do to bits of the globe beyond the purview of Yale. (Eagleton 1998: 157-8)

His satirising of the focus of interest is well made, raising as it does the issue of the social and professional investments in attending to some categories of bodies rather than others, of privileging certain discursive formations over others, for example, that of psychoanalysis over the sociological or sociohistorical. But the representation of the "labouring body" within contemporary culture may indeed provide a problem, the result of complex changes in the nature and organisation of work experienced during the twentieth century. In the final passage of his conclusion, titled "The Obsolescence of the Body", American social historian Anson Rabinbach articulates the problem as follows:

> The displacement of work from the centre to the periphery of late twentieth century thought can thus be understood by the disappearance of the system of representations that placed the working body at the juncture of nature and society – by the disappearance of the "human motor". (Rabinbach 1990: 300)

This essay will return to the early twentieth century with its accelerated modernisation programme, where some avant-garde artists were attempting to forge representations which could accommodate that experience of modernity.[1] It will consider some of the prevailing discourses on the theorising of the body as machine and its shift to that of the body as motor, on the rationalisation of work and of the human body, as found in scientific work management (Taylorism) and mass-production and the division of labour (Fordism). The prosthetic, both as concept and as reality (its referencing by artists as a critical tool, as in the work of Dadaists such as Dix, Grosz and Heartfield) will be addressed. In its widest sense, it can be theorised as follows: "The universal laws of energy applied equally to the movements of the planets, the forces of nature, the mechanical work of machines and the work of the body [...]. The cosmos, the factory and the worker were all extensions of the 'human motor'", where the implication of prosthetic as extension is clear (Rabinbach 1990: 290). Although this was positivist science with its calibration of response to stimulus and measurement of reaction and movement, there were also dimensions to it which seemed to accord it a less scientific materialist complexity, what Rabinbach characterises as "trans-sensual", "the manifest forms of energy belonged to the world of the senses, but energy itself was a hidden, invisible and secret substance embedded in all these forms, 'like the Platonic idea over things'", a quasi-metaphysical thickening, fashioned by scientific mapping of the working body, focusing on the factory worker's body (Rabinbach 1990: 289).

18. Otto Dix, Kartenspieler, *1920*

The scientific tracing of this source of energy, occasioning the conceptualisation of the body no longer in the image of the machine but in that of the motor, also had wider cultural implications. The new science "dissolved the anthropomorphic body as a distinct entity and made the individual body a sophisticated analytics of space and time" (Rabinbach 1990: 87). The figures of the philosopher Bergson, the artist Duchamp and the scientist Marey come into conjunction here. Marey's investigative practices realised in a sense those analytics of space and time, concerned as they were with raising questions about the performance of the body in this newly theorised spatiotemporal world. He was physician, physiologist, pioneer of medical measurement, student of hydraulics and, interestingly in this context, a pioneer in elaborating photographic and cinematic techniques to chart such performance, complex instruments of graphic description and inscription, "a sort of automatic writing [that] united the body's own signs (pulse, heart rate, gait) with a language of technical representation" (Rabinbach 1990: 97). Although it will not be pursued further in this text, the impact of Marey's chronophotographic studies of the human body in motion, together with Bergson's ideas of the *élan vital* set out in his *Creative Evolution* (1907), was to influence work by Futurists and the early work of the future Dadaist Marcel Duchamp, for example, his *Nude descending a Stair, Sad Young Man on a Train* and other works.[2]

Having sketched out briefly the shift in the conceptualisation of how the potential of the human body and its performance could be understood under the imperatives and conditions of early twentieth century technological modernisation, the remainder of the essay will be concerned with how some of these ideas contained within the general category of the prosthetic, filtered through to and impacted on the world of visual culture. Initially, in order to gain purchase on the critique encountered in the work of German Dadaists, a context will be established in rehearsing some of the ideas addressed by Hal Foster's "Prosthetic Gods".

1. Prosthetic Gods

Marinetti's delirious description of the interactions of man and machine may be seen as a precursor to what Eagleton identifies as a contemporary obsession, that with the libidinalisation of the body at the expense of other bodies, such as the labouring body. This is given theoretical expression in "Multiplied Man and the Reign of the Machine", in which he propounds a man/machine hybrid type, that augmented concept of the prosthetic quoted above in Rabinbach, a fantasy construction in which "we must prepare for the imminent, inevitable identification of man with motor, facilitating and perfecting a constant interchange of intuition, rhythm, instinct, and metallic discipline of which the majority are wholly ignorant" (Poggi 1997: 37).[3] In his "Technical Manifesto" of 1912 Marinetti celebrates this man/machine binding and bonding, with particular reference to the experience of an airplane flight which, as Jeffrey Schnapp writes, took place in 1910. Schnapp details the occasion, at the Brescia International Air Meeting, and relates the type of aircraft with its limited accommodation for the human body and the consequent immediate impact of the technology on that body – the reverberations of the engine coursing through Marinetti's body as he was seated against it. He writes of its importance for Marinetti's programme and draws a cruical distinction between that and the programme of the theorists of scientific work methods outlined above:

> All three attributes – power, danger, and unreliability – are advantageous from Marinetti's viewpoint, since they permit the

> development of a body/machine complex founded on notions of
> struggle, sacrifice, feverish effort, and expenditure: an aesthetic
> (i.e. non-productivist) body/machine complex that runs counter
> to the complexes being devised within the domains of scientific
> management (Taylor) and the "science of work", which were
> founded instead on notions of body/machine harmony, energy
> conservation, and freedom from fatigue. (Schnapp 1994: 161)

Both approaches, however, despite their differences, involved instrumentalisation of the body, its subjection to the requirements and the
demands of technological modernisation, Taylorisation through an impoverished process of rationalisation, Marinetti by way of a technological romanticism.[4]

Foster prefaces his essay on Marinetti (and Wyndham Lewis)
with a quote from Freud, which might be seen as preliminary to a
psychoanalytic gloss on the Futurist's rhapsodising: "Man has, as it
were, become a kind of prosthetic God. When he puts on all his aux-
iliary organs he is truly magnificent, but those organs have not grown
on to him and they still give him much trouble at times" (Foster 1997:
5).[5] He extends the concept of the prosthetic from the work of Mark
Seltzer, borrowing from it the idea of "the double logic of the prosthesis" (Foster 1997: 5). The Seltzer passage quoted follows his comment on a statement by Henry Ford and the kind of bodies required for
producing his cars: Seltzer writes: "If from one point of view, such a
fantasy projects a violent dismemberment of the natural body and an
emptying out of human agency, from another it projects a transcendence of the natural body and the extension of human agency
through the forms of technology that represent it. This is precisely the
double logic of prosthesis and it is also the double logic of a sheer
culturalism that posits that the individual is something that can be
made" (Seltzer 1992: 157).[6] This "double logic" Foster sees as "an
addition to the body that threatened a subtraction from it" (Foster
1997: 5). Although he recognises "[t]he fundamental difference between a Marxist project to *overcome* technological self-alienation
dialectically (for all) and a protofascist desire to elevate this self-
alienation into an absolute value (for a select few) as a form of ego
ecstasy", his theoretical imperative is to explore the putative psycho-
analytical implication of the double logic of the prosthesis rather than
materialist ones.[7] Technological modernisation in this provocative and
psychoanalytically well informed account is conceived of as a kind of

primal scene, where the double logic of the prosthesis negotiates the experience as follows: "the machine as a castrative trauma *and* as a phallic shield against such trauma" (Foster 1997: 8). Foster ingeniously proposes that this reaction formation, as traced in Marinetti's texts, is a way of overcoming "the old bourgeois idea of a non-technological subject", in favour of an imagined "new ego that can withstand the shocks of the military-industrial, the modern-urban, and the mass-political, indeed that can forge these stimuli into a protective shield, even convert them into a hardened subject to *thrive* on such shocks" (Foster 1997: 9).[8] In the Marinetti model, then, the double logic works "to extrapolate the human toward the inorganic-technological", on the one hand; on the other "to trope the inorganic-technological as the epitome of the human", a reading supported by much that is to be found in the Futurist's manifestos (Foster 1997: 15). Foster characterises Marinetti's projection through the libidinalised drives of what can be termed a "technological unconscious", traces laid down in the sedimentation of a modernist tradition from Jarry to the French Dadaists Picabia and Duchamp, in which the human/machine nexus had been eroticised, from Jarry's *Surmâle* and its insatiable machine to the less destructive human/machine entanglements in Duchamp's *The Bride Stripped Bare by Her Bachelors, Even.*[9] Given such aestheticisation, it is not surprising that Marinetti suggested the Italian Fascist party "would solve the social problem artistically" (Foster 1997: 18).[10] Reading Marinetti in a more direct manner in the 1930s, Benjamin saw his programme differently: "fascism [...] as Marinetti admits, expects war to supply the artistic gratification of a sense perception that has been changed by technology". Mankind's "self-alienation has reached such a degree that it can experience its own destruction as an aesthetic pleasure of the first order. This is the situation of politics which Fascism is rendering aesthetic" (Benjamin 1982: 244). Although written after the end of Dada, Benjamin's articulation reflects their critique of the technological, where the prosthetic is only too present as a reminder of technology's collusion with the military-industrial complex during the war, or of its potential for reinforcing worker alienation in the process of rationalisation.

2. Homo Prostheticus

Commenting on the standard psychotechnical books which addressed the German war-wounded during the 1914–18 conflict, Peter Sloterdijk writes: "In the textbooks on the maimed and the writings of the medical-technical industry, a highly apposite image of the human being emerges: *Homo Prostheticus*, who is supposed to say a wildly joyful Yes to everything that says No to the 'individuality' of 'individuals'" (Sloterdijk 1988: 446). He quotes from one such primer. Heroic precedent is referred to in order to encourage the injured and then,

> whoever has done his share with two sound arms in the field against the enemy will be able to master his fate and himself with one arm [...]. The present booklet wants [...] to show him [...] that one armedness is not the worst thing by a long shot [...]. How favourably the war-wounded is situated. [...] Even the single working hand cannot be done without. [...] After a diligent stay at a school, some get on better than they did before the injury. (Sloterdijk 1988: 446)

Consolation is obtained through recognition, "[m]ost people view the war-injured person as a living monument [!] of our hard times to whom we give thanks silently".[11] Accommodation to loss will naturalise it: "Some experienced one-armers say they would not know what to do with a second arm if suddenly, through a miracle, they were given back the lost arm".[12] This was not an isolated instance but part of a wider discourse on the subject. Another source referenced by Sloterdijk is the *Contributions to the question of equipping war damaged who have lost an arm for employment*: the "polite" address seems to be to a middle-class readership ("You see, ladies and gentlemen") and the passage goes on to list those helping the wounded,

> doctors and first-aid helpers, engineers and manufacturers [...] officers of our emergency services, all strive *in the same way* to place their experience at the service of our cause and to replace the loss of hand and arm [...]. And for the injured the poet's words are apt: Whoever always strives to make an effort/ Can be redeemed by us. (Sloterdijk 1988: 449)[13]

It is in the context of such a discourse that the presence of the prosthesis in Dada work must, in the first instance, be considered. There
are no "Prosthetic Gods" here. The first two images being addressed
will be considered in the context of the following quotation from
Sloterdijk:

> War loosens the tongue of the latent cynicism of domination,
> medicine and the military. Under its influence, the military and
> production apparatuses admit their claim to use up the lives of
> individuals in their service. The human body in the society of
> labour had already been an artificial limb even before one had to
> replace damaged parts with functioning parts. (Sloterdijk 1988:
> 447-8)

19. Otto Dix, Pragerstrasse, *1920*

Dix's collage of 1920 *Pragerstrasse*, Dresden's most fashionable
street and site of recent bitter fighting between workers and *Freikorps*
troups visualises the world of the prosthetic, a world inflected here by
class as much as any other part of the social world. Dix was, of
course, himself a war veteran. A prosthetic-looking hand, but in fact a
well-gloved cane-carrying one (bottom left), leads us into the socially
layered world of the prosthesis. The two crippled males are not bene-
ficiaries of that rehabilitation programme set out above, making do as
best they can with primitive prostheses in front of a shop window
offering sophisticated and expensive artificial limbs. In the left-hand

window two fashionable-looking truncated lower arm prostheses seem to participate gratuitously in the general circulation of limbs; in the right hand window, artificial limbs more elegant and more expensive than those possessed by the crippled ex-soldier nearer the window are ironically displayed in the company of corsets, bust improvers and slimming pads – the newspaper collaged behind the female torso refers to "beautiful breasts" ("hübschen Büsen"). As against Marinetti's rhetorical flights (and Foster's theoretical contextualising), Dix's representation of the economy of the prosthesis is altogether more grounded. The artificial feet in the window lie upon two fragments of collaged paper, the right one on an advertisement for "American condoms", the left on one advertising surgical tools used for abortions. With the aim of replacing losses on the war front – for example, these two casualties – contraception had been banned in Germany in 1915, and consequently women turned to abortion, which was also illegal – concerns which ironically point up the condition of the former soldiers.

20. *Otto Dix,* Die Skatspieler, *1920*

Although Sloterdijk's comments on those bodies in the "society of labour", that "[s]ome in any case, could say nothing about the reassembling of humans in modernity; they no longer had mouths", do not literally apply to the "Skat Players" (*Die Skatspieler*, 1920) –

some forms of mouths are in place – the general point is taken.[14] The prostheses here are not the products of technology as proclaimed in the brochures referred to above, but are more the bizarre results of bricoleuring – Dix himself constructs the lower jaw of the player on the right sporting the Iron Cross, advertising, and using his own image, the "lower jaw prosthesis brand Dix" ("Unterkiefer Prosthese Marke Dix"), a prosthesis whose quality is only guaranteed when accompanied "by the image of the inventor" ("nur echt mit dem Bild des Erfinders"), as in the photograph.[15] Dix's deployment of the prosthetic was one level at which this motif was mobilised as a critique of the effects of technological modernisation, here in the immediate aftermath of the war, when its physical presence and presence in discourse was overt and unavoidable.

For a brief period in 1920, during their Dada period, Grosz and Hausmann engaged with the technologically-extended (prosthetic) figure in an attempt to represent a new human subject, in representations that were critical of the claim to interiority made by the bourgeoisie, particularly in the realm of culture – the artist as an inspired creator. In Hausmann's striking "Mechanical Head" (*Mechanischer Kopf*) also ambivalently titled "Spirit of Our Time" (*Der Geist unserer Zeit*)[16] there is no interior, everything is on the outside, the instruments of measurement upon which the bourgeois economy depends but which also threaten its culture and bourgeois self-understanding. The technological extensions here raise questions about human agency: "what is the purpose of spirit in a world that processes mechanically, what is man? (He is an instance, formed and spoken through his mode of production, his milieu. [...] You believe you thrive and make decisions, you believe yourself to be original [...] and what happens? The milieu has thrown the soul-machine into gear and the whole thing runs itself" (*Der Dada* 3 1920: n.p.).[17] This conceptualisation of the man/ machine interaction questions both the ambiguous relationship of the bourgeoisie with its technology and the technological romanticism of Marinetti. Dada irony allowed serious questions to be addressed to technology's potential to extend human agency. In *Daum marries her pedantic automaton "George"* (Grosz), the latter is, as "automaton" suggests, a fully prostheticised figure assembled literally from machine parts. Grosz published six works, executed in watercolour, pen and ink, in an article on his new painting, in which the subjects are "sportsman, engineer and machine, but devoid of Futurist romantic dynamism", in a style which has "the concreteness and clarity of an engineer's drawing" (*Das Kunstblatt* 1921: 10-16) .

Among them is one titled "The New Man" (*Der neue Mensch*), possibly even the new artist constructor, again as a type of automaton striding across the studio floor towards an easel containing not a painting but a blueprint. But, as he insisted, his objective is not the apparent melding of man and machine aspired to by "Futurist romantic dynamism". As with the focus of Dix's work the target is more immediate, a different conceptualisation of the post-revolutionary subject, here the artist: "Man is no longer an individual to be examined in subtle psychological terms but as a collective, almost mechanical concept".[18] That he only saw the more obvious surface of the social order was admitted to by Grosz in a long 1925 essay he co-authored with Wieland Herzfelde, editor of Dada journals and left-wing magazines, and brother of John Heartfield (also Grosz's sometime collaborator). The essay, ironically titled "Art is in Danger. An Investigation", is not concerned with saving it, but with arguing for a more engaged art. They defend the challenge Dada offered to the culture of the period – "Dada was the only genuine art movement in Germany in decades", but "we saw the lunatic end products of the social order and broke out into laughter. As yet we did not see that this lunacy was the system itself" (Schneede 1979: 134).[19] When John Heartfield montaged his 1927 work on industrial rationalisation, he saw exactly where the madness lay. Benjamin recognised the revolutionary strength of Dada and wrote that "[m]uch of this revolutionary attitude passed into photomontage. You need only think of the works of John Heartfield [...]" (Benjamin 1977: 94). *"Die Rationalisierung marschiert!"* ("Rationalisation is on the march!"), embodies that revolutionary strength of Dada.[20]

By the time Heartfield produced this montage, the Americanisation of the German economy, financed by the American Dawes Plan of 1924, and the rationalisation of industrial production had ushered in the era of New Objectivity and its obsession with the surface appearance of the technological world. Taylorist ideas of the fragmentation of the work experience through time and motion studies were known in prewar Germany, and the publication of Henry Ford's autobiography in Germany in 1923 augmented the discourse on mechanisation and rationalisation. Although there were differences between the theories of Taylor and Ford, it is with a quote from the latter that I am providing an initial context for the reading of the Heartfield image – it is from his thinking about the production of the 1923 Model T car, which required 7882 distinct operations: he estimated that only twelve percent of the tasks required "strong able-bodied and practically physically perfect men": "670 operations could be filled by legless men; 2637 by one-legged men; two by armless men; 715 by one-armed men, and ten by blind men" (Ford 1923: 108-9).[21]

21. John Heartfield, "Die Rationalisierung marschiert!", 1927

The calculus of the human motor is finely calibrated and tuned here in this grotesque dismembering of the human body. In this passage we see clearly what Mark Seltzer has termed the "double-logic of the prosthesis", agency removed from the body but simultaneously the body's functioning apparently extended through technology. This is a very different site for the deployment of the concept than that of Foster's reading of Marinetti's romantic engagement (carrying its brutalising espousal of violent application). The Heartfield "new man" is the post-Dawes Taylorist worker, part stopwatch, part work-study spread sheet, part machine elements, a disarticulated body. A sense of what is involved in this unromantic reductivist "metallisation" of the body may be intimated in Kracauer's observation that "only as a tiny particle of the mass can the individual human being effortlessly clamber up charts and service machines" (Kracauer 1975: 69). That extended prosthetic world proposed by Rabinbach above, "the cosmos, the factory, the worker" as a common force-field of energy, finds a literalisation here, although as a quotation from Seltzer suggests, not one in which all elements are equal. He refers to an earlier observer of the scientific work study method, a reference in which the presence of the Panopticon may be felt: "The men felt and often remarked that the eyes of the company were always on them through the books [...] the process of production is replicated in paper before, as and after it takes place in physical form" (Seltzer 1992: 159). The torso of Heartfield's paradigmatic *homo prostheticus* bodies forth these calculations. Heartfield represents a situation that Benjamin speculates on in a passage in his "The Work of Art in the Age of Its Technical Reproducibility" – he is reflecting on the prevalence of scientific work study practices in all spheres of social life, the role of statistics in relation to perception and the structuring of reality:

> Thus is manifested in the field of perception what in the theoretical sphere is noticeable in the increasing significance of statistics. The alignment of reality with the masses and of the masses with reality is a process of immeasurable importance for both thinking and perception. (Benjamin 2003: 256)

In his representation of the experience of rationalisation, Heartfield engages with that level of abstraction articulated by Benjamin – unlike other left-wing artists the worker, heroic or immiserated, is not depicted; instead, we are presented with the concept of how rationalisation works. An earlier version carries the inscription "A spectre is haunting Europe" ("Ein Gespenst geht um in Europa"); for Heartfield, a ghost still haunts the machine but one, in that it is "as much for thinking as for perception", which became palpable in this artist's hands.

3. Conclusion

The particular nodal points around which this study was structured may be abstracted in the following manner. There is Rabinbach's observation on the obsolescence of the body through the "displacement of work" to the periphery of interest and "the disappearance of the systems of representations that placed the working body at the juncture of nature and society", a challenge posed at least to one tradition of representation since mid-nineteenth century Realism to late nineteenth century Naturalism and into politically engaged art in the first three decades of the twentieth century.[22] Eagleton expresses a related concern but coming from a different perspective, that of a cultural politics, noting the ideological propensity to privilege the libidinalised, desirous body over that of the labouring body, essentially that of the private body over that of the social. Seltzer, among other issues, proposed a dialectical operation of the prosthetic in the body/machine relationship, with its "double logic", as that which extends the capacity of the human being but can also appear to diminish it. Both Rabinbach and Seltzer, the former more so, trace in a Foucauldian-type manner the disciplining of the human body through theories of a science of work (*Arbeitswissenschaft*) and scientific work-study (Taylorism) in the pursuit of defining energy and its deployment. More particularly, injuries sustained in war introduced the search for more efficient prostheses, inflected chauvinistically by nationalistically driven advocates. This was the context into which the concerns of some artists with these issues were introduced, particularly during the early modernist period, where Futurism and Dada were prime candidates for consideration.

Although the arguments have moved on as we enter the third stage of technological modernisation, where the more complex image of the cyborg has displaced that of the earlier prosthetic figure in whatever guise, the conceptualisation and representational strategies of Futurism and Dada still possesses important "archaeological" dimensions in the Foucauldian sense. They rehearse in striking visual form the socio-cultural concerns raised by the major studies of Rabinbach and Seltzer. The enthusiastic embrace of the technological as espoused in the writings of Marinetti has been reread above, through Freudian and Lacanian discourses, where the prosthetic has been proposed as a process of ego hardening, a self-armouring, against the massification of society implicit in modernisation. The German Dadaists were not concerned with the fashioning of such a protective shell: the issues they raised across their practices, if not in the same form, about how the system works and how human beings are shaped within it are still relevant, as Eagleton suggests. Although the modes of representation may have been superseded, the double registers of "kynical" (the laughter of Diogenes, whose presence Grosz recounts in his 1925 essay, quoted above) and cynical reason deployed by the Dadaists are still very much with us as cultural tools.

Notes

Translations from the German in the text are by the author, unless otherwise acknowledged.

[1] In "Between Taylorism and Technocracy: European ideologies and the vision of industrial productivity in the 1920s", Charles S. Maier attempts a connection between these ideas on scientific work methods (Taylorism) and avant-garde art. Of England he writes: "Conversely, those places where the cultural avant-garde showed little response displayed less interest in the new doctrines in general. In England, before the war, schemes of scientific management awoke scant interest among engineers and managers" (p. 37). Compared with Germany this is the case, but using the expanded definition of the prosthetic beings proposed below, Hal Foster includes the founder of English Vorticism among his "Prosthetic Gods". *MODERNISM/modernity*, 4, no. 2, 5-38, 1997. This text will be further considered below.

[2] Duchamp's early work, c. 1913-14, on the *"Bride"* theme, culminating in his unfinished iconic *The Bride Stripped Bare by Her Bachelors, Even*, c. 1915 - c. 1923, could be seen to be informed by the emerging discourse briefly mapped out above.

[3] Quoted by Christine Poggi, (1997: 37). A "fleshing out", as it were, of Marinetti's somewhat frenetic embrace of the machine can be attempted with reference to Theodor Veblen's work, as found in Mark Seltzer's *Bodies and Machines*, where he writes of "Veblen's concern with 'the vague and shifting line' between the 'animate and inanimate' in turn of the century American culture". For Veblen "the interpretation of the market in 'sensuous terms' [...] is directly at odds with 'the metaphysics of machine technology'". Pessimistically, Veblen saw the end of the "radiant body", "the natural body as charismatic", under the conditions of modern culture. The Veblen work, *Theory of the Leisure Class*, was published in 1899. (Seltzer 1992: 61).

[4] German critics of the rationalisation process, such as the social theorist Siegfried Kracauer or philosopher Ernst Bloch, condemned the capitalist system's rationalisation programme: the former characterised the *ratio* of capitalism as "not reason itself but a reason rendered dreary [...]. It does not rationalise too much but rather too little. The thought which it bears resists the completion of reason which speaks from the foundations of humanity".

[5] Quoted from *Civilisation and Its Discontents*, 1930, in "Prosthetic Gods", p. 5. Marinetti uses this conceit in his own writings: "We believe in the possibility of an incalculable number of human transformations and without a smile we declare that wings are asleep in the flesh of man [...]. From now on we can foresee a bodily development in the form of a prow from the outward swell of the breastbone, which will be the more marked the better an aviator the man of the future becomes" (Poggi 1997: 37).

[6] The Ford passage itself will be returned to below in the context of German Dada.

[7] In the context of the journal *October*, whose values as a contributor Foster shares, it may be more accurate to say a psychoanalytic reading with materialist pretensions. He is aware of those "Left Fordist positions", represented by, amongst others, "Antonio Gramsci, Siegfried Kracauer and Walter Benjamin" which would propose materialist readings.

[8] Marinetti's prewar "techno-transformational" fantasies of the man/machine prosthetic embrace are confirmed for Foster in the postwar writing of Ernst Jünger, where the armoured body is foregrounded in that of the worker-soldier, steeled in the fire storms of the trenches, in a "struggle for power in battles in which events mesh together with the precision of machines", men whose faces are "metallic [...] galvanised". "Struggle as inner experience" (*Kampf als inneres Erlebnis*), 1922, and "The Worker" (*Der Arbeiter*), 1932, quoted in Herf (1984: 107-8; 133).

[9] I have traced this laying down of a "technological unconscious" in "The Diagrammatic as Abstractive Representational Mode in New York Dada" (2003).

[10] Picabia and Duchamp, of course did not subscribe to Marinetti's technological romanticism. Picabia, diagnosed as "neurasthenic", could be regarded as being opposed to any such inclination: "neurasthenia is a kind of inverted work ethic [...] an ethic of resistance to work or activity in all its forms" (Rabinbach, 1990, p. 167). Although the Zürich Dadaist Hans Richter did not conceal the group's indebtedness to Futurism, "in fact we had swallowed Futurism, bones, feathers and all", there is no prosthetic extending of the body, rather the opposite in a protest against such incorporation: their performance has been described as "spontaneous phonic ejaculations [...] underscored by brawn and bone, in jitter and gyration" (Richter 1965: 33). War experience would produce a cleaner focus on technology for the Berlin Dadaists.

[11] George Grosz satirises such recognition in his drawing, "You are assured of the people's gratitude" (*Des Volkes Dank ist Euch gewiss*) published in the Dada journal *Der Blutige Ernst* (Deadly Serious) vol. 1, no. 5, December 1919, a weekly issue, edited by the critic Carl Einstein and Grosz himself. A crippled bemedalled soldier, legless and noseless, squatting on a street corner, holds a box of matches in his primitive artificial hand, offering it for sale to conspicuously bourgeois types passing by.

[12] The source quoted is the *The One-arm Primer* (*Einarm-Fibel*) 1915, by a university teacher, one Dr Eberhard Freiherr von Künzberg, ennobled as the name indicates. Huelsenbeck's claim that everyone was a Dadaist might be ironically employed here!

[13] *Beiträge zur Frage der Ausrüstung armverletzer Kriegsbeschädigter für das Erwerbsleben*, ibid. p. 449. In *Germania ohne Hemd* ("Germany Uncovered"), a dense collage commenting on contemporary politics and culture, published in *Der Blütige Ernst*, no. 6, January/February 1920, Grosz includes an advertising image for *Dörflinger-Bein* (leg), "the best artificial leg in the world" (*bestes Kunstbein der Welt*). It is naturalised among a number of jostling discourses, including those of the recently deposed emperor, Wilhelm II.

[14] Photographic images of such injuries and disfigurement were circulated in left-wing journals after the war. A famous collection, *Krieg dem Kriege* (War against War) was published by Ernst Friedrich in 1924.

[15] The parodying of the advertising world was a Dada trope – the Berlin Dadaists established an advertising bureau as part of their cultural war. References are to be found in their publications.

[16] See reproduction in Scheunemann 2000: 63.

[17] "Wozu Geist haben in einer Welt, die mechanisch weiterläuft. Eine bald lustige, bald traurige Angelegenheit, die von ihrer Produktion, von ihrem Milieu gespielt und gesungen wird. [...]. Sie glauben original zu sein – und was geschieht? Das Milieu [...] hat den Seelenmotor angeworfen und die Sache läuft vorn allein". Hausmann, "Dada in Europa" in the Dada journal, *Der Dada* no. 3, Berlin, 1920. n.p., Kunst-bibliothek, Berlin.

[18] "Zu meinen neuen Bildern", *Das Kunstblatt*, 1921, 10-16. "Der Mensch ist nicht mehr individuell, mit feinschürfender Psychologie dargestellt, sondern als kollektiv-istischer, fast mechanischer Begriff".

[19] "Die Kunst ist in Gefahr. Ein Orientierungsversuch", reprinted in *Die Zwanziger Jahre. Manifeste und Dokumente Deutscher Künstler*, herausgegeben und kommentiert von U. M. Schneede, Köln, 126-137; "Der Dadaismus war die einzige wesentliche künstlerische Bewegung in Deutschland seit Jahrzenten [...] wir sehen damals die irrsinnigen Endprodukte der herrschenden Gesellschaftsordnung und brachen in Gelächter aus, noch nicht sahen wir, dass diesem Irrsinn ein System zugrundelag " (134).

[20] The immediate politics of the image is not being considered here. As a member of the Communist party (*KPD*) Heartfield is criticising the Socialists' espousal of the rationalising free market. The newspaper *Vorwärts* is the official Socialist (*SPD*) paper: it carries the policy statement "Back to the free market" ("Zurück zur freien Wirtschaft").

[21] Former members of the Cologne Dada group around Max Ernst, Franz Seiwert and Heinrich Hoerle, who founded the "*Progressiven Gruppe*", produced many images which could be meaningfully placed in the context of Ford's statement. One is reproduced on the cover of Sloterdijk's *Critique of Cynical Reason*.

[22] I have addressed the problematisation for representation in, "'A progressive de-materialisation of labour power': a problem for visual representation in Germany in the 1920s" (2000).

References

Benjamin, Walter
      1977   "The Author as Producer". In *Understanding Brecht*. Anna
                Bostock (tr.). Introduction by Stanley Mitchell. London: New Left
                Books.

      2003   "The Work of Art in the Age of Its Technical Reproducibility"
                (Third Version). In Howard Eiland and Michael W. Jennings (eds)
                and Edmund Jephcott (tr.) *Walter Benjamin: Selected Writings,
                vol. 4, 1938–1940*. Cambridge: Belknap Press.

Eagleton, Terry
      1998   Review of *Body Work* by Peter Brooks. In *London Review of
                Books*, 27 May 1993: 7-8. Reprinted in Stephen Regan (ed.). *The
                Eagleton Reader*. Oxford: Blackwell.

Foster, Hal
      1997   "Prosthetic Gods". In *MODERNISM/modernity*, 4 (2): 5-38.

Gaughan, Martin Ignatius
      2000   "'A progressive dematerialisation of labour power': a problem for
                visual representation in Germany in the 1920s". In *Work in
                Modern Times. Visual Mediations and Social Processes, Work
                and the Image*. 2. Valerie Mainz and Griselda Pollock (eds).
                Aldershot: Ashgate.

      2003   "The Diagrammatic as Abstractive Representational Mode in New
                York Dada". In *Dada New York: New World for Old*. M. I.
                Gaughan (ed.). New York: G. K. Hall & Co., vol. 8, *Crisis and
                the Arts: The History of Dada*.

Grosz, George and Herzfelde, Wieland
      2002   "Art Is In Danger. An Investigation" (1925). In *Art in Theory
                1900–2000: An Anthology of Changing Ideas* (Second edition)
                (eds Charles Harrison and Paul Wood). London: Blackwell.

Hausmann, Raoul
      1920   "Dada in Europa". In the Dada journal *Der Dada* 3: Berlin.

Kracauer, Siegfried
      1975   "The Mass Ornament". Reprinted in *New German Critique* 5
                (Spring).

Poggi, Christina
    1997   "Dreams of Metallised Flesh: Futurism and the Masculine Body".
                In *MODERNISM/modernity*, 4 (3): 19-43.

Rabinbach, Anson
    1990   *The Human Motor. Energy, Fatigue and the Origins of*
                Modernity. New York: Basics Books.

Scheunemann, Dietrich (ed.)
    2000   *European Avant-Garde: New Perspectives*, Avant Garde Critical
                Studies 15. Amsterdam and Atlanta: Rodopi.

Schnapp, Jeffrey
    1993   "18BLI Fascist Mass Spectacle. In *Representations* 43 (Summer):
                89-125.

    1994   "Propellor Talk". In *MODERNISM/modernity*, 1 (3): 153-178.

Schneede, Uwe M.
    1979   *George Grosz: Life and Work*. New York: Universe Books.

Seltzer, Mark
    1992   *Bodies and Machines*. New York: Routledge.

Sloterdijk, Peter
    1988   *Critique of Cynical Reason* (tr. Michael Eldred). London: Verso.

Montage and Totality: Kurt Schwitters's relationship to "tradition" and "avant-garde"

Curt Germundson

Abstract: Kurt Schwitters discussed his work in terms associated with traditional concepts of art, while at the same time adhering to the non-traditional technique of collage. Peter Bürger's influential *Theory of the Avant-Garde* is limited in that it does not allow an artist like Schwitters to be considered avant-garde. A productive theory of the avant-garde is one that accounts for artists such as Schwitters, who do not simply oppose tradition, but transform it in their work. Within the critical literature there is still a tendency to focus on Schwitters's supposed separation and isolation from society at large. A discussion in this essay of works from drawings and paintings to the collages demonstrates how Schwitters transformed nineteenth and twentieth century ideas concerning the Gothic cathedral, leading to the merging of "private" and "public" in the *Merzbau*.

1. Introduction

Peter Bürger in his 1974 *Theory of the Avant-Garde* (English translation published in 1984) discusses montage as being the "fundamental principle of avant-gardiste art", as it "breaks through the appearance of totality", by making it clear that the work is made up of reality fragments (Bürger 1984: 72). This essay will examine the way Kurt Schwitters searched for a non-conventional art while adhering to concepts that Bürger associates with the "organic" work of art. Schwitters and the evolution of his idea of the "autonomous" and "organic" work of art serve to expose the limitation of Bürger's theory of the avant-garde, for the latter sees the avant-garde purely in terms of opposition. Starting with early works by Schwitters, this essay argues for a reevaluation of his move into abstraction, by showing the importance of the Gothic cathedral and its accompanying discourse in early twentieth century Germany, making it clear that any theory of the avant-garde must allow for an artist such as Schwitters, whose work is situated in a complex inter-relationship to tradition. The assemblage *Cathedral of Erotic Misery* (also known as the *Merzbau*) is the culmination of Schwitters's search to create within the guise of an "autonomous" work of art a new kind of collective, a constantly evolving space in which ideas of the private and the social become reconciled.

22. *Kurt Schwitters,* Baum und Kirche (Z 124), *1918*

2. Schwitters and tradition

The majority of the scholarly literature discusses Kurt Schwitters's move into abstraction and collage within the context of his relationship to the Sturm gallery. In a pivotal early essay, John Elderfield focuses on the paintings called "expressions" and "abstractions" (1971). According to Elderfield, the Sturm gallery made Schwitters

develop a more Cubist style, getting away from Expressionist influences. Werner Schmalenbach similarly implies that Kandinsky and the
Sturm gallery were important for Schwitters's explorations of "expressions" and "abstractions" (1967). But Elderfield, Schmalenbach
and others downplay some very important drawings, which show
another major influence on Schwitters: the Gothic cathedral. The first
volume of the Schwitters *Catalogue Raisonné* is filled with drawings
by Schwitters that show the degree to which he dealt with the
cathedral/church as a formal theme. The church spire and clock turn
into triangle and circle in the drawing *Baum und Kirche* (Tree and
Church). It is not coincidental that Schwitters uses the shape of
churches to commit the jump into abstraction. There is a plethora of
images of cathedrals in German art of the early nineteenth and
twentieth century. Romantic artists such as Schinkel associated the
Gothic cathedral with community and the search for the total work of
art, leading to the idealising of a supposed "German" style. The early
twentieth century and the reaction to increasing industrialisation
brought with it a renewed emphasis on Gothic-derived imagery.
German Expressionist artists used concepts associated with the Gothic
cathedral for their explorations of anti-materialism and spirituality. It
is this essay's contention that the many drawings of cathedrals are
Schwitters's response to the *Zeitgeist*. He was familiar with the
discourse surrounding Gothic art, but wanted to go beyond religious
and nationalist subject matter. Schwitters's use of the term "autonomous" or "absolute" art is best seen within the context of his attempt
to free art from any shackles.

23. Kurt Schwitters, Die Sonne im Hochgebirge (G Expression 2), *1918*

2.1. The influence of Wilhelm Worringer

Between 1918 and 1919 Schwitters completed a series of paintings he labeled "expressions" and "abstractions". As examples, let us look at the works *Die Sonne im Hochgebirge* (Sun in the Mountains), which was subtitled *G Expression 2* and *Hochgebirgsfriedhof* (Mountain Graveyard), which was subtitled *Abstraktion*. Kandinsky was important as a source for the terms "expression", "abstraction" and "composition", but another name also needs to be mentioned: Wilhelm Worringer. In 1910, several years before this series, Schwitters began a manuscript entitled "The Problem of Abstract Art" while still a student at the Dresden Academy. He quotes from books by Goethe, Peschkau, Naumann, and others, focusing on the relationship between colour and music. This apparent interest in abstract art is not reflected in the paintings of 1910. There is no hint of the colours of the Brücke Expressionists, who were very well known in Dresden at the time. But years later, on 28 February 1918, Schwitters returns to the manuscript on abstract art and elaborates on his notes. Gwendolen Webster suggests it was Worringer's lecture at the Kestner Gesellschaft in Hanover on 11 February that prompted Schwitters to go back to his 1910 notebooks on abstract art (1997: 28). Schwitters made drawings on the back of these updated notes on abstraction that are very close to the style of *Baum und Kirche* of 1918, spires and churches simplified into triangles and rectangles, strengthening the argument that such drawings were an important aspect of his move into abstraction.

24. Kurt Schwitters, Hochgebirgsfriedhof (Abstraktion)*, 1919*

The lecture that Worringer gave to the *Kestner Gesellschaft* (the Hanover Kestner Society) was on contemporary art. Ever since the publication of *Abstraction and Empathy* (1908) and *Form in Gothic* (1912) Worringer was seen as an expert on modern German art movements such as Expressionism and Cubism and the way modern artists used a spiritual language akin to Gothic art. In *Abstraction and Empathy*, Worringer claims that the urge to abstraction in cultures such as the Egyptian and Gothic developed out of a need to "create resting points, opportunities for repose, necessities in the contemplation of which the spirit exhausted by the caprice of perception could halt awhile" (1908: 34-35). Empathy, on the other hand, was connected by Worringer to the naturalism or materialism of the Greeks. According to Geoffrey Waite, the ideas of Worringer and their apparent espousal of the anti-material and transcendent were used as an "open sesame to the modern movement as a whole" (1995: 16). However, Waite does not consider this to have been the original intention of *Abstraction and Empathy*, arguing instead that Worringer wanted to represent the Northern Gothic as a synthesis of naturalistic tendencies (empathy) and abstraction (1995: 22). The lecture by Worringer was discussed in the *Hannoverscher Kurier* on 12 February 1918: "A new worldview gains strength, opposing the old one based on materialism". The Worringer lecture was sponsored by the Kestner Society, an exhibition society that tried to expose the citizens of Hanover to more current styles of art than that displayed at the local *Kunstverein* (art association). The director of the Kestner Society, Paul Erich Küppers, used Worringer's connection between abstraction and Gothic notions of community in order to assure nervous collectors that such modern styles as Expressionism were not French and foreign, but anchored in the German spirit. The Kestner Society encouraged Hanover artists, including Kurt Schwitters, to form the Hanover Secession, a group that would show works independently from the annual art association exhibitions. *Die Sonne im Hochgebirge* and *Hochgebirgsfriedhof* were displayed together with other works by Schwitters, including the abstract painting *Eisenbetonstimmung* at the second exhibition of the Hanover Secession at the Kestner Society, from March until April 1919. The titles of exhibited works by various artists demonstrate the emphasis on religious themes: *Entry of Christ into Jerusalem* (Herbert Anger), *Crucifixion* and *Descent from the Cross* (Max Burchartz).

Siegfried Lang points out that Worringer created two alternative models to an aesthetic in which empathy was connected too closely to naturalism: "geometric abstraction" (as seen in Egyptian art) and the "expressive abstraction" of the Northern Gothic (2002: 116). It is my contention that Schwitters's series of "expressions" (see illustration 22) and "abstractions" (see illustration 23) are related to Worringer's legitimising of a visual vocabulary that distanced itself from pure naturalism.

25. *Caspar David Friedrich,* Kreuz im Gebirge (Tetschener Altar)*, 1808*

Schwitters's friend and Hanover art critic Christof Spengemann wrote an article in *Cicerone* XI, 18, 1919, in which he used *Die Sonne im Hochgebirge* as one of the illustrations. The year 1919–20 is crucial, for this is the period during which Schwitters turned away from religious subject matter and instead focused on abstract shapes. The *Cicerone* article solves a problem that Schwitters was still grappling with at this point: how to continue with the expression of feelings without having to rely on religious symbolism (such as crosses). Spengemann solved this problem by discussing Schwitters's abstract work in terms similar to those used in describing the Romantic painter Caspar David Friedrich's *Kreuz im Gebirge* (Cross in the Mountain): "With Circles, ovals, cubes, curves, and through dissolving colours, without centre, expanding out of eternity, these images convey the great thought of unity and cosmic harmony"[1] (1919: 576). According to Spengemann, Schwitters does not relinquish the religious language, but the "worship" is aimed at art itself, not at Christian religion and ideology. Hans Belting claims Friedrich's *Kreuz im Gebirge* "consecrated nature", creating a pure landscape in which any kind of religious or spiritual feeling came across through the landscape itself (1999: 72-73). According to Spengemann, Schwitters tries to create a pure art without conventional symbolism: "Artists working abstractly have no goal. What should the goal be? They follow their law and hover in the boundless. They glance the pinnacle and do not find the words. That is how great God is! Restlessly they must search for a form that is worthy of their feelings. The conventional is not enough"[2] (1919: 576). Spengemann uses this argument concerning unconventionality to state the legitimacy of Schwitters's use of objects in an assemblage such as *Merzpicture 1B with Red Cross*: "These objects have merely artistic value and are used naïvely: a windowpane as surface, wire as line, wire-mesh as glaze, cotton wool as softness" (1919: 578).[3] Spengemann's article is important because it shows that Schwitters's collage work developed out of Worringer's confrontation between empathy as naturalism and the use of abstraction as expression. Schwitters himself clarifies the debt he owed to Worringer's notion of abstraction in a quote from the essay "Merz", published in 1921 in *Ararat*:

> I abandoned all reproduction of natural elements and painted only with pictorial elements. These are my abstractions. I adjusted the elements of the picture to one another, just as I had formerly done at the academy, yet not for the purpose of reproducing nature but with a view to expression. Today the striving for expression in a work of art also seems to me injurious to art. (Schwitters 1921a: 76)[4]

Annegreth Nill employs the Schwitters story *Zwei Leinwände* (Two Canvases) in order to explain that for Schwitters "the contemporary artist is just as deliberate in saying something by using an abstract vocabulary as the old masters were in saying something using a figurative vocabulary" (1990: 15). In the story, Schwitters describes an artist (Smith) painting an abstract work: "Finally, the trembling yellow line completely disappeared, because Smith had gained full confidence in himself. The picture was like the forces at play in a Gothic cathedral, controlled, mystical, thorough, and deeply serious"

(Nill 1990: 14). Even though the story itself was written late in his life (most likely between 1941 and 1947), the quote is informative, for it shows the way Schwitters writes about the Gothic cathedral within the context of abstract art.

This section has contended that Schwitters moved into abstraction both through the use of formal elements of cathedrals and a working through of Worringer's ideas regarding abstraction and empathy. The following section elaborates on the aforementioned connection between Schwitters and nineteenth century Romanticism.

2.2. Romantic irony

Much of Wilhelm Worringer's theory of "abstraction and empathy" is influenced by Romantic philosophy. Schwitters too reflects notions of Romanticism, for example in a 1921 text in which he elaborates on the importance of experiencing nature and how this led him into abstraction: "In 1910, while hiking during winter alone in the *Böhmische Schweiz*, I saw the eternal laws of nature. I recognised that art could only derive from the total grasp of these laws" (Schwitters 1921a: 83).[5] It is significant that 1910 was also the year during which Schwitters started writing the aforementioned manuscript on abstract art. Although it is an exaggeration on Schwitters's part to say that he painted abstractly since 1910, it is significant that he connects this budding interest in the notion of abstraction to the experience of nature. The *Böhmische Schweiz* (borderland area between Germany and the Czech Republic) is the same place where the Dresden Romantic artist Friedrich most likely found his subject matter for his 1808 *Kreuz im Gebirge* (also known as *Tetschener Altar*). Schwitters would have seen works by Friedrich during his time as a student at the Dresden Academy, for the Dresden *Gemälde Galerie*, associated with the Academy, owned nine works by Friedrich around the time that Schwitters was a student. Iain Boyd White deals with the increasing use of sublime imagery in the early twentieth century:

> There was ... in the first decade of this century a climate of ideas that was sympathetic to the aesthetic concerns and artistic production of Romanticism. Friedrich, for example, emerged as the undisputed star of the centenary exhibition held at the National-

galerie in Berlin in 1906, which launched a reappraisal of Romantic painting. (2001: 120)

In a 1927 catalogue, Schwitters claims that he transitioned from painting representations to painting "specific atmospheres, for example the
feeling of infinity. But the goal is the general, the whole" (1927:
252).[6] This "feeling of infinity" is very much related to the Romantic
notion of the sublime. *Kreuz im Gebirge* was Friedrich's first oil
painting, completed in 1808. A Classicist art critic, Friedrich Wilhelm
Basilius von Ramdohr, accused it of going against all conventions, for
example by not having a clear fore, middle, and background. Friedrich
himself responded, saying that conventions do not have to be followed
and that if Ramdohr did not understand the work, it was his own fault.
This sounds very similar to the way Schwitters himself (and Spengemann; see previous section) discussed Schwitters's move into abstraction. Another similarity is that both Friedrich and Schwitters were
looking for harmony in their work. Gertrud Fiege says the following
about Friedrich's interest in harmony: "Nature symbolised a harmony
that was missing in society" (1977: 68).[7] Schwitters also writes about
harmony, a harmony created by the strategy of "valuing" various
elements against each other. Another parallel is that Friedrich claimed
that it was not important to "copy" nature, but rather he wanted to
"work" like nature. Fiege discusses the connection between Friedrich
and the Romantic philosopher Schlegel: "It is not the copying of nature that is important, but rather the distilling of the essential. Schlegel
too opposed the copying of nature, demanding that the artist remove
himself from representing nature, in order to create like the spirit of
nature" (1977: 72).[8] It is thus interesting to note that Friedrich did not
depict directly what he saw in front of him, but used drawings made
from different localities and points of view, combining them in his
paintings.

Besides harmony and nature, another important element that
connects Schwitters to Romantic artists such as Friedrich is the
concept of Romantic irony. According to Beatrix Nobis, Romantic
irony is all about being "stuck" between the finite and the infinite, the
dialectic between scepticism and idealism (1993: 26). Nobis mentions
in her book on Schwitters and Romantic irony that Carola Giedion-
Welcker was one of the only people who discussed the connection
between the two. Welcker saw Romantic irony as the victory of wit
over the heaviness of life (1973: 285). She published her text on

Schwitters in an August 1947 issue of the *Weltwoche,* comparing Schwitters's work and Romanticism: "While Romanticism was able to be ironic about the magical and the ideal at the same time, we see in Schwitters work how the ordinary is taken on with the ordinary" (1973: 286).[9] After reading the article, Schwitters wrote to Giedion-Welcker on August 19, 1947, saying that he especially loved her definition of Romantic irony as being about the sovereignty of the spirit. The following is the sentence that Schwitters appreciated so much: "Romantic irony in a general and timeless sense means the sovereignty of the spirit, humor as a weapon, and its victory over the heaviness of life" (Welcker 1973: 285).[10]

26. *Kurt Schwitters,* Das Merzbild, *1919*

Nobis looks at the pivotal Schwitters collage *Das Merzbild* from 1919, seeing irony in the way Schwitters uses trash in his works. Trash shows an endless potentiality of form, but at the same time it questions this endlessness, for the damaged aspect of used objects already implies the destruction of this "endlessness". Nobis paraphrases the Romantic philosopher Schlegel, saying that according to Schlegel an artist's work is "sharply delineated, but within the borders it is borderless and endless ... true to itself, everywhere the same, but at the same time towering above itself" (1993: 26).[11] Paraphrasing Schlegel, one could say that Schwitters uses formal valuing of collaged elements in order to "delineate" or limit the heterogeneity of the elements.

2.3. Toward a different kind of church: *Das Merzbild* and *Haus Merz*

This section will address Schwitters's relationship to religious ideas connected with churches and cathedrals. The previous sections discussed the way in which Schwitters embraced the formal language of circles and triangles, and began to form with objects. Looking at the work *Das Merzbild* one realises quickly that he is using in this collage a similar formal language as in the drawing that originated from the shape of a church spire (illustration 22). Schwitters, like Romantic painters such as Friedrich, is looking for an organic whole, the only difference being that he does so through the use of everyday materials, including wire mesh and newspaper cut-outs. *Das Merzbild* resembles Lyonel Feininger's famous woodcut depicting the "Cathedral of Socialism", in which three star-topped spires symbolise the unity of the three arts: painting, sculpture, architecture. Ingeborg Prange says the following about Feininger's woodcut, which was used for the Bauhaus Manifesto in 1919: "The formalised cathedral conveys the dissolving of perspective rules, and the synthesis of subject and space within the crystalline surface turns into the materialisation of the spiritual, i.e. the transcending of the material" (1991: 172).[12] The same can be said about Schwitters's church spire and *Das Merzbild*, but the "transcending" takes place in the *process* of "deforming" or "de-materialising" the materials. The key is not the purely visual connection between the church drawings and the collages, but rather the *process* of transforming the material into a harmonious composition. This emphasis on transformation is close to the way the cathedral was used by both the Romantics and the Expressionists to infuse their art with the "spiritual" and "supra-individual". Feininger's woodcut is about the loss of tradition within a materialist society, conveying nostalgia about the medieval workshops (*Bauhütte*). Gropius in the Bauhaus manifesto and Feininger in his woodcut envisioned a future in which architecture, sculpture and painting would be embraced in one unity. Schwitters in *Das Merzbild* is also searching for a way to correct the loss of tradition. But instead of celebrating socialism and the anonymous collective of workers as the element that will make the future total work of art possible, Schwitters uses the idea of valuing elements against each other. Dorothea Dietrich puts it this way: "Art, in Schwitters's terminology, becomes a substitute totality, compensating and correcting for the loss of tradition" (1993: 69).

27. Kurt Schwitters, Haus Merz, *1920*

    The work *Haus Merz* exemplifies Schwitters's view toward conventional worship and church ideology. The art critic Spengemann wrote an article in *Der Zweemann* (June 1920) discussing *Haus Merz* as an "anti-church", for it is non-functional, being filled with wheels and gears and cannot be used for religious worship. Spengemann claims that the *Haus Merz* is an "absolute" work of art: "I see in the *Haus Merz* the cathedral: THE cathedral. Not the church structure. No, the building as expression of a truly spiritual view of what lifts us into the eternal absolute art. This cathedral cannot be used" (1920: 41).[13] Schwitters used this quote in his own 1921 article titled "Merz", published in *Ararat*. It is my contention that Spengemann and Schwitters put the emphasis on the autonomous aspect of art because they wanted to free the idea of art and the cathedral from any subservience to nationalism or religion, or even socialism. This is similar to the way in which Hugo Ball with his sound poems tried to free words from any commercial connotations. Schwitters would probably criticise Feininger's "Cathedral of Socialism" (as the woodcut was known by members of the Bauhaus) for its alignment with a particular class, in this case the proletariat. The following quote from Schwitters's 1923

"Manifest Proletkunst", clarifies his view concerning art: "Art as we would have it is neither proletarian nor bourgeois: the forces it develops are strong enough to influence the whole of civilisation, rather than let themselves be influenced by social conditions" (1923: 413).[14]

28. Kurt Schwitters, Merzbau, *c. 1930*

3. Cathedral of Erotic Misery (*Merzbau*)

From the drawings to the series of "expressions" and "abstractions", through the collages *Das Merzbild* and *Haus Merz*, Schwitters works through Romantic and Expressionist notions of empathy, transforming the conception of art and the cathedral. The culmination of Schwitters's reevaluation of the cathedral idea is the *Cathedral of Erotic Misery* – the *Merzbau*. He worked on this assemblage in his home from 1923 until 1937, when he went into exile first to Norway, then to England. The *Merzbau* itself was destroyed during an air raid in 1943. The structure started with various assembled "columns", which later became interconnected. By the early 1930s, when the photograph was taken, the structure was covered by a "skin" of plaster and wood.

3.1. The *Merzbau* and the issue of private and public

The *Merzbau* began as a single "column", upon which Schwitters stuck various printed items such as newspapers and periodicals, but also smaller objects like a toy house and a rabbit's foot. After constructing several such columns, Schwitters created connections between them, merging them into one larger structure. By the later 1920s a "shell" of plaster and wood "covered up" the columns, leading to the creation of "grottoes", which were depositories of objects. Schwitters wrote the following about the contents and meanings of several of these grottoes:

> All the grottoes are characterised by some major features. There is the Nibelungen hoard with its gleaming treasure; the Kyffhäuser with the stone table; the Goethe Grotto with one of Goethe's legs as a holy relic and his many pencils poetry-worn to stub-end; the sunken "personal union-city" of Braunschweig-Lüneburg with houses from Weimar by Feininger, Persil advertising, and the heraldic sign of Karlsruhe designed by me. (1931: 423)[15]

Schwitters mentions the Kyffhäuser, alluding to the Barbarossa legend. According to this legend, emperor Barbarossa, who drowned during a crusade, is sleeping in a cave within the Kyffhäuser mountain range, ready to wake up when Germany becomes an empire again. This myth obtained Nationalist proportions when Germany became an empire in 1871 and emperor Wilhelm I was celebrated as fulfilling the visions of Barbarossa. Exhibition installer Harald Szeemann believes that Schwitters exorcises forces of nationalism in his grottoes (1995: 536). Schwitters clarifies what he thinks about nationalism in the text "Nationalitätsgefühl", which he published in 1924 in *Der Sturm*. He makes the point that there is no reason why the nation Germany should be valued any more than, for example, the nation France. Schwitters writes that based on the conventional ideas regarding patriotism, he might as well decide that the people across his street are his enemy; thus putting up a machine-gun and shooting them all down.

There were also grottoes containing objects connected with his friends. Kate Steinitz, for example, recalls that Schwitters incorporated one of her keys and a small pillbox into the *Merzbau*. Hans Richter explains that Schwitters cut off a lock of his hair and put it into a grotto. Another of these "friendship-grottoes" included a pencil taken from Mies van der Rohe. The critical literature often places emphasis on the supposed private aspect of the *Merzbau*. Elderfield, for example, claims that "[t]he *Merzbau* is an unsullied and unfettered abstract reality removed from the pain of everyday existence" (1977: 21). But this point of view neglects the various ways in which Schwitters used this structure to interact with society at large, and with tradition. Dietrich on the other hand points out the interrelationship between the "public" and the "private" in Schwitters's work: "[t]he grottoes achieved on a small scale what the *Merzbau* set out to do on a grand scale: the interpenetration of the street and the bourgeois interior" (1993: 203). Dietrich separates the grottoes into ones symbolising either *Kultur* or *Zivilisation*, "for they use as themes eros, friendship, and historical or political events" (1993: 189). Dietrich believes that Schwitters's work "enacts the contentious relations between the organic and the inorganic, the traditional and modern" (1993: 208). Within this context, Dietrich sees the *Kultur* (concerned with nationalist issues) and friendship grottoes not as polar opposites, but as building blocks for a greater whole. For Dietrich, the fragments placed within the friendship grottoes become important: "[t]hey are presented as alternative, positive fragments, symbolic of the desirable transformative processes brought about through collaboration and the disregard of nationalist concerns" (1993: 198). In a recent article, Dietrich sums up her ideas concerning the relationship between Merz and tradition: "Schwitters's Merz does not break with tradition but rather formulates paths to its redemption" (2005: 177). Beat Wyss, in the article "*Merzpicture Horse Grease*: Art in the Age of Reproduction", makes an instructive point about the issue of privacy concerning Schwitters's work: "A work of art is not made in order for its beholder to feel entitled to peek under the creator's bedcover. We will not understand the private sphere in Schwitters's work properly until we perceive it as a symbolic form of cultural technique" (Wyss 2004: 75). These arguments by Dietrich and Wyss question the idea of looking at Schwitters's work in terms of a narrow view of "privacy" and "autonomy".

Another way that Schwitters merges the personal with the societal is through his use of a guestbook, the *Säulenbuch* (Column Book). Rudolf Jahns describes a visit to the *Merzbau* in 1927:

> Schwitters asked me to go alone into the centre of the grotto and,
> after a few moments of immersion, report my thoughts in a book
> deposited there on a wooden table. I entered the site, which re-
> sembled with its many turns both a snail-shell and a cave. The
> path leading to the center was very narrow, since new sections
> and constructions, together with the already existing Merz-reliefs
> and caves, grew into the empty space. Immediately to the left of
> the entryway hung a bottle with Schwitters's urine in which float-
> ed Immortelles. Then came grottoes of different types and sizes,
> whose entries were not always on the same level. When one had
> walked all the way around, one finally came to the center, where
> there was a seat on which I sat down. I was overcome by a strange
> sensation of rapture. This room had its own special existence. The
> steps one took were barely audible, and all around was total si-
> lence. Only the grotto's form circled around me and led me to
> write words about the absolute in art. (In Dietrich 1993: 204)

Jahns describes the experience of Schwitters's *Cathedral* as a kind of
ritual, but it is one not connected to the ideology of the church or
nationalism. What Jahns describes as "the absolute in art" thus serves
to expand the idea of community. The transactional element of the
column book is underlined by Schwitters's habit of taking comments
written in it, and incorporating these into tours he gave to his friends,
who served as extensions of the community at large. In a letter of
1956, Friedrich Vordemberge Gildewart wrote that he and Sigfried
Giedion took part in such a tour that lasted three hours (1997: 323).
Katherine Dreier explains in a letter of 1930 that she is holding on to
the guestbook into which she was asked the previous year to write
about the *Merzbau* and will bring it back to Hanover when she visits
again. Dreier's letter implies that she was planning to visit Hanover in
1931.[16] But indications are that Dreier came to Hanover only in the
spring 1937, by which time Kurt Schwitters had already left Germany
for exile in Norway. It is possible that Dreier brought the *Säulenbuch*
with her at that time and that Helma Schwitters then placed it into the
Merzbau. It is most likely that this guestbook was destroyed together
with the structure itself during the bombing raids of October 1943.

Around 1930/31 Schwitters wrote a text called "The Great E",
referring to parts of the *Cathedral of Erotic Misery*, calling for sub-
missions: "Please donate objects for the Great E, objects from your
beloved working sphere, including art, kitsch, whatever you want"
(1931: 339). It is unclear why Schwitters did not publish this text, but
it shows that he was thinking about integrating objects from the com-

munity "at large" into his Cathedral, turning it into a communal project, unified by art. Schwitters's cathedral thus becomes as encompassing as Worringer's ideal of the Gothic as a "total work of art". But
Elizabeth Burns Gamard explains that there is a major difference in
the way Worringer and Schwitters use the cathedral: "In Schwitters,
however, the ideological component of Worringer – the author's projection of a unique and exclusive German identity – is inverted by the
inclusive nature of Merz" (2000: 123).

Besides the idea of "community" and "ritual", another element that Schwitters takes from the discourse on the Gothic cathedral is
that of "great unifier". Formally speaking, a Gothic cathedral unites
the various elements into a total work of art. Schwitters writes a lot
about the way elements within the *Merzbau* relate to each other,
playing shapes off each other. Schwitters opposes the nationalistic
idea of the Gothic cathedral as unifying a nation. Iris Klein discussed
the "aesthetic behaviour" of German avant-garde artists like Schwitters as replacing a "confessional-doctrinaire" type of religion (1990:
108). One can thus say that in place of the myths associated with
cathedrals and/or national monuments, Schwitters created his own
mythical site by expanding the idea of community within the
Cathedral of Erotic Misery. Hanne Bergius makes the point that the
Merzbau was meant to take up the importance associated conventionally with the cathedral and its rituals during which the present,
memory, and expectation intermingled into one revelation (1989:
205). Bergius paraphrases Schwitters's idea that to engulf oneself in
art (i.e. "sich versenken in Kunst") resembles a church service. But instead of a church service based on religious ideology, the *Merzbau* is
based on the inclusive power of Merz art to incorporate all objects,
experiences and ideas. The existence of the guestbook shows that
Schwitters was not interested in the differentiating between public and
private. It is my contention that society becomes an integral part of the
Merzbau, turning it into a "communal" and "ritualistic" space, one
that does not worship a particular religious doctrine, but instead follows the open-ended and inclusive "rules" of Merz art. Thus, Schwitters's *Cathedral*, which might at first seem purely individualistic and
subjective, actually expands the idea of community, merging the personal and the societal, setting up the experience of art as an alternative
to an art and architecture tied up with religion and nationalism.

3.2. *Merzbau* and romantic ideas concerning living systems

Leah Dickerman compares the *Merzbau* to a living body: "Yet the body invoked in the *Merzbau* is clearly very different from the one at the centre of the humanist tradition, which is whole, inviolable, and guided by the rational mind (2005: 111). She continues, discussing the structure as a grotesque body (using Bakhtin) in which the boundaries between the body and the world disappear. But instead of looking toward the "grotesque" as a possible model for Schwitters's reaction against humanist rational tradition, one could focus on the Romantic concept of the cathedral as a living and "antirational" structure. The previous section discussed the way in which the interrelationship between "private" and "public" within the *Merzbau* expands the idea of the cathedral, Schwitters himself being less interested in an ideological-religious revelation. This section will compare Schwitters's *Cathedral* to Romantic notions concerning living systems and the organic whole. Gamard describes cathedrals as organic (living) systems: "As religious edifices devoted to the intrinsic relationship of daily life and faith, cathedrals were programmed to function *as* living systems, rather than function following form, form and functions were intertwined, wedded in a unified whole" (2000: 122). Similarly, the *Merzbau* is an organic structure. Karin Orchard writes that the *Merzbau* was "not inanimate matter but living and enlivened architecture, an active space" (2004: 43). Schwitters's *Cathedral* was an active space, one that relied on the visitor's experience. Another element that relates the *Merzbau* and Schwitters's work in general to Romantic art is the fact that Romanticism also relied on the idea of process and the idea that a work is never complete. August Wiedmann points out that the Romantics believed in change and the dynamic (1979: 14). Nobis sees the *Merzbau* as a Romantic search for pure form, in which all elements of existence become part of a never-ending creation (1993: 97). She disagrees with authors such as Elderfied, who discuss Schwitters's work in terms of pure autonomy and subjectivity. Another way to put this is that Schwitters is looking for the "objectivity of the subjective" (Nobis 1993: 93). Nobis sees the *Merzbau* as the culmination of the idea of Romantic irony, for it combines the perishable with the eternal. Equally related to the concept of irony is the way Schwitters works within the contradiction between abstraction and signs of the times. Isabel Schulz has expressed it succinctly:

> Schwitters defended abstraction, when the political environment
> demanded a different form of art; only abstraction was able to re-
> flect for him his own time. Like no other, Schwitters was able to
> make the contradiction between abstraction and the manifestations
> of his own time artistically fruitful. (2004: 203)[17]

Another Romantic element is Schwitters's interest in colour and light.
Szeemann compared Schwitters's *Cathedral of Erotic Misery* to the
work of the Romantic artist Philip Otto Runge, who had "reduced the
cycle of the seasons to the experiences of a day, of its 'four times'"
(1995: 536). Schwitters had an electrician install several small bulbs,
thus "[t]he *Merzbau* shone with a morning, afternoon or evening light
at those times of day" (1995: 536). Schwitters claims in a letter to
Suse Lutter-Freudenthal from July 20, 1935, that he is interested in the
music that is played by the light within the *Merzbau*. This is reminiscent of what he wrote about the importance of colour and light in his
aforementioned 1910 notes on abstract art. Schwitters, like Runge,
was interested in creating for the beholder a "total experience". It is
also interesting that Schwitters collected articles within the *Schwarzes
Notizbuch VI* (Black Notebook VI) dealing with the healing power of
the same colour of light that he used within his *Cathedral*.

As discussed in section 2.2, Romantic philosophers such as
Schelling believed that artists needed to remove themselves from representation and instead create in the way the spirit of nature does.
According to Goethe, the cathedral possesses "inner form" and grows
naturally like a tree. Goethe alluded to the legend that the idea for the
Gothic cathedral developed out of the grove of trees, but he is using
this legend to emphasise that the laws underlying nature are the same
as those that underlie art. The following anecdote indicates that
Schwitters was aware of the Romantic notion that the original form of
the cathedral came from the shape created by a grove of trees.

> Mies van der Rohe tells that once Schwitters was on a train, carry-
> ing great roots from trees with him [the work was called *Schloss
> und Kathedrale mit Hofbrunnen*]. Someone asked him what the
> roots were, and he replied that they constituted a cathedral. *"But
> that is no cathedral, that is only wood!"* the stranger exclaimed.
> *"But don't you know that cathedrals are made out of wood?"*
> Schwitters replied. (Motherwell 1989: xxvii)

It was Schlegel who added the idea of the "crystal" to the discourse of "Gothic and nature", the idea of the forest already existing. The crystal for Schlegel symbolises the "inner geometry of nature" (Prange 1991: 9). Ingeborg Prange sees Schlegel's letters from 1804–5 as important because he describes in them the way a cathedral resembles an organism: "[t]he result of Schlegel's text consists in the dissolving of the separation between art and natural form" (1991: 10).[18] This is another link between Schwitters's *Merzbau* and Romanticism, for Schwitters also sees the *Merzbau* as a kind of organism. Isabel Ewig, in "Hans Arp und Kurt Schwitters, oder wie die Natur zur abstrakten Kunst kam" (2004), compares the *Merzbau* to the famous "needles" in the *Sächsisch Böhmische Schweiz*, which are natural phenomena. According to Ewig, the *Merzbau* grows like a crystal and the growing process is never complete. White has pointed out the importance of the concept of the crystal for Expressionist artists: "As a symbol of messianic reform, the German Expressionists turned, as their Romantic forebears had before them, to the biblical symbol of purity, order, and indivisibility: the crystal" (2001: 126). But within Schwitters's *Cathedral*, the "biblical symbol" changes into a model of open-ended transformation. Dietrich discusses the way destruction and construction become one:

> Lines, planes, cubes, and spirals – the architect's complete vo-
> cabulary – are brought together in one totality in a process that
> sees destruction and construction as interdependent. Transform-
> ation is the key; it is dynamic and organic. Comparing Merz to a
> shell that has grown out of different materials within, Schwitters
> declares Merz as a comprehensive project of organic transform-
> ation. The *Merzbau* is indeed a model for societal reorganisation.
> (1993: 198)

In the *Cathedral of Erotic Misery*, Schwitters updates the topos of the cathedral by merging the personal and the societal. Instead of religion and nationalism, what is worshipped is art and the experience of art. In the same way that a visit to a Gothic cathedral is supposed to transport the visitor to a transcendental realm, so the visitor to the *Merzbau* is meant to transact with this living and constantly changing space, experiencing for example the juxtaposition between grottoes of nationalism and those dedicated to friends and community.

3.3. Bürger's concept of autonomous art

The previous sections have demonstrated that the *Merzbau* was both autonomous and related to society at large. Peter Bürger cannot accept such a case within his definition of "avant-garde", because for him autonomy immediately means that the work of art forfeits the power to affect society. Bürger cannot tolerate the idea that art might be autonomous and affect society at the same time, which is why he is unable to consider Schwitters's art as "avant-garde", for it does not distance itself from the label "art". According to Bürger's theory of the avant-garde, montage is used by avant-garde artists to oppose the idea of an organic whole:

> The organic work of art seeks to make unrecognisable the fact that
> it has been made. The opposite holds true for the avant-gardiste
> work: it proclaims itself an artificial construct, an artifact. To this
> extent, montage may be considered the fundamental principle of
> avant-gardiste art. The "fitted" work calls attention to the fact that
> it is made up of reality fragments; it breaks through the appear-
> ance of totality. (1984: 72)

But as the preceding discussion on irony sought to clarify, Romantic artists too acknowledged art as a construct, being something of the times, while simultaneously alluding to the timeless. Friedrich, for example, combined drawings from different time periods and loca-tions when painting his landscapes, a painting method that resembles the concept of collage/montage. Schwitters, similarly, is interested in the concept of the "organic" work of art, but at the same time he does not hide the fact that his collages are artifices, made up of parts.

Bürger uses Adorno to make the point that the "man-made or-ganic work of art that pretends to be like nature projects an image of the reconciliation of man and nature" (Bürger 1984: 78). So Bürger:

> The avant-gardiste work neither creates a total impression that
> would permit an interpretation of its meaning nor can whatever
> impression may be created be accounted for by the recourse to the
> individual parts, for they are no longer subordinated to a pervasive
> intent. [...] Shock is aimed for as a stimulus to change one's
> conduct of life, it is the means to break through aesthetic imma-
> nence and to usher in (initiate) a change in the recipient's life
> praxis. (1984: 80)

But, as discussed earlier, Romantic irony as expressed by Nobis indicates that Schwitters uses the formal language of "valuing elements against each other" to create a "total impression" or "pervasive intent" (as Bürger would put it), while at the same time creating a shock, through the use of romantic irony, referring to destruction and endlessness at the same time. Dietrich discusses the difference between Schwitters's idea of collage and the one advocated by Brecht, whose concept of montage as transforming power is close to Bürger's:

> Defining collage as a process of organic transformation, Schwitters offers a collage theory radically different from that of Bertolt Brecht, who also saw collage and montage as means for societal reform but like the Berlin Dadaists defined the method in strict opposition to organic modes of representation. (1993: 203)

Schwitters uses a notion of autonomy that is close to Romanticism and ideas coming out of the reception of Gothic art immediately before the First World War. But the previous discussion of the transactional elements of the *Merzbau*, such as the guestbook, demonstrated that Schwitters's emphasis on "autonomy" was not meant as an isolation and separation from society "at large", but rather was meant as a space expanding what constitutes community.

4. Conclusion

The idea of autonomous art as developed by Kurt Schwitters needs to be understood as a reaction against the religious and nationalist instrumentation of art. This essay argues for a reevaluation of Schwitters's move into abstraction and his relationship to the Gothic and Romantic revivals. This is important, because it demonstrates the limitations of Bürger's arguments. Bürger sees the "avant-garde" purely in terms of opposition, instead of looking at the way the avant-garde was positioned problematically, even intrinsically, to tradition. The cathedral appears in Schwitters drawings and becomes a compositional device in collages such as *Das Merzbild*. The assemblage *Haus Merz* demonstrates that Schwitters opposed religious ideology. The *Cathedral of Erotic Misery*, also known as the *Merzbau*, is the culmination of his search for an open-ended and transactional concept of art and community. In the same way as Romantic writers such as Goethe wrote about Gothic cathedrals in terms of the organic, so Schwitters saw his own *Cathedral* as a living structure. The *Merzbau* became a site in which the personal and the private merged, constituting thus an alternative type of community.

Notes

Translations from the German in the text are by the author, unless otherwise acknowledged.

[1] "In Kreisen, Ovalen, Kuben, Kurven, in steigenden, fallenden, gegenseitig sich hebenden, Spannung lösenden, traumhaft verlöschenden Farben, ohne Mittelpunkt, ausgeströmt aus der Unendlichkeit: grosser Gedanke der Einheit klingen diese Bilder die kosmische Harmonie."

[2] "Abstrakt schaffende Künstler haben kein Ziel. Wo sollte es sein? Sie folgen ihrem Gesetz und schweben durchschüttert im Grenzenlosen. Sie schauen das höchste und finden die Worte nicht. So gross ist Gott! Rastlos müssen sie suchen nach Form ihres Fühlens würdig. Bisheriges reicht nicht aus."

[3] "Sie haben lediglich künstlerische Werte. Werden naiv benutzt: eine Scheibe als Fläche, Draht als Linie. Drahtnetz als Lasur, Watte als Weichheit."

[4] Translation from *Kurt Schwitters: Die Literarischen Werke*, vol. 5, 406. Quote in the original: "Ich verzichtete auf jede Wiedergabe von Naturelementen und malte nur mit Bildelementen. Dieses sind meine Abstraktionen. Ich stimmte die Element des Bildes untereinander ab, immer noch wie damals in der Akademie, aber nicht zum Zwecke der Naturwiedergabe, sondern zum Zwecke des Ausdrucks. Jetzt scheint mir auch das Streben nach Ausdruck im Kunstwerk schädlich für die Kunst zu sein."

[5] "1910 auf einsamer Wanderung in der Böhmischen Schweiz, im Winter, sah ich die ewigen Gesetze der Natur. Ich erkannte dass nur restloses Erfassen dieser Gesetze Kunst sein könne. Seitdem male ich Abstraktionen."

[6] "[…] ganz bestimmte spezielle Stimmung, etwa das Gefühl der Unendlichkeit. Aber das Ziel ist das Allgemeine, das Ganze."

[7] "Die Natur erschien als Sinnbild einer Harmonie, die in der gesellschaftlichen Umwelt vermisst wurde."

[8] "Nicht auf das Abschreiben der Natur kommt es an, sondern – so hatte schon Schlegel gefordert – auf das Herausarbeiten des Wesentlichen. Auch Schelling lehnte die Nachahmung der Natur ab und forderte, dass der Künstler sich von den Naturerscheinungen entfernen müsse, um wie der Naturgeist schaffen zu koennen."

[9] "Während die Romantik das Märchenhafte, die Idealität gleichzeitig ironisieren konnte, wird hier das Alltägliche mit Alltäglichkeit vorgenommen."

[10] "Die 'romantische Ironie' bedeutet aber ganz allgemein und zeitlos: die Souveränität des Geistes, die Waffe des Witzes und sein Sieg über die Trägheit und Schwere des Lebens". Schwitters's letter to Carola Giedion-Welcker is reprinted in Welcker 1973: 506-507.

[11] "[…] scharf begrenzt, innerhalb der Grenzen aber Grenzlos und unerschöpflich … sich selbst ganz treu, überall gleich, und doch über sich selbst erhaben."

12 "An dem trotz Formalisierung des Bildganzen erhalten gebliebene Sujet der Kathedrale wird die Auflösung perspektivischer Gestaltungsgesetze demonstriert, die Synthese aus Stoff und Raum in der kristallinen Fläche dabei zur Materialisierung des Geistigen bzw. transzendierung des Stofflichen überhöht."

13 "Ich sehe in *Haus Merz* die Kathedrale: *die* Kathedrale. Nicht den Kirchenbau. Nein, das Bauwerk als Ausdruck wahrhaft geistiger Anschauung dessen, was uns in das Unendliche erhebt: der absoluten Kunst. Diese Kathedrale kann nicht benutzt werden."

14 Translation in *Kurt Schwitters: Das Literarische Werk*, vol. 5, 413. Quote in the original: "Die Kunst, wie wir sie wollen, die Kunst ist weder proletarisch noch bürgerlich, denn sie entwickelt Kräfte, die stark genug sind, die ganze Kultur zu beeinflussen, statt durch soziale Verhältnisse sich beeinflussen zu lassen."

15 Translation in *Kurt Schwitters: Das Literarische Werk*, vol. 5, 423. Quote in the original: "Alle Grotten sind durch irgend welche hauptsächlichen Bestandteile charakterisiert. Da gibt es den Nibelungenhort mit dem glänzenden Schatz, den Kyffhäuser mit dem steinernen Tisch, die Göthegrotte mit einem Bein Göthes als Reliquie und den vielen fast zu ende gedichteten Bleistiften, die versunkene Personalunionstadt Braunschweig-Lüneburg mit Häusern aus Weimar von Feininger, Persilreklame und dem von mir entworfenen Zeichen der Stadt Karlsruhe."

16 The letter from Katherine Dreier and the response written by Helma Schwitters are located in Yale University Beinecke Rare Book and Manuscript Library among the Katherine S. Dreier Papers, Box 31, Folder 925.

17 "Schwitters hat die Abstraktion verteidigt, als das politische Umfeld eine andere Form der Kunstausübung forderte; nur die Abstraktion vermochte ihm die eigene Zeit zu spiegeln. Wie kaum ein anderer hat er den Widerspruch zwischen abstrakter Form und der Manifestation eigener Zeitbedungungen künstlerisch fruchtbar zu machen gewusst."

18 "Die Konsequenz des Schlegelschen Textes besteht in einer Aufhebung des Bruches zwischen Kunst – und Naturform."

References

Belting, Hans
    1999   *Identität im Zweifel: Ansichten der Deutschen Kunst.* Cologne: DuMont Verlag.

Bergius, Hanne
    1989   "Aspekte zum Merzbau von Kurt Schwitters". In *Architektur Experimente in Berlin und Anderswo.* Julius Posener (ed.). Berlin: Konopka.

Bürger, Peter
    1984   *Theory of the Avant-Garde* (tr. Michael Shaw). Minneapolis: University of Minnesota Press.

Dickerman, Leah
    2005   "Merz and Memory: On Kurt Schwitters" in *The Dada Seminars* (ed. Leah Dickerman). Washington: Natinoal Gallery of Art.

Dietrich, Dorothea
    1993   *The Collages of Kurt Schwitters: tradition and innovation.* Cambridge: Cambridge University Press.

    2005   "Hannover" in *DADA: Zürich, Berlin, Hannover, Cologne, New York, Paris* (ed. Leah Dickerman). Washington: National Gallery of Art.

Elderfield, John
    1973   "The Early Work of Kurt Schwitters". In *Artforum* 10(3).

    1977   "On a Merz-Gesamtwerk". In *Art International* 21(6): 21.

    1985   *Kurt Schwitters.* London: Thames and Hudson.

Ewig, Isabel
    2004   "Hans Arp und Kurt Schwitters, oder wie die Natur zur abstrakten Kunst kam". In *Schwitters-Arp.* Basel: Kunstmuseum: 159-168.

Fiege, Gertrud
    1977   *Caspar David Friedrich.* Reinbeck bei Hamburg: Rowholt Verlag.

Gamard, Elizabeth Burns
    2000   *Kurt Schwitters's Merzbau: The Cathedral of Erotic Misery.* New York: Princeton Architectural Press.

Klein, Iris
    1990   *Vom kosmogonischen zum völkischen Eros: Eine*
                sozialgeschichtliche Analyse bürgerlich-liberaler Kunstkritik in
                der Zeit von 1917 bis 1936. Munich: tuduv-Studien, Reihe
                Kunstgeschichte, Band 42.

Lang, Siegfried
    2002   "Wilhelm Worringers *Abstraktion und Einfühlung*: Enstehung und
                Bedeutung" in *Wilhelm Worringers Kunstgeschichte* (ed. Hannes
                Böhringer). Munich: Wilhelm Fink Verlag.

Motherwell, Robert
    1989   *The Dada Painters and Poets: An Anthology.* Cambridge:
                Belknap Press.

Nill, Annegreth
    1990   *Decoding Merz: An Interpretive Study of Kurt Schwitters's Early*
                Work 1918–1922. University of Texas at Austin: Ph.D.
                dissertation.

Nobis, Beatrix
    1993   *Kurt Schwitters und die Romantische Ironie: Ein Beitrag zur*
                Deutung des Merz-Kunstbegriffes. Alfter: Verlag und Datenbank
                fuer Geisteswissenschaften.

Orchard, Karin
    2004   "Kurt Schwitters's Spatial Growths". In *Merz: A Total World*
                Picture. Basel: Tinguely Museum.

Prange, Ingeborg
    1991   *Das Kristalline als Kunstsymbol: Bruno Taut und Paul Klee.*
                Hildesheim: Georg Olms Verlag.

Schmalenbach, Werner
    1970   *Kurt Schwitters.* New York: Harry N. Abrams.

Schulz, Isabel
    2004   "Die Kunst ist mir viel zu wertvoll, um als Werkzeug missbraucht
                zu werden: Kurt Schwitters und die Politik". In *Schwitters-Arp.*
                Basel: Kunstmuseum: 197-204.

Schwitters, Kurt
    1921a   "Herkunft, Werden und Entfaltung". In *Kurt Schwitters: Die*
                Literarische Werke, vol. 5, 83. Originally published in *Sturm*
                Bilderbücher IV: Kurt Schwitters.

1921b   "Merz". In *Ararat* II, 1 (January 1921): 3-9. See *Kurt Schwitters: Die Literarische Werke*, vol. 5, 74-82.

1923   "Manifest Proletkunst". In *Merz* 2. See *Kurt Schwitters: Die Literarische Werke*, vol. 5, 143-144.

1924   "Nationalitätsgefühl" Der Sturm.

1927   "Kurt Schwitters". In *Merz* 20. See *Kurt Schwitters: Die Literarische Werke*, vol. 5, 250-254.

1931   "Ich und meine Ziele". In *Merz* 21. See *Kurt Schwitters: Die Literarische Werke*, vol. 5, 340-348.

Spengemann, Christof
1919   "Kurt Schwitters". In *Der Cicerone* 11(8): 573-582.

1920   "Merz – die offizielle Kunst". In *Der Zweemann* 8 (June 1920): 41.

Szeemann, Harald
1995   "Kurt Schwitters". In *Kurt Schwitters*. Valencia: IVAM Centre Julio Gonzalez.

Vordemberge-Gildewart, Friedrich
1997   "Letter to Carola Giedion-Welcker" (1956). In *Friedrich Vordemberge-Gildewart: Briefwechsel*, vol. 1 (ed. Dietrich Helms). Nürnberg: Verlag für moderne Kunst.

Waite, Geoffrey
1995   "Worringer's *Abstraction and Empathy*: Remarks on Its Reception and on the Rhetoric of Its Criticism". In *Invisible Cathedrals: The Expressionist Art History of Wilhelm Worringer* (ed. Neil Donahue). University Park: Pennsylvania State University Press.

Webster, Gwendolen
1997   *Kurt Merz Schwitters: A Biographical Study*. Cardiff: University of Wales Press.

Welcker, Carola Giedion
1973   *Carola Giedion-Welcker: Schriften 1926–1971*. Cologne: DuMont Verlag

White, Iain Boyd
2001   "The Expressionist Sublime". In *Expressionist Utopias*. Timothy Benson (ed.). Los Angeles: Los Angeles County Museum of Art.

Wiedmann, August
1979   *Romantic Roots in Modern Art.* Surrey: Gresham Books.

Worringer, Wilhelm
1908   *Abstraktion und Einfühlung.* Munich: Piper. Translation used: *Abstraction and Empathy*, 1953, New York: International Universities Press.

Wyss, Beat
2004   "*Merzpicture Horse Grease*: Art in the Age of Reproduction". In *Kurt Schwitters MERZ: A Total Vision of the World.* Basel: Tinguely Museum.

IV. Thinkers on Stage

The Mortality of Roles:
Johannes Baader and spiritual materialism

Stephen C. Foster

Abstract: The assumption of roles among figures from the early twentieth-century avant-garde, specifically figures associated with Dada, is all too often discussed in the misleading terms of deliberate attempts at synthesising roles. Attempting to understand such a figure as the Berlin Oberdada Johannes Baader, however, demands both a critique of and departure from any notion of him as a synthesiser of roles; any role that Baader assumed became useful to him only in its assumption of relationships to other roles, and in certain key instances in its equation with other roles. This essay develops a study of Baader that not so much collapses distinction between the roles of architect, artist and God, as to preserve the distinction of each in order to work through the others. Whilst maintaining the overarching and pivotal identity of Architekt Baader, Johannes Baader could maximise his application of a conceptual model for the reformulation of all dimensions of cultural activity and reorganisation of cultural mechanics. The effect, as argued in this essay, was not to provide a synthesis of truths but to constitute Baader's truth in the disclosure of culture.

Anyone seriously pursuing a study of modernism cannot avoid formulating certain assumptions concerning the development of roles in twentieth century art and literature; above all, that roles, as we typically understand them are, in some special way, endemic to modernism and that they are transmitted culturally through modernism's institutions. It is therefore surprising that the subject has received so little attention in the literature, where cases of roles are typically presented first through categories and then through specific instances of those categories. That is, the abstract concept of the "role" is most often embodied by paradigmatic "kinds" of roles and, within them, further embodied by historically specific content.

I suspect that our concept of role may be historiographically overdetermined in these ways and that too little attention is being given to the self-definition of roles by artists, and the motives that command attention to them as starting points rather than as end results for the twentieth century concepts of artists and authors. Put another way, I think we too easily discount the historical agent's self-consciousness of role "as role", and the facts of role *per se*, conceived of independently from their realisation in any particular form.

In order to clarify some of these issues, I should like to challenge some of the operations characteristic of past work on roles and some of the assumptions latent in the historical and critical literature on the twentieth-century avant-garde as a whole. In qualifying them, I shall discuss one particular individual for whom roles became primary in the execution of his career as artist and author. In the following remarks, then, I wish to focus the questions on the nature and instrumental value of roles understood apart from any particular manifestation of roles.

The achievements of Johannes Baader rested on the fact that his acceptance, adoption or projection of roles was conceived primarily as means for a theoretical disclosure of roles. Architect, pacifist, politician, philosopher, author, theologian, scientist, prophet, historian, artist, deity and madman, among many other things, Baader's genius lay in his identification of this "instrumental" value of roles in their management. Leaving nothing to the spectator or receiver, it was precisely his indiscriminate adoption and deployment of every imaginable role, for the navigation of specific situations, that revealed the character of roles as essentially transactional. Roles were clarified less in their revealment than in their exploitation. Actions formulated by Baader and Raoul Hausmann serve as adequate examples of their intentions. The 1917 creation of the Jesus Christ Club (with Franz Jung), organised around an all-Berlin parade, was to serve as the occasion for the distribution of bibles to the population as preparation for Baader's discussions of the new era of world peace. Employing a role characteristic of Baader's early career as a prophet, one could purchase, for the modest sum of fifty marks, certification of themselves as Christ and thereby claim exemption from service in the war. Baader served as president of the Club (he was given a purple cloak by Hausmann as a sign of his office) much as he had for the Inter-Religious League of Humanity ten years earlier (Hausmann 1980: 55).

In such cases, it is the artist or author that projects the roles, but not so much as a means of explaining something, either through role types or through their content specifics, so much as a means of creating or configuring something. I wish to maintain that in Baader's case, relationships in a situation are re-structured by the adjustment forced through the "placement" or "deployment" of a role.[1] Roles were designed to provide the artist with highly self-conscious, theoretical approaches in their use. This invocation and manipulation of conventional roles sought not to validate the content of the role, but to assert its operational parameters in strictly artistic and more broadly cultural situations.

Baader's divergent objectives can be located in his different concepts of culture. And it is Baader, for this reason, I would maintain, and not the usually exemplary Duchamp, who responds best to our own concerns with "role" – but he does so less as a constituted element of culture than a constitutive basis of culture. Roles are typically as useful as they are believable, and they are normally made believable by the authority of the culture as a whole; that is, the culture understood as a whole thing or as a world composed of a compatible and stable set of world-views. Whether this compatibility or stability is real or imagined is irrelevant. Indeed, it is probably as real as it is successfully imagined, a fact accounting for Baader's easy adoption of a variety of roles, including that of Jesus. For Baader, then, the question of roles was inseparable from questions of cultural politics (of which God and the Kaiser are outstanding examples), and their consequences were decipherable through their determination of that politics. Reduced to the level of materials for composing alternative authority and power, the truth value claimed by any specific role was neutralised in favour of its largely structural purposes in the reconfiguration of culture as a whole.

Das ist die Erscheinung des Oberdada in den Wolken des Himmels illustrates the point on both the literal and figurative levels, and both in the pictorial and textual components of the work. Social realities are presented largely through media evidence, fragmented to the point of near complete dissolution. Yet, through the mirroring of the wartime chaos, the organisational structure of the society is discerned through roles accounting for its then present condition and the role(s) through which it would be reconstituted; that is, Architekt Baader, whose photograph sits in the centre of the universe, a clear reference to one of Baader's early visions in which a voice from the heavens had ordered the world to "mobilise around Baader". Further indications of Baader's roles include reference to Baader's attempt to stand as Reichstag candidate in September 1918, for instance. The cultural invisibility of the roles as roles – typically hidden behind the culture specific content of the roles – was dispelled, and roles were revealed as the means for recreating individuals, nations and worlds.

29. *Johannes Baader,* Das ist die Erscheinung des Oberdada in den Wolken des Himmels, Der Dada *no. 2, Berlin, December 1919*

Understandably, such a use of roles depended precisely on their disembodiment of any culturally specific content; that is, the cancellation or nullification of content became the necessary condition of role value in formulating and transacting concepts of culture. In the course of this, the artist's concepts of truth, power and authority become no more than the cause for identifying and configuring useful concepts of role. In no case was the truth, power or authority derived from the role itself. New or better truths are not secured through advancement of the content of the role. Rather, preferred truths are substantiated by means of reconsidering the nature and cultural location of the roles embracing them. Short of this, roles are disempowered as a constitutive basis in structuring culture. What Baader may have believed was never the issue; the constitution of these beliefs as truth and their cultural empowerment was forever the issue.

Despite the artist's devaluation of a role's content (as truth, power or whatever), he or she had to be perceived as a truth-teller, power-base, or authority figure – had to be seen therefore as a figure in whom one believed. Baader's *Author at Home* pictures are, on one level, the artist in his studio and, on another level, "God in his Heaven" at the moment of the "Creation".[2] The cosmic principles and revisionist platforms of the earlier works are now entirely assimilated into his "role" as artist – the artist as creator, and the artist as God. What has occurred is the complete aestheticisation of his role, the content it carries, and the means by which it is constituted. The success of this was to rest in the "truth" of the strategy of truth (which may or may not be true) and the "power" of the transaction of power (which may or may not be powerful); where the "role of the authority" is transformed into the "authority of role".

Baader sought nothing short of a new world-view achieved through the aesthetic management of roles. Intersecting at sur-roles, characteristic of "whole" cultures, Baader's alternative was bodied forth and given the appearance of substance through its constant rehearsal (in his visual works, texts and actions) where Baader played all the roles. Events became the unfolding of his roles and the exercise of their content, both the "creations" of responses to reconstituted truths. Their authority, won through their interception of and projection onto conventional events, acted parallel to conventional culture but never in its service.

The theory of roles implied in Baader's overall activities were made explicit in his pictorial, performative and textual works. Nowhere in the twentieth century do we get such a clear image of role, or such a compelling image of the artist as role. Neutralised in terms of their conventional content, the specific roles are stated in terms that can best be described as structural, where the structural is made to coincide with the aesthetic, and where both are made to coincide with the political. Ranging through the liberal, the conservative and the reactionary, these roles nevertheless persuade our belief – in the truth of their "strategy of truth", and the power of their "transaction of power". Baader's alternative culture rests on political fictions (understood broadly), no different in kind than the fictions of all cultures; its wholeness on the creation of high-level abstractions characteristic of all cultures; its prosecution in the restructuring of the role patterns by which the new culture is played out.

It would be as wrong to see Baader as a collection of roles as it would be to see him as a synthesis of roles, although there were roles that he frequently adopted.[3] Baader was never content to assume roles. They found use only in the relationships they assumed to other roles. Baader's greatest overall project, his daybook HADO, was literally a daily recreation of his life as he understood it at any given point. In no way cumulative, virtually devoid of any comprehensible narrative, and conceived of independently of his beliefs (which he frequently parodied as "mere" beliefs), the whole point seems to rest in the establishment of an order, recollaged daily, of which his own actions and deeds (as well as those of others) became the source, but not the point. Witness to his creations, but not "of" his creations, he gives proof of the mortality of roles and of his own godliness ("Dieses Buch ist weder Koran, noch Bibel, noch Tipitakam, sondern HADO").[4]

30. Johannes Baader, HADO, announcement, Berlin, 1919

Far exceeding the mere formulation of social worlds (the business of De Stijl and Constructivist reformers), Baader's ambitious project demanded nothing less than the role of roles to which, strictly speaking, there could be only one claimant (although we know, historically speaking, this was not the case). The period threw up a number of messianic leaders who preached redemption and attracted bands of believers, sometimes dressing in robes and sandals in imitation of Christ and wandering from place to place; such were Johannes Guttzeit and his "Bund fur volle Menschlich-keit" of the Bavarian Diefenbach. Such figures became models (roles) for characters by Conrad, Hauptmann, and Th. Mann whose prophets are artists and bohemians who, according to Roy Pascal, "put religious roles to a sophisticated misuse" (1973: 172-173, 161ff).

If there was any place in need of a God, it was surely post-1918 Germany. Politically thrown into a state of complete chaos, morally bankrupt and culturally disgraced, it provided fertile ground for any further deconstructing of culture not already accomplished by the First World War. Between 1917 and the impending loss of the war, and Weimar's stabilisation (or appearance of stabilisation) in the early twenties, countless schemes were hatched for rehabilitating culture in ways that would provide a fair and just society. Roles were assumed in the name of responsibility to culture and include many or all of the cases discussed in other contributions to this literature; that is, genius, hero and seer, cultural anthropologist, psychoanalyst, social engineer and political activist. Yet most of them, derived from the far reaches of the politically and culturally right or left, contented themselves with reenacting roles too familiar for comfort; roles that were only marginally less predictable than those of pre-1914 Germany. Their conventionality and stereotypicality became the target of much of the Dadaists' most cutting criticism. Indeed, it was in defeating such roles that Berlin Dada defined itself, particularly through the "role" of the Oberdada (Baader's execution of his role somewhat exceeded the expectations of Club Dada – his willful and preemptive actions caused some of the members real concern for their own safety).

Raoul Hausmann, looking back on the Dada movement, had proclaimed that "Baader was the right man for Dada" (1980: 55). What made him right was his identification of a sur-role located outside conventional human affairs; a role that assiduously avoided the normalcy, advocacy and partisanship that roles, as we typically understand them, involve. *Dada Milchstrasse*, a photocollage dating from 1920, presents Baader's programme, worked out, for the most part, in terms of the roles it configures (roles familiar from the *Das ist die Erscheinung des Oberdada in den Wolken des Himmels*, discussed above). Baader becomes the principle by which the chaos of wartime Germany is reconstituted into a new order – a new era of world peace which, significantly enough, commenced on the occasion of Baader's death and resurrection on April 1 and April 2, 1919! Historical roles, as they are reflected in the texts and images incorporated into his works, are repositioned, structured according to substantially new terms, and made the "mere" materials of an aesthetically conceived re-creation of the world.

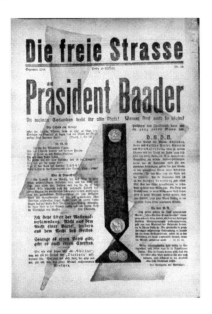

31. Johannes Baader, guest editor, Die freie Strasse *no. 10, Berlin, 1918*

It is scarcely surprising that the architect of the universe exerted his authority, over human affairs as well, absorbing as his subjects (as he had historical figures in *Das ist die Erscheinung des Oberdada in den Wolken des Himmels*) the roles of Weimar's political leaders. Subsumed under the same authority and subjected to the same structure, the society of temporal affairs is cast in the image of universal order; that is, Baader himself. Issue number 10 of *Die freie Strasse*, and *Dada Milchstrasse*, betray the visible outlines of culture within which roles quietly take their place. The texts from which the works are collaged, in both the photomontage and the paper, are nothing less than the cultural texts of roles salvaged from his own and others' pasts. They sit together not as a synthesis of truths of culture but as a constitution of the truth of culture. His configuration of roles disclosed his concept of culture.

Sophisticated in his understanding of twentieth-century culture, Baader clearly recognised that roles, insofar as they were assumed by people who were essentially media constructions, are likewise media constructs, the subjects of cultural texts. The *Commemorative Page to Gutenberg*[5] focuses on the source and production of the texts by which we come to understand ourselves as roles. The pictorial works (which we too summarily dismiss as "collage") provide the blueprints of a fundamentally reconceived culture.

32. Johannes Baader, "Dadaisten gegen Weimar"
broadside manifesto, Berlin, 1919

Everything, whether it was its original author's intention or not, is made a role. It is true of monuments, beliefs, systems and professions, and it is true of actions; for example, Dada's declamation of Weimar, given voice by the authority (role) of the Oberdada, or the *Grüne Leiche*,[6] the text for Baader's extravagant behavior at Weimar's first National Assembly. The former, the 1919 document *Dadaisten gegen Weimar*, well indicates Berlin Dada's creation of a remarkable

role for Baader that surpassed all other roles – "Oberdada als Präsi-
dent des Erdballs". Although a mock role designed to be filled by a
fool, it satisfied Baader's platform perfectly. His skillful execution of
this role, made easier by his 1917 certification as insane and the im-
punity that entailed, provided him with a power base and capability
for sensation greatly appreciated by the media which followed his
activities with enthusiasm. To all his other roles Baader added those of
"personality" and "celebrity". All these actions are only important to
the degree that they assume roles or reflect the roles which bear them
in the overall design of a new culture to which they are made to
submit.

Baader was not unaccustomed to heavy responsibilities. In
1905–06 he had projected plans for what would have been the largest
structure in the world. A utopian city built by a labor force of all humanity over a construction period of one thousand years, the project
was to be organised and financed by the Inter-Religious League of
Humanity of which he, Baader, was president (Bergius, Miller, Riha
1977: 181-191).[7] Assumed out of his role as prophet, the enterprise
fell victim to the insensitive horde of mediocrity, which five years
later first tried to commit him to an asylum, and which ten years later
succeeded. It was only with the total collapse of German culture that
Baader regained his footing; but even then, not without the total transformation of his role as artist from prophet to Godhead.

Assessing Baader's activities is a difficult business. Richard
Huelsenbeck, fellow Dadaist, acting out of his roles as psychoanalyst
and poet, brushed aside Baader as a clown and a fool, a task made
easier by the facts that Baader had been legally certified insane, that
he exhibited, in the International Dada Fair of 1920, the luggage he
used in his first escape from an insane asylum, and that he penned a
card to Tristan Tzara declaring he had discovered in German a new
and beautiful name for genius – "fool".[8] But, of course, such an explanation will not do. It is precisely Baader's role as fool that underscores the role basis of charges brought against him.

As mortuary architect, Baader enjoyed considerable success
through 1906–07; as a pacifist he was minor; as a politician ineffect-
ive; as an author unimaginative; as a theologian idiosyncratic; and as a
prophet marginal, measured even by the peculiar standards of early
twentieth-century Germany. Yet, as a creator, he commands our serious respect. Baader never required the concept of art or artist. Indeed,

the latter was only an available metaphor for what he conceived to be his real position; artist was a role that he freely absorbed, as he did all others, into his constructions of culture. At his best a culture-maker, conventional roles are trivialised by Baader into something like their real stature in culture. The image of maker is nowhere in twentieth century art better realised than in *The Author of the Fourteen Letters from Christ in his Home*, and its three-dimensional realisation in the *Dada-Dio-Drama* of 1919–20, works that imply a sophistication in his understanding of culture rarely rivaled by his contemporaries. Con-structed of the very stuff of culture, the texts of its roles, Baader was surely justified in thinking that his insights would be rewarded; that after fifteen years, people would, in his own words, "mobilise around Baader".

33. Johannes Baader, Dada-Dio-Drama, *1919–20*

In 1918, Baader, with the blessings of Club Dada, nominated himself for the Nobel Prize.[9] The document, an open letter to poet Paul Ernst, carefully explained the limits of specialised knowledge – that, for example, of science or any other knowledge proscribed by roles – and its inability to guarantee its own constructive and creative use. This was his, Baader's, responsibility, and the clear justification for being made the award. The unkind reception of his proposition by the press left him basically undaunted. Tantamount to Baader's crucifixion, the whole affair was simply consigned to his work; an event among other events ... a role played, among other roles played.

Notes

[1] For a description of such a case, Baader's dissemination of the broadside *Grüne Leiche* and how roles can fold into events, see Stephen C. Foster, "The Prerequisite Text", *The Avant-Garde and the Text* (Providence: *Visible Language*, 1987), pp. 327-331.

[2] See reproduction in Scheunemann 2000: 59.

[3] In the open letter to Paul Ernst ("Ein Brief an den Dichter Paul Ernst", typeset letter, Berlin, 1918) Baader faults science, interpreted narrowly, as a wrong or inadequate kind of knowledge as it fails to address ultimate things. The solution, claims Baader, rests with the synthesiser of fields, or dilettante, who is capable of whole world views. This is "a role", however, no less than his other roles.

[4] Long ago dispersed, the appearance of the HADO was announced for June 28, 1919. The document is signed "Der Verfasser: dada".

[5] See reproduction in Scheunemann 2000: 61.

[6] See reproduction in Scheunemann 2000: 57.

[7] See also Stephen C. Foster, "Mediale Wahrnehmung und stadtische Realitat: Die Kunst des Johannes Baader", *Die Zunkunft der Metropolen* (Berlin: Dietrich Reimer Verlag, 1982), pp 528-531.

[8] The card is reproduced in *Johannes Baader: Oberdada*, p. 72, document number 55.

[9] The letter is reproduced in Stephen C. Foster, "Johannes Baader: The Complete Dada", *Dada/Dimensions* (Ann Arbor: UMI Research Press, 1985), p. 256, figure 11-2).

References

Bergius, Hanne; Miller, Norbert; Riha, Karl (eds)
    1977   *Johannes Baader: Oberdada*. Giessen: Anabas Verlag.

Foster, Stephen C.
    1982   "Mediale Wahrnehmung und stadtische Realitat: Die Kunst des
               Johannes Baader". In *Die Zunkunft der Metropolen*. Berlin:
               Dietrich Reimer Verlag.

    1985   "Johannes Baader: The Complete Dada". In *Dada/Dimensions*.
               Stephen C. Foster (ed.). Ann Arbor: UMI Research Press.

    1987   "The Prerequisite Text". In *The Avant-Garde and the Text*.
               Providence. *Visible Language* 21: 3/4.

Hausmann, Raoul
    1980   *Am Anfang War Dada*. Karl Riha and Günter Kämpf (eds).
               Giessen: Anabas Verlag.

Pascal, Roy
    1973   *From Naturalism to Expressionism*. New York: Basic Books.

Scheunemann, Dietrich (ed.)
    2000   *European Avant-Garde: New Perspectives*, Avant Garde Critical
               Studies 15. Amsterdam and Atlanta: Rodopi.

To Be or Not To Be ... Arthur Cravan:
subject, surface and difference

Dafydd Jones

Abstract: This essay addresses the question of the counter-appropriation of cultural pose, identity and persona, and its symbolic nature, around the instance of the proto-dada poet and boxer Arthur Cravan. The individual subject is read as an effect of the social system preceding it, and so it is the same system that gives the subject its identity. The subject comes into being as a signifier active within and identified by the system – the late twentieth century expansion on structural marxism that constructs a logic of consumption around the sign then charts our movement within the intricacy of relations between sometimes replaceable if not interchangeable signs, struggling with and problematising the systematicity of subject-object relations. Artistic engagement with and breakdown of the analytical truth of the object, the world and the social sphere, is exercised by deconstructing their appearances; deconstructive arrest then becomes the condition for reconfiguring the object, the world and the social sphere, to constitute in the process new "truths" in new appearances.

In Paris, on June 10, 1909, the leading column of *L'Echo des Sports* carried a short article signed at the bottom by one Fabian Lloyd. Fabian Avenarius Lloyd was the "real" name of the cultural itinerant, poet and boxer soon to spring out of his corner as Arthur Cravan. The article, "To Be or Not To Be ... American" concluded a formative phase for the writer spent "masticating space" and roaming the globe, and set out strategic indicators for Cravan's movement over the following decade, up until his disappearance in 1918. Assuming pose, the article argued, counted for everything as it would emerge in avant-gardist exploitation of cultural situations, exploitation of the social field as marked according to an exchangist model that would posit individuals as unified, autonomous agents. The article, which functioned effectively as Cravan's proto-manifesto, presented pose, appearance and the adoption of role as a strategic principle of cultural agency and engagement – specifically in this instance in order to *be* American, "or at least to look like you are one, which is exactly the same thing" (Cravan 1995d: 33). For the next ten years, Cravan would practice a mode of action that he ironically foregrounded in his article, there addressing a constituency regarded variously as his audience, colleagues and accomplices – the readership and interested parties of sports journals and newspapers, that is to say "everyone who is slightly sporty and capable of being of interest to us" (1995d: 33). His action was founded on a fundamental belief in the disunity and disharmony of the subject and of individual identity, from which position he mounted his exploitative, yet sincere, assault on society.

34. *"To Be or Not To Be ... American"*, L'Echo des Sports, *Paris, 10 June 1909*

"I am here," said Cravan, "because life has no solution." Wherever "here" might have been, conceptually or in the most literal terms, Cravan's conviction regarding individual disunity would again deliberately be voiced as, in contemplative mood, he dreamed of distant places and other poses from the Parisian evening gloom. So he continued:

> I can make merry in Montmartre and a thousand eccentricities, since I need them [...]. I, who dream myself even amid catastrophes, I say that man is only so unfortunate because a thousand souls inhabit a single body. (1995b: 51)

The body takes form as the site of contesting forces, a thousand struggling souls, a disassembly in effect constituted as an assemblage through infinite connections. Thus the dream of Cravan produced monsters, "under the pseudonym of *The Mysterious Sir Arthur Cravan*, the world's shortest-haired poet, *Grandson of the Chancellor to the Queen*, of course, *Oscar Wilde's Nephew*, likewise of course, and *Alfred Lord Tennyson's Great Nephew*, once again of course" (Cravan 1995c: 62). The stream of credentials continued as he announced his arrival in the boxing ring, invoking the poses – sometimes imagined, sometimes real – of confidence man, sailor, snake charmer, hotel thief, lumberjack, chauffeur, and nephew to the Royal Commissioner into Welsh Sunday Closing. What those outside the ring looking in saw unfolding before their eyes was not a roll call of characters under the direction of one authorial consciousness – let's say of Directeur Cravan and his Paris periodical *Maintenant*[1] – but rather "a plurality of consciousnesses, with equal rights and each with its own world ... [which] combine but are not merged in the unity of the event" (Bakhtin 1984: 6-7). The event, as consciousnesses combined, empties roles of their perceived content, setting up simultaneously their cultural visibility and cultural transparency in critical engagement with concepts of culture; the body's assemblage, as Bakhtin's observations here indicate, gives us the polyphonic body (1984: 6-7).

Without content, roles are made redundant in their former function of structuring culture, and assume new authority in relating to other roles and in mirroring cultural contexts. In the occurrence of the event, transformation makes the value of a role contingent always upon its cultural location, and no longer does role rely on any former content for truth currency or authority. When Mina Loy looked back and wondered "how it was that I had been able to recognise any identity behind his frequent transformations" (1986: 108), structured meaning for her (by then) lost husband Cravan appeared as an impermanent effect, as for the philosopher there is no identity, or being, behind doing – the deed is everything.[2] So the suspension of a notion of truth permits the pursuit of systematic scepticism of the environment and of its structures; truths disintegrate, genealogies are exposed, and truths are revealed to be, precisely, untruths. Cravan responded to his environment with the realisation:

> "At once I knew that everyone was lying to me – that Life was not *like that*." His own interpretation of truth was so precious that he safeguarded it with lies, as others presented their lies with a semblance of truth. (Loy 1982: 321)

So, even in his own interpretation of it, "truth" became an unstable notion to play with, "without any moral additive, in forever equal innocence" (Nietzsche 1987: 62). His strongest objection was to being told *what* to do and *how* to think, and that objection was most forcibly demonstrated in his categorical refusal to accept what he took to be orders from others, even at the most mundane and menial level:

> He got a job at Brentano's and threw all the books in his first client's face because she said, *"allons, allons!"* when he fumbled with tying up the string. He considered it outrageous that a mere little French actress should say *allons, allons* to *Him*, and he walked out. (Loy 1982: 317)

In refusal and rejection of conditions imposed by others, Cravan was reacting against stratification, the process of reciprocal sedimentation and setting up of stable functional structures, the continuous "passage from sediment to sedimentary rock" (Deleuze and Guattari 1988: 40-41). It is the stratification that Deleuze and Guattari engage with and struggle against theoretically:

> You will be organised, you will be an organism, you will articulate your body – otherwise you're just depraved. You will be signifier and signified, interpreter and interpreted – otherwise you're just a deviant. You will be a subject, nailed down as one, a subject of the enunciation recoiled into a subject of the statement – otherwise you're just a tramp. (1988:159)

We might nonetheless concede that Cravan was more or less perceived in these very terms, as a depraved, deviant, itinerant tramp, even by the *belle époque* Parisian constituency to whom he proudly

proclaimed, "Je mangerais ma merde!" (Conover 1995: 27) – a plebeian figure in whose very stance the stable orders of state sensed
some challenge and threat to continued, uninterrupted, stability. De-
siring always to maintain or, when put under threat, to resume
"normal" service, the state consolidates its boundaries and raises its
city walls. It is by his proximity to these walls that Cravan assumes
the qualities elsewhere ascribed to the ancient Greek kynic Diogenes,
"the plebeian outsider inside the walls of the city who challenged the
state and community through loud satirical laughter and who lived an
animalist philosophy of survival and happy refusal" (Huyssen 1995:
165). In retrospect, then, it is hardly surprising that Cravan, this
paradoxical stateless citizen, was rudely ejected from another city,
Berlin, by the city police in 1905, for the crime of being "too
noticeable" (Conover 1982: lviii) – a modern equivalent perhaps for
the poets that Plato would have expelled from the Republic for the
crime of yielding deleterious effects in singing of appearances and of
surfaces.

1. Enabling constraints

The struggle we encounter in the poet and boxer is the struggle of subjectification, between the unformed, or form-resisting, subject matter
of Cravan, and the external form of the state. Subjectification sees the
body being fixated by the state, being given a precise form, and then
being held accountable to that form. Actively to forget that such a
process takes place is surely itself a component in that process, and
underlies Althusser's famous assertion that "those who are in ideology
believe themselves by definition outside ideology ... ideology never
says, 'I am ideological'" (1971: 175). Hence, the body that resists the
appellation "body" militates resistance to the unthought (and therefore
unstated) reproduction of the subjectifying procedures of state agen-
cies of power. The refusal of orders fundamentally appeals to the
possibility of finding escape routes and of stepping outside prescriptive behavioural and thought patterns, because, inevitably, "[t]ruly,
what man of the State has not dreamed of that paltry impossible thing
– to be a thinker?" (Deleuze and Guattari 1988: 376).

    Posing the question alerts us to closures and obstructions to
the possibility of thinking or existing without state-imposed con-

straints; they are the closures and obstructions that bind the individual to the social, the subject to the state, as "a human being alone is an impossibility, not just *de facto*, but as it were *de jure*" (Taylor 1985: 8). It is an impossibility, however, which does not deny the critical function of recognition, as again Althusser describes how

> the formulation of a *problem* is merely the theoretical expression of the conditions that allow a *solution* already produced outside the process of knowledge ... to *recognise itself* in an artificial problem manufactured to serve it both as theoretical mirror and as a practical justification. (1977: 231)

Indeed, and accordingly, the subject's recognition that he or she is placed in ideology does not lead to a release from ideology, but the recognition of ideology as "a process of *repetition*" itself entails the subject's perception of his or her own subjectification (Badiou 1967: 49). The impossibility of a human being alone, then, fails to prohibit the possibility that existence without the regulation of the state apparatus can, under certain conditions, be negotiated by the individual who always remains a state subject. The notion of the outsider inside the city walls is instructive, proposing relatively unconstrained movement that is nonetheless responsive to state structures when it comes up against them – effectively, it proposes a notion we might provisionally term an *interior* exteriority, analogous in this sense to the idea of "indirect discourse" or notions of subjectless subjectivity.

To pursue this, we would note that by constituting his truth in the disclosure of culture, Cravan was blissfully unconcerned with any synthesis of truth in the unified, sovereign subject. His truth was rather constituted at that point where the functioning of external forces is admitted, that is where sovereignty wanes and agency begins. As agent, the individual who yields sovereignty acts "to the extent that he or she is constituted as an actor and, hence, operating within a linguistic field of enabling constraints from the outset" (Butler 1997: 6). The enabling constraints that Judith Butler here names demarcate the stage of the performative, the stage upon which action becomes perlocutionary, to the extent that what is initiated is a set of consequences distinguishable from their origin by an emerging interval. The consequences are not the same as the act, which means that progress for the perlocutionary act is achieved by way of consequences; the interval, as a temporal distinction, accommodates a less defined space that in turn allows movement *in-between* the act and the effect.

This in-between, *un entre-temps*, is where the event occurs (Deleuze and Guattari 1994: 158) – it is where Cravan occurs as an assemblage constituted through the connections between parts. The notion of the assemblage, or body-assemblage, however, deceptively advances a sense of itself as being a complete and fully formed thing, when we ought initially to address Deleuze's question:

> What is the body? We do not define it by saying that it is a field of forces, a nutrient medium fought over by a plurality of forces. For in fact there is no "medium", no field of forces or battle. There is no quantity of reality, all reality is already quantity of force. (1983: 39-40)

As expressive therefore of the relationships between forces, the body is an idea that is implicated through a plurality of elements, a series of *possible* selves, even disposable selves, which takes us beyond the address of a sequence of poses in the recovered Cravan narrative, where we encounter the poet and boxer giving himself as a representation that always implies his absence rather than his presence, reminding us of the confusion of the body with the subject. In the implication that Cravan's presence is somewhere outside the representation given to us, such otherness is to be taken as highly affirmative of the polysemy of representations, positing the self as always in excess of what we have (re)presented to us. Here, representation is located not in sameness but in *difference*, so in Nietzschean terms proposing repetition that does not generate copies but rather traces of an original that has itself never existed, through multiplicities and disjunctions asserting that "difference is behind everything, but behind difference there is nothing" (Deleuze 1994: 57). In a particular sense, Cravan recedes from focus as the embodiment of the object of any enquiry, as we witness in him an acting out of the *idea* of Cravan.

*

The idea, inevitably, impacts against state structures, just as the outsider runs into the city walls. Indeed, the collision is demonstrably to be found in the bizarre sequence of events that started in 1909 in Paris, for instance, when Cravan signed up for his first formal boxing lessons at the club Cuny, on the rue du Faubourg du Temple. With his proto-manifesto "To Be or Not To Be" under his belt and having already stated his intention – "Americans are feared since they know how to box – or at least are supposed to" (1995d: 34) – he was shaping up for competition at the start of 1910, and in February won his way through to the final of the Second Annual Championship of Amateur Boxers. There, in anticipation of what was to unfold, the first default of his boxing career promoted him to the light-heavyweight division champion, when his opponent withdrew. Cravan was back in the ring in March, in the same weight division, for the Eighth Meeting of the Boxing Championships for Amateurs and Soldiers. Then followed the almost if not farcical accumulation of defaults as a string of opponents fell by the wayside, either through disqualification, withdrawal or resignation, leading to the supremely proto-dada occasion of Cravan becoming the French Amateur Light-Heavyweight Boxing Champion without once stepping into the ring:

> His life was unreal, or surreal, in that he never *was* the things he became. [...] For instance, he became *champion de Boxe amateur de la France* without boxing, because all the challengers sat in a row and he was presented and they all resigned. Nobody would box him so he was champion. (Loy 1982: 317)

Which is, as Cravan would no doubt argue, exactly the same thing. In retrospect, the necessary fluidity of movement by which Cravan could quite literally become a boxing champion is understood; the principle had been publicly stated since at least June 1909, when Cravan wrote how "[c]aps with outrageous peaks are tolerable only for boxers or those who wish to pass as such, which is exactly the same thing" (1995d: 36).

The body-assemblage, drawing upon the "fatal plurality" with which Cravan grappled, articulates both critical and creative function, with its fluid form making its "meaning" even more so. Critically, the body evaluates existing values, and creatively it engenders new ones, as "[t]he point of critique is not justification but a different way of feeling: another sensibility" (Deleuze 1983: 94). This process of engendering new values posits the notion of the perpetually creating, ever unfinished, ambivalently dual image of the body from which a new body always emerges in another form. The image is one that finds its only accommodation in unofficial culture, in those forbidden

spots and unaccepted places, for instance, that Cravan would invariably be drawn to:

> Arrived at a new town he would give it a glance and assess its
> population – then tramp through every street ... wherever one
> went with him one was sure to arrive sooner or later in some
> forbidden spot – so intuitively did he separate himself from the
> accepted places. (Loy 1982: 320)

Cravan's perceived intuition is generated from his defiant aversion to
and refusal of "all possible lines of conduct presented to him as en-
gagements with untruth" (Loy 1982: 321), and advances his resistance
to stratification. Such resistance, however, should deliberately exercise its own resistance against destroying strata altogether, in acknow-
ledgment of strata as enabling means to proceed and operate in the
world. As Deleuze and Guattari caution:

> you have to keep small supplies of signifiance and subjectifi-
> cation, if only to turn them against their own systems when the
> circumstances demand it ... and you have to keep small rations of
> subjectivity in sufficient quantity to enable you to respond to the
> dominant reality. (1988: 160)

Still, the significance of the resistance exercised by Cravan was deliberately brought into effect as the means to defer fixed, stable, pathetic
completion.

*

The ambivalent form of the body-assemblage derives partly, in the
case of Cravan most certainly, from the fluid passage between personae – and, in appropriation of a description given to Nietzsche, "the
combination of talents this man possessed caused him to lead the life
of an obscure outsider on the fringes of organised life" (Sloterdijk
1989: 10). Continuing this thought, Sloterdijk suggests that there is
significantly more at stake than the coexistence of multiple roles in
one body; each role functions *through* another and, as in Nietzsche's
example, Cravan "did not practice the one discipline alongside the
other, but practiced the one *by* practising the other" (1989: 10). The
unfolding of each role is seen to take place in contest with another,
and in this struggle, indeed, honouring the other becomes an essential

component in the process of liberating the one. The liberation here in question must be recognised as liberation from prescribed and state-imposed behavioural and thought patterns, liberation whereby thought can be radicalised while the level of discipline becomes greater, and as the struggling forms "consistently take the wrong step ... [they] thereby proceed upward!" (1989: 12). Here we depart from notions of progressive dialectic as Sloterdijk's use of the ambivalent, dual image of the centauric body capitalises on open hostility between distinct personae, successfully negotiating the condition that he specifies in terms of "intellectual dismemberment", in that whole expression of what cannot be totalised. Cravan, like Nietzsche,

> with his effortlessly effective double-natured observations ... found himself caught in the position of representing an unclassifiable curiosity, which is at home nowhere because it could belong anywhere. (Sloterdijk 1989: 12)

Out of curiosity emerges critical vigilance, distrust and interrogation, manifesting itself without recognition of any imposed limits, and indeed possessing "an imperturbable lack of respect for limits" (Sloterdijk 1989: 13). As those outside the ring looked in, Cravan's working of one role through another was tempered always by the hostile distinction of each, and so too the distinction between inside and outside the ring – as he remains on the margin of things, we might suggest, "he compels others to create him, while denying their values" (Camus 1951: 48). Sloterdijk is insistent on the importance of limits and boundaries in negotiating the significance of what is at stake for a figure like Cravan, in relation not only to Cravan's Parisian constituency but also to the broader implications within a western cultural constituency. Perspectives are multiplied under a motive force characterised as the "general eloquence of intelligent minds who seem to see the only value in limits as lying in the fact that these limits afford us the opportunity to exceed them" (Sloterdijk 1989: 13). Cravan's movement and double movement around the ring brings forth a moment in which he generates the people outside *and* incorporates those who would create him into himself: "the people is internal to the thinker because it is a 'becoming-people', just as the thinker is internal to the people as no less unlimited becoming" (Deleuze and Guattari 1994: 109). His emphatic claim that he was all things, all men and all animals (Cravan 1995a: 46) magnifies his cultural ring into a cultural stage, "a stage for exceptional disclosures ... [and] for cultural reevaluations of the most menacing sort" (Sloterdijk 1989: 14), upon which the performer exposes himself to those who would create him.

2. Insult and injury

Cravan set up his observation point in Montparnasse suitably enough on the avenue de l'Observatoire, and nightly rolled out of his apartment there to confront the people he found and generated on the street. His confrontation was always combative, though he seemed on occasion to possess an overriding congeniality to the confrontational pose. Alternatively, the fight was the whole point:

> He once went to the Closerie des Lilas bar-restaurant ... and re-marking what stupid faces everybody had, expressed his emotion by challenging, then beating up the whole place. When the police arrested him, the people he had beaten up insisted that the police set him at liberty, because, they said, "C'est Cravan et il est si sympathique". (Loy 1982: 317)

Critical to this confrontation, patently crowned with arrogance, is the appropriation and counter-appropriation of the offensive pose, the linguistic gaming and revaluation that restages the confrontation. The final verdict by the regulars at the Closerie des Lilas, within crawling distance of Cravan's apartment, suggests that his speech and action undergo a certain transformation, returning to him as speaker and actor, eventually to be cited against the initial purpose as the effect is reversed. This transformation is marked by what Butler refers to as a discursive performativity, "that is not a discrete series of speech acts, but a ritual chain of resignification whose origin and end remain unfixed and unfixable" (1997: 14).

Revaluation in these terms is freed from being tied to the future tense only, and moreover we admit the possibility that the act can resignify and transform the past tense also – transform it according to the distance between the prior context of the act and the effects produced by it. Further, we can pursue the Bakhtinian position, which holds that "meanings are not completely formalisable because the context of any utterance can never be fully specified" (Sprinker 1986:

122). Bakhtin conceives of the transformation that takes place in the interval, the "radical otherness" of intersubjectivity, in terms of the negotiation of the context of signs in the spaces in-between utterances, a notion that can be termed deconstructive therefore when it is recognised that there is neither a first word nor a last word: "[t]he contexts of dialogue are without limit. They extend into the deepest past and into the most distant future" (Sprinker 1986: 127). The act retains the potential for revaluation, and as Butler goes on to describe it, it is "not a momentary happening, but a certain nexus of temporal horizons, the condensation of an iterability that exceeds the moment it occasions" (1997: 14). Increasingly, for the poet and boxer, acts stand outside of any predictable expectation as the perceived threat that is posed returns to the actor in a different form; intentions are overtaken by the accumulation of meanings and effects. So we can look at Cravan's actions and public pronouncements as *acting upon* his people, or his audience, contributing to their social constitution and so to the process of social interpellation. Their position is distinct from the one that he occupies, to the extent that the people/audience becomes synonymous with its social position, fixed in hierarchical relation to other positions.

35. Arthur Cravan, Maintenant *no. 4, Paris, March-April 1914*

The demarcators may have been the ropes around the boxing ring or the covers of *Maintenant,* but the effect always was to place

Cravan's people/audience in a position of reception – in the case of
the boxer, it was the reception of the sucker punch; in the case of
Maintenant, it was the sustained reception of insult and injury from
the words and actions of the performer, speech acts that in turn enjoin
the subject to reoccupy a subordinate social position. At times, the
motive – confrontational and mercenary – was explicit:

> I write to infuriate my colleagues; to get myself talked about and
> make a name for myself. [...] With such intellectual readers as
> mine, I am obliged ... to say that I consider a man intelligent only
> when his intelligence has a temperament, since a *really intelligent*
> man resembles millions of *really intelligent* men. Therefore, as far
> as I am concerned, a man of subtlety or refinement is nearly al-
> ways nothing but an idiot. (1989: 3-4)

The effect that the words and actions of the performer have is to re-
invoke and to reinscribe structural relations of domination, so to constitute the reconstruction of that structural domination in linguistic
terms. More physically and more forcefully, at one notorious performance lecture,

> [Cravan] fired several pistol shots in the air, then, half in jest, half
> seriously, made the most insane pronouncements against art and
> life. [...] He read standing, balancing first on one foot and then on
> the other, and from time to time he insulted the audience. His
> listeners seemed enthralled by this bizarre performer. Things al-
> most went too far, however, when this Cravan threw his briefcase
> into the audience. It was only by accident that no one was hit.
> (Conover 1982: liii)

Beyond the reflection of a relation of social domination, here there is
an *enacting* of domination, and with that a rehearsal of the procedure
by which a social structure is reinstated. The people/audience is constituted at the moment of address by the performer, rather than being
described or produced as a consequence of words and actions: if injurious, it is in the performance of the injury that the injury is understood as social subordination.

　　When accounts of the subordinating consequences of words or
actions are given in advance, they may foreclose the possibility of a
critical response to that subordination, whose totalising effect is confirmed by the account. Still, discursive means hold the finality of the
subject's constitution open to renegotiation, suggesting that the effects

of words and actions can always be disrupted and subverted, effect-ively to undo any discursive constitution. We should question whether words and actions reduplicate fixed, static notions of social structures in their enactment of domination and subordination, and in turn propose that the effect of repeated, reiterated and rearticulated words and actions might in fact dismantle such structures. The injurious effect of subordination is tempered, and opens up to alternative innov-ation and subversion when we allow for the impermanence of *any* structure enunciated in words, actions or speech acts.

*

With the suggestion that permanence of structure is to be understood in terms of *continuity* of structure, it is instructive to recognise that continuity relies at all times upon the enunciation of speech; with that, we can ask whether there is potentially an enunciation that will discontinue or subvert the structure through its repetition in speech. If injurious speech proceeds as an act that recalls prior acts and future repetition for confirmation of its permanence/continuity, then there is potentially always a repetition that will sever the act from a structured stability, effectively so that continuous repetition can indeed under-mine rather than affirm the injurious efficacy of the act. By default, the form of such repetition will be familiar, as a recognised pose, to the extent that its subversive potential is derived from the studied use and shared recognition of means of communication, rather than sever-ing those means.

Recognition of the pose was conditional in allowing Cravan to execute the operational mode outlined in "To Be or Not To Be", where the undermining of gravity in the striking of different poses fuelled the critique; the performance lecturer, it was reported, though fully aware "that he was not in a position to be taken seriously ... [was able] to loathe the condition he found himself in and at the same time to defy his public with it" (Conover 1996: 104). That defiance sig-nalled, inevitably, the interaction between Cravan and others exterior to himself, others with whom he entered into a process of dialogism that functioned "to sustain and think through the radical exteriority or heterogeneity of one voice with regard to any other" (de Man 1986: 109-110),[3] and so to defer completion or consummation of the rela-tionship between the one and the other. For the one to be oriented within ideology is, in marxist thought at least, an orientation within a representation of what is the imaginary relation between the *determining* "I" and the *determinable* "I".[4] So ideology is an objective reality, which, it is argued, can be apprehended but not surpassed, and in turn theoretical ideology is understood as a form of recognition rather than cognition, as Althusser has already observed.

The parameters of ideology consequently indicate the limits that Cravan lacked any respect for, and in which the only perceived virtue was the opportunity to exceed them. His wilfully transgressive stance engaged in "play as artists and children engage in it ... coming-to-be and passing away, structuring and destroying" (Nietzsche 1987: 62), to activate *will to power* as the differential between forces, and so estimate "the quality of force that gives meaning to a given phenomenon, or event" (Deleuze 1983: 53). With the relation itself being an effect of chance, it follows that the body is constituted as an arbitrary relation of force with force and, in Deleuze's reading of Nietzsche, existence too is an effect of chance – radically innocent because of its necessity, and purely just because of its release of all things from having a purpose. Necessity transforms the game of chance into a serious game indeed, as it is positively identified "with multiplicity, with fragments, with parts, with chaos: the chaos of the dice that are shaken and then thrown" (1983: 25-27). In affirmation of innocence, necessity and multiplicity, Deleuze, we read, is emphatic in his criticism:

> [t]o abolish chance by holding it in the grip of causality and finality, to count on the repetition of throws rather than affirming chance, to anticipate a result instead of affirming necessity – these are all the operations of a bad player. (1983: 27)

Entering the ring, affirming chance, Cravan takes the stage as the supreme player, as unimpeded by causal motives as he is by the idea of a goal.[5] Without any experience of cause, as Nietzsche goes on to observe, "we have combined our feeling of a will, our feeling of 'freedom', our feeling of responsibility and our intention to perform an act, into the concept 'cause'" (1968: 295-97). Cravan acts without the idea of a goal and, in welcoming "every moment of universal existence with a sense of triumph" (Nietzsche 1968: 36), each act and each pose initiates an ethic of joy to the sound of the regenerative and universal laughter that "frees human consciousness, thought, and imagination for new potentialities" (Bakhtin 1984b: 49).

*

The body-assemblage itself can be recognised in the manufactured "artificial problem" that functions as reflexive (Althusser 1977: 23), pointing towards a solution that is generated outside thought and the process of knowledge. As an open totality, no single component of the body-assemblage can be changed without affecting and changing the whole, though it remains always the sum of an infinitely variable and mutable set of relations between relations. The effect is not closure or completion, but rather the opening up of the body-assemblage and the subsequent intermingling of reactions to other body-assemblages, "of incorporeal transformations attributed to bodies", within the context of the territorial or reterritorialised plane against which the body-assemblage is thought and thinks itself (Deleuze and Guattari 1988: 88). As it moves, acts and speaks, the body-assemblage is always collective even though its form may be the singularity of Cravan; thus, what makes its statement collective, even as it is emitted by the one singularity, is that it does not refer back to a subject and neither does it refer back to a double: "there isn't a subject who emits the statement or a subject about which the statement would be emitted". In this sense, the collective nature of the statement forces us critically to question the usual apprehension of Cravan as individualist, when the statement itself cannot be connected to a subject by any definition, "doubled or not, divided or not, reflected or not" (Deleuze and Guattari 1986: 83).

Further, the concept of difference drives against completion and unifying forces, and it is precisely in thinking about systems in terms of compositions of series, with each series defined on the basis of difference, that Deleuze employs the term "singularity"; here, the delineation of Cravan as singularity is derived from the image of the actor who plays a role, which, Deleuze suggests, is in fact beyond and greater than the personal – Deleuze's fourth person, therefore:

> What is neither individual nor personal are, on the contrary, emis-
> sions of singularities insofar as they occur on an unconscious sur-
> face and possess a mobile, immanent principle of auto-unification
> through a *nomadic distribution*, radically distinct from fixed and
> sedentary distributions as conditions of the syntheses of con-
> sciousness. (1990b: 102-103)

Difference in this sense is instructive and constitutive, and crucially confounds any unifying force that would preclude difference; indeed, it further confounds any theoretically guiding principle that might itself militate as a unifying force. To think in terms of difference becomes affirmative of surfaces and surface phenomena, philosophically to abandon thoughts about surfaces as secondary to something that resides beneath or outside of them: "[t]he philosopher is no longer … Plato's soul or bird, but rather the animal that is on a level with the surface – a tick or louse" (Deleuze 1990b: 133). So, with Deleuze's philosophy of surfaces and differences, what is preserved is the integrity of surfaces of difference, irreducible to any unifying principle. Thinking in this way gives centrality to the idea of *expression* as the relation among elements that allows each to be conceived as distinct from and simultaneously part of the others: "expression accounts for the real activity of the participated, and for the possibility of participation. […] Expression appears as the unity of the multiple, as the complication of the multiple, and as the explication of the one" (Deleuze 1990a: 176). The idea appeals always and only to surfaces and, for the declaiming poet and boxer, "what is expressed has no existence outside its expressions; each expression is, as it were, the existence of what is expressed" (Deleuze 1990a: 42).

3. Specific variability

Cravan, the one, expresses and *is* the multiple – all things, all men and all animals – as the multiple expresses and is the one. In 1909, his inaugural public address set the cultural stage for his declaration of intent, his manifesto of surfaces and differences, his affirmative expression of multiplicity, fragments, parts and chaos. The free mobility expressed between roles or parts occurred within the context of a social system formulated first in terms of "a socius of inscription where the essential thing is to mark and to be marked" (Deleuze and Guattari 1984: 142), returning us subsequently to the principle of nomadic distribution of body parts and the body-assemblage, marked, inscribed, and reincorporated into the social code. The encounter of Cravan is the encounter of the nomadic movement of the body-assemblage, distributing itself and making its appearance on surfaces, "at home nowhere because it could belong anywhere".

36. Littérature *no. 11/12, Paris, 15 October 1923*

Everyone, Cravan then wrote, accords to a certain posturing, "but more or less convincingly" (1995d: 35), as every body forms new connections between itself and its surrounding environment, which includes other roles, other people, other bodies. In exceeding himself, Cravan's movement is inclusive as it extends in rhizomatic form, connecting beyond any hierarchical predetermination. Connections are made on the unstated proposition that if the body wants something then it must be good – the same proposition reformulated by Deleuze (after Spinoza) as he observes that "[d]esire does not 'want' revolution, it is revolutionary in its own right, as though involuntarily, by wanting what it wants" (Deleuze and Guattari 1984: 116). The logic of Deleuze's reformulation proceeds to condemn as counter-revolutionary any restriction (by state or otherwise) on the nature of the connections that a body may make. The connections, in turn, remain scattered as fragments throughout the alleged physical and spiritual apprehensions that continued to be made of the poet and boxer – in the pages of *Littérature* and elsewhere – long after his known movement ceased in the autumn of 1918, when he sailed off in his little boat into the sunset of the shark-infested Caribbean; of the man who sometimes spoke of suicide and who many believed would one day step back into the cultural ring. Legend now surrounds the corpse in the jungle, the desert island life off the Argentine coast, and her husband's bloodied moneybelt sent to Mina Loy in Paris by one of Cravan's old girl-friends; suspicion surrounds the vendor of forged Oscar Wilde manu-scripts during the 1920s, who claimed to be the homosexual secretary of André Gide; ether surrounds the situationist model and the spec-tacular Arthur Cravan, the laughing revolutionary, whose critique and recreation of everyday life was undertaken in oppressive conditions in order to destroy those conditions, through the explosive politics of the body whose signal is its always specific variability.

Notes

[1] "Directeur Cravan" was the ringmaster of *Maintenant*, the irregular periodical published by Cravan in Paris between 1912 and 1915, calling upon contributors W. Cooper, Edouard Archinard, E. Lajeunesse, Robert Miradique and Marie Lowitska each in turn – all Cravan under a different name. As an instructive notion, we might parallel "Directeur Cravan" with the instance of Berlin Oberdada Johannes Baader, described as maintaining the overarching and pivotal identity of "Architekt Baader" as a means to maximise the application of a conceptual model for the reformulation of all dimensions of cultural activity and reorganisation of cultural mechanics. See Stephen C. Foster, "The Mortality of Roles: Johannes Baader and spiritual materi-alism", in the present volume.

[2] Nietzsche's words are quoted in full on page 20 of the Introduction to this volume.

[3] "Dialogism" is not to be confused with "dialogue": dialogue comes after dialogism as the cognitive-ethical event resulting from the interaction referred to here.

[4] See Deleuze 1988: 61. The imaginary relation specified is that between the homo-geneous speaking self and the subject. See also Jacques Lacan. 1977. *Écrits: A Selec-tion*. London: Routledge: 23.

[5] Žižek observes how, ironically, "for Deleuze, *the* sport was surfing ... no longer a sport of self-control and domination directed toward some goal but just a practice of inserting oneself into a wave and letting oneself be carried by it". Slavoj Žižek. 2004. *Organs Without Bodies: On Deleuze and Consequences*. New York and London: Routledge, p. 184.

References

Althusser, Louis
1971   "Ideology and Ideological State Apparatuses (Notes Towards an Investigation)". In *Lenin and Philosophy and Other Essays*. New York: Monthly Review Press.

1977   *For Marx*. London: New Left Books.

Badiou, Alain
1967   "Le (re)commencement du materialisme dialectique". *Critique*, 240.

Bakhtin, Mikhail
1984a   *Problems of Dostoevsky's Poetics*. Minneapolis: University of Minnesota Press.

1984b   *Rabelais and His World*. Bloomington: Indiana University Press.

Butler, Judith
1997   *Excitable Speech: A Politics of the Performative*. New York and London: Routledge.

Camus, Albert
1951   *The Rebel*. Harmondsworth: Penguin Modern Classics.

Conover, Roger
1982   Introduction to Mina Loy, *The Last Lunar Baedeker*. Highlands: Jargon Society.

1995   "Wanted: Arthur Cravan 1887–?". In *Four Dada Suicides*. London: Atlas Press.

1996   "Arthur Cravan: Stances of the Century". In *Boxer: An Anthology of Writings on Boxing and Visual Culture*. London: Institute of International Visual Arts.

Cravan, Arthur
1989   "Exhibition at the Independents". In Robert Motherwell (ed.), *The Dada Painters and Poets: An Anthology*. Cambridge: Belknap Press.

1995a   "Hie!" In *4 Dada Suicides*. London: Atlas Press.

1995b   "Oscar Wilde Lives". In *4 Dada Suicides*. London: Atlas Press.

1995c   "Poet and Boxer". In *4 Dada Suicides*. London: Atlas Press.

1995d   "To Be or Not To Be ... American". In *4 Dada Suicides*. London:
         Atlas Press.

Deleuze, Gilles
1983   *Nietzsche and Philosophy*. New York: Columbia University Press.

1990a   *The Logic of Sense*. London: The Athlone Press.

1990b   *Expressionism in Philosophy: Spinoza*. New York: Zone Books.

1994   *Difference and Repetition*. London: The Athlone Press.

Deleuze, Gilles and Guattari, Félix
1984   *Anti-Oedipus: Capitalism and Schizophrenia*. London: The
         Athlone Press.

1986   *Kafka: Toward a Minor Literature*. Minneapolis: University of
         Minnesota Press.

1988   *A Thousand Plateaus: Capitalism and Schizophrenia*. London:
         The Athlone Press.

1994   *What is Philosophy?* London and New York: Verso.

De Man, Paul
1986   *The Resistance to Theory*. Minneapolis: University of Minnesota
         Press.

Huyssen, Andreas
1995   "Postenlightened Cynicism: Diogenes as Postmodern
         Intellectual". In *Twilight Memories: Marking Time in a Culture of
         Amnesia*. New York and London: Routledge.

Loy, Mina
1982   "Arthur Cravan is Alive!" In *The Last Lunar Baedeker*.
         Highlands: Jargon Society.

1986   "Colossus" (extracts). In Roger Conover, "Mina Loy's
         'Colossus': Arthur Cravan Undressed". In *New York Dada*.
         Rudolf E. Kuenzli (ed.). New York: Willis Locker & Owens.

Nietzsche, Friedrich
1968   *The Will to Power*. New York: Vintage Books.

       1987   *Philosophy in the Tragic Age of the Greeks*. Washington DC: Regnery Gateway.

Sloterdijk, Peter
       1989   *Thinker on Stage: Nietzsche's Materialism*. Minneapolis: University of Minnesota Press.

Sprinker, Michael
       1986   "Boundless Context: Problems in Bakhtin's Linguistics". In *Poetics Today* 7(1), Tel Aviv: The Porter Institute for Poetics and Semiotics.

Taylor, Charles
       1985   *Human Agency and Language: Philosophical Papers 1*. New York: Cambridge University Press.

V. Philosophy, Theory and the Avant-Garde

Ernst Bloch and Hugo Ball:
toward an ontology of the avant-garde

Joel Freeman

Abstract: This essay argues that Zürich Dada, in particular as expressed through the work of Hugo Ball, contains a latent ontologically grounded and systematic aesthetic theory. This claim may appear counter intuitive. Famously Dada, like the name itself, was meant to flout cultural and conceptual norms and break the stranglehold of theorisation typical of many "classical" avant-garde art movements. One of the few things that unified Dadaists such as Hugo Ball, Hans Arp, Marcel Janco and Tristan Tzara was a communal rejection of the title "school" and a deliberate refusal to offer a programme or clear structure for Dada. Dada portrayed itself as anti-theoretical; an arbitrary, anarchistic, chaotic celebration of art and life that freely incorporated Expressionism, Futurism and Cubism, to name just a few, without holding allegiance to any of them. According to Ball, to systematise Dada would be to succumb to the very mechanisms of control (social, artistic, political, conceptual) that Dada endeavours to overthrow. But a closer look at Hugo Ball's work, especially *Das Wort und das Bild* reveals that Dada was guided, sometimes unconsciously, by a philosophical system; it is however a unique system because it has an open and fluid structure. The structure of the philosophical system latent in Dada closely mirrors the aesthetic features of Ernst Bloch's ontology of not-yet-being. Thus a comparison of Ernst Bloch's aesthetic theory and Hugo Ball's diary/autobiographical work between 1916 and 1919 makes explicit the structure of "Dada as philosophical system". Bloch's thought and Dadaism *via* Hugo Ball share a common goal; to break through the static, reified mould of social interaction. Both Bloch and Ball saw the arena of the aesthetic as the place where this was possible. The incoherence of Dada in practice reflects the psychic incoherence that emerges out of a repressive and mechanised social system. It does not reflect true internal incoherence. This is true of Bloch's philosophy as well. The essay itself will support these claims by laying out the structure of Bloch's aesthetics and demonstrating its presence in Dada.

"Die Normaluhr einer abstrakten Epoche ist explodiert."
– Hugo Ball, *Die Flucht aus der Zeit*, 1926

1. Introduction

There are a number of striking correspondences in the lives of Hugo
Ball and Ernst Bloch. The parallels reached a brief but noteworthy
highpoint in Bern and Zürich in the years 1917–1919 when they worked together for the anti-war paper *Die Freie Zeitung*. Both Bloch and
Ball came from the Rheinland Pfalz region of Germany. Ball was born
in 1886, Bloch in 1885. Both studied philosophy and literature in Munich in the years 1905–1906. Bloch wrote his dissertation in Würzberg
in 1908 under Oswald Külpe, titled *Critical Analyses of Rickert and
the Problem of Modern Epistemology*.[1] In 1909 it was given limited
publication. Ball was close to receiving a doctorate with a work that
probably would have been titled either *Nietzsche in Basel* or *Nietzsche
and the Renewal of Germany*, but broke from academia to take up a
career in the theatre. They both came of age immersed in Expressionist literature and art.[2] Their intellectual development, Ball's Dadaism,
Bloch's ontology of not-yet-being and his *Geist der Utopie* (The Spirit
of Utopia) bear the indelible imprint of the Expressionist era. Ball and
Bloch shared, like many of their contemporaries, a chiliastic and utopian vision of history. Both Ball and Bloch went into exile as radical
pacifists at the start of the First World War and met for the first time
through their work for *Die Freie Zeitung*.
    In addition to the biographical correspondences, they share a
set of common aesthetic, philosophical and political concerns. Bloch
and Ball were two of the most sophisticated thinkers to advance, contribute to and participate in an aesthetic theory of the avant-garde
while the "classical" avant-garde was in its bloom in the early part of
the twentieth century. They shared a vociferous, militant, pacifist opposition to the German war machine and its self-destructive imperial-
ist "logic of death". Much of Ball's polemics against the "machine",
like Bloch's polemics against "die Technische Kälte" has to be seen
against the backdrop of the war. They saw in the mechanised destruction brought on by the war the power of rationalisation gone mad.
They both saw theology and history as inseparable discursive fields.
Strikingly, shortly after the end of the war and the Russian Revo-

lution, when they had gone separate ways, they both authored works on Thomas Münzer. Each was an attempt, broadly speaking, at revising accepted understanding of German theological and political history by motivating Münzer to counteract the cultural dominance of Martin Luther.[3]

Ball's involvement in Dadaism was short lived – eight months to be exact – but he remains in many respects the founding figure of Dada. The fame and attention he receives rests on the role he played in igniting Dada as an international movement in the arts. Ball's sudden and abrupt break from Dada, his conversion to strict orthodox Catholicism and the study of mystical religious texts, served to cement his reputation as a paradigm of Dadaism and one of the most important figures in the development of the "classical" avant-garde.

Throughout his life, Bloch was perhaps Germany's most vocal philosophical defender of the avant-garde. Bloch's thought developed in tandem with the avant-garde of the early twentieth century and he can be seen as putting into practice, in style and content, some of the latent principles that inform Dada. Bloch is the only thinker who ever attempted to provide the avant-garde with an ontologically grounded philosophical system, one that attempts to give conceptual coherence to its political and aesthetic ambitions. The final stages of this essay will excavate Bloch's aesthetic theory and Ball's Dadaism, paying particular attention to the question of finitude. The project of an "ontology of the avant-garde" like Bloch's philosophy itself is radically temporal in nature. Bloch and Ball share a deep seated, theoretically grounded aversion to the "instrumentalised" and "reified" model of time that dominated European culture and they both make a concerted effort to rethink the temporal nature of human existence. This issue makes a comparison of them at the level of a history of ideas fruitful. Further, an appreciation of the contextual significance of their critiques of instrumentalised time is essential to understanding the new ontology that drives Bloch's thought and which is latent in Dada.

2. Traditional ontology, Utopia and the ontology of not-yet-being

For the sake of clarity, I offer here a brief preliminary remark on what the term ontology means for Bloch, and how it relates to the central question of Utopia in his philosophy. *Ontos* is the Greek word for *being*. In the German tradition, ontology was often difficult to separate from metaphysics and theology, especially in scholasticism. Christian Wolff, the chief representative of German scholastic philosophy, gave ontology a modern academic valence in the seventeenth century. According to Wolff, ontology is the "science of being in general", whereas metaphysics is the science of that which transcends nature. In traditional ontology, the borders between these two "sciences" blur when ontology begins to investigate the timeless essence of Being. Traditionally, despite their many differences, both metaphysics and ontology were informed by the presupposition that the ultimate focus of investigation is eternal unconditioned truth, the realm of the absolute.

Bloch's ontology breaks with the presupposition that the focus of ontology is ultimately a realm of a-temporal absolute essences. His ontology follows Marx's example. In place of the absolute, Bloch investigates the fundamental features of being in terms of historical processes that the human being engages in and through work (*Arbeit*). Rather than preclude the finite, it attempts to forge an ontology that grasps the fundamental dialectical role that the finite nature of human existence (*Dasein*) has in shaping being. For Bloch, the work of art reveals, through production, the historically conditioned nature of being. He does not reject wholesale that there is a timeless essence to Being, but his system of thought requires a reworking of the concept of time according to his principle of the not-yet. Bloch's take on temporality requires a concept of time that is open to the finite but forward moving, potentially latent in the intentional structure of being itself. Simultaneously, Bloch views time as in some respects eternal. For Bloch, organic being in general, and especially the human being, are both finite and part of a process of becoming that is in a constant state of dialectical self-actualisation and renewal. In this process, particular beings take embodiment through a variety of temporal structures. For instance, the time of the plant is different to inorganic time and the time of the human being. No individual human being shares absolutely the time of other human beings. Further, a proper understanding of the historically and culturally conditioned temporal structure of the human being requires new and differentiated modes of theoretical and sociological analysis. Bloch's concepts of simultaneity (*Gleichzeitigkeit*) and non-simultaneity (*Ungleichzeitigkeit*) emerge, purely terminologically, as early as his 1908 dissertation. The concept of non-simultaneity plays a central role in his philosophy of history, and he applies it in a thorough fashion in his cultural analyses in *Erbschaft dieser Zeit* (Heritage of our Times) in the 1930s. They are concepts designed to meet some of the challenges that arise when ontology attempts to grasp the finite structure of concrete existent being. On the other hand, for Bloch, Being, construed in the largest and universal sense, is a radically concrete inexhaustible and infinite material substrate to finite particular being. Bloch sees the idea of a "concrete Utopia" as *the* carrier of the infinite within the finite.

Bloch derives his concept of Utopia from the ontological principle of the not-yet. Again, his ontology of not-yet-being is shaped by a radically temporal concept of being. For Bloch the being of the temporal now is intrinsically unfixed and can only be expressed through approximation and negation.[4] Being does not have itself; it is ontologically ungrounded and incomplete. However, it is driven by a desire to overcome this fundamental incompleteness. He stresses constantly that there is no static, fixed mode of Being underlying existence. Without the lack that drives being forward and orients it to the future, *Dasein* would not exist. Hope and (concrete) Utopia are names for this drive and for the intrinsic incompleteness of being. Utopia and hope are ontological categories that describe the fundamental urge, the motor, for becoming. Bloch radically reverses the position of Utopia. Utopia is not an abstract event that will occur at the end of history. It is inscribed in the fundament of *Dasein* itself and he reshapes it into the ontological principle that drives the human being (but is also manifest in the material world). The human being senses first its hunger, the lack inscribed in its fundament and attempts to fill this lack. The drive to survive, to feed oneself, is coterminous with Bloch's utopian principle. Hope for completion, for an end to the hunger, is for Bloch always already inscribed in this originary phenomenon. His philosophical system describes an open process of movement toward an unknown that cannot be described in positive terms.

Concrete Utopia, the desire to successfully fill the material lack, is the start of human history, not necessarily its end. For Bloch, Being as such and the human being in particular are essentially becoming. Neither Being in the largest sense, nor *Dasein*, has itself. *Experimentum Mundi* opens with the words, "Ich bin. Aber ich habe mich noch nicht" ("I am, but I do not-yet have myself"). Here *Dasein*

and material being are in themselves driven forward by what he calls
Sehnsucht, a desire for completeness. He expresses this in the formula
S is not yet P: the Subject is not yet its Predicate. The subject aims
toward the predicate, it wants to have the predicate and achieve a
complete, whole identity. This desire drives human movement and
struggle. In this way, Bloch is fundamentally a thinker of a future
oriented intentionality.

3. Notes on Bloch's aesthetic theory
in relation to the avant-garde

Bloch's analyses of literature, music, film, individual art works,
movements in the arts, pop culture and the interrelationship of the aesthetic and the political, to name just a few, appear eclectic and seem to
move improvisationally across vast cultural and historical chasms.
This tendency has put off many readers. His work on aesthetics is best
known in English *via* the Expressionism debate in "Das Wort" in the
late thirties, part of which was documented and translated, with an
afterward by Fredric Jameson, in the collection *Aesthetics and Politics*
in 1977.[5] The volume has become a standard work in courses on the
Frankfurt School and western marxism. Yet it does not touch on the
interconnections between his aesthetic theory, his philosophy and the
specific context in which the debate arose.

     The rise of Nazism, the ban on "Degenerate Art" and the
internal dynamics of German marxism around 1938 conditioned the
Expressionism debate and shaped Bloch's politically motivated defence of Expressionism. Key to the debate were the public disagreements between Bloch and Lukács. In the teens and twenties, they were
close friends, personally and intellectually, and their disagreements in
"Das Wort" reflects discussion, intellectual collaboration and tensions
that passed between them over the prior decades of their association.
Bloch met Lukács in 1911 in Berlin at a private seminar held by
Georg Simmel. For several years, they developed in a state of intense
philosophical symbiosis. In addition, by 1938 Bloch had had longstanding personal relationships with Adorno, Brecht and Benjamin.
Ball introduced Bloch to Benjamin in 1918 in Switzerland, where
Benjamin was writing his dissertation.[6] At the time, Bloch was living
primarily in Zürich, but also in Bern and Interlaken, writing polemical

political essays for the journal *Die Freie Zeitung*, and reworking the recently published *Geist der Utopie*. During the Expressionism debate in the late thirties and throughout his life, Bloch uses the term Expressionism to indicate groundbreaking modes of artistic practice during the period 1910–1933. In Bloch's repertoire, the term is often a stand-in for the avant-garde in general. However, despite his loose application of terminology, Bloch is wary of static modes of "aesthetic" classification.[7] In contrast to Lukács, when it comes to the avant-garde, he emphasises the necessity of giving attention to specific art works and their individual creators. Bloch's critique of Lukács's reading of Expressionism is typical of how he came to view the work of Lukács as a whole. For Bloch, the philosophy of Lukács, at its weakest, was a closed, totalising and potentially repressive system. Early on, Bloch was alert to what he saw as a dogmatic impulse in Lukács. Despite their intense philosophical collaboration, he became wary of the tendency of Lukács to read philosophical and cultural phenomena purely as socially conditioned events determined by broad, undifferentiated historical categories.[8] This, according to Bloch, is what allowed Lukács to read Expressionism as bourgeois subjectivism fused with implicit fascist impulses, and he dismisses it wholesale.

The strength of Bloch's defence of Expressionism lies in his emphasis on the diversity within Expression, its diffuse character and its differentiated manifestations across artistic genres. What does not come through in the debate is that his defence of Expressionism is a broad defence of the avant-garde, and at the same time it is part of an ontology of the ground-breaking, experimental, incomplete and unpredictable impulse that gives rise to and drives art forward. Inquiry into the origin and structure of this fundamental impulse is the starting point for Bloch's ontological aesthetic of the avant-garde. Bloch's aesthetic is one of emergence, one that excavates the originary impulse that gives rise to works of art. The degree to which Bloch's ontology is inseparable from his aesthetics and the degree to which his aesthetics cannot be understood without reference to his ontology is already apparent in *Geist der Utopie*. A definite aesthetic theory drives the wild, improvisational expressiveness of *Geist der Utopie*, an aesthetic theory integral to his philosophical system as a whole. In some respects this is also true for Dada; neither Bloch nor Ball, nor Dada generally, are as arbitrary and self indulgent as they appear. The disorientation induced by Bloch's philosophical style and by Dada practice gives expression to levels of experience that are repressed, often to specific ideological ends. Their shared goal is that of breaking open static and reified social and intellectual discourses. It is obviously a political project, one that demands a fundamental reshaping of dominant modes of social interaction and it requires an underlying theoretical structure to join normally discreet spheres, the political, the aesthetic, and the ontological, in a convincing way. It requires methods for breaking open and moving beyond the boundaries intrinsic to dominant social discourses. The incoherence of Dada praxis reflects the psychic incoherence that is a product of a repressive and mechanised social system. As such, Dada is not in truth internally incoherent. A deliberate system underlies the fragmentary appearance of Dada, and this is true of Bloch's aesthetic as well. In what follows, I attempt to discern the structural correspondences in Bloch's aesthetic and in Dada artistic practice. This will allow the outlining of an avant-garde ontology.

4. Breaking ground: Bloch's ontology of the work of art

During his exile in Switzerland, core structural elements of Bloch's ontology of not-yet-being were beginning to emerge. Yet his philosophy, as a developed system, does not begin to find full expression until the mature works such as *Das Prinzip Hoffnung* (1949), *Das Materialismusproblem, seine Geschichte und Subtanz* (1972) and especially *Experimentum Mundi* (1974). Although used widely in the second edition of *Geist der Utopie*, Bloch does not give the term sharp definition until much later in his work. Nevertheless, some fifty years earlier while in association with the radical anti-war political and artistic fringe in Switzerland, Bloch laid the groundwork for an explosion of publication toward the very end of his life. In 1919 he published the short essay "Das Noch Nicht Bewusste Wissen" in *Die Weissen Blatter*, a Swiss journal that was friendly to avant-garde writers. Hugo Ball also contributed to *Die Weissen Blatter*. "Das Noch Nicht Bewusste Wissen" is an introduction to Bloch's discovery of the not-yet, which he made initially at the age of twenty-two and by the time of the writing of *Geist der Utopie* was already long overdue.[9] It contains, in cryptographic form, Bloch's attempt to overturn both Freud and Husserl and an outline of his future oriented philosophy. At the same time, he was reworking *Geist der Utopie* to include an introduction to the ontology of not-yet-being and give his work (through no easy comprehensibility) a degree of systematic coherence. Not coincidentally, the period was just as crucial with regard to the development of his aesthetic stance. It was a time when he developed a mine of ideas that he would spend the rest of his life reworking and developing, much of which came about in a period of friendship with Zürich Dadaists, especially Hugo Ball and Emmy Hennings.

Bloch's aesthetic is in essence a further development and unfolding of the basic positions that drive his philosophy as a whole. Aesthetics for Bloch is not a matter of objectifying, analysing and categorising works of art in order to distill a set of formal organising principles. Rather, Bloch's aesthetic stands in the tradition of theoretical aesthetics that followed in Baumgarten's wake. In this tradition, aesthetics attempts to understand works of art in terms of the original meaning of the Greek word *aisthesis*, the science of sense perception. Baumgarten redefined *aisthesis* to create aesthetics as a discipline meant to overcome the strict opposition between art and philosophy, and open up metaphysics and epistemology to questions related to the work of art. Its object of study is the aesthetic dimension of reality in relation to human consciousness, and not simply art as object. However, Bloch is not simply offering a furthering of traditional philosophical aesthetics as conceived by Baumgarten and taken up by Kant and Hegel, among others. He reworks this tradition through the modifying power of the ontology of not-yet-being. This is what makes Bloch's aesthetics actually a distinct development, a break from rather than a continuation, of the German tradition of philosophical aesthetics.

Bloch refers to Hegel constantly in his aesthetic work, but he does not view art in a strictly Hegelian light. For Bloch, art does not reflect a metaphysically structured historically determined truth. Building on the basic centrality of the category of the not-yet, Bloch views Hegel's aesthetics and indeed all prior philosophical aesthetics as flawed by anamnesis, by a static structure that looks exclusively to the past for its truth content. For Bloch, art is not primarily a cipher for understanding the past; rather, its futurial intentional content reveals the truth in art. The power of art is that it reveals the ways in which being, the being of human subjects and the being of the objective material world, are unsettled, incomplete and in a process of be-

coming something that is not-yet actualised. In this sense, the future as
much as the past structures aesthetic experience, and the work of art.

Thus, in opposition to Hegel, Bloch sees the truth in art in its
intentional structure, or to use a Husserlian term, protentionality. Protentionality indicates the intentional directedness toward the future
that structures human consciousness. Bloch, *via* his concept of the not-
yet-conscious ("das noch nicht bewusste Wissen"), and more generally in his wide ranging analyses of anticipatory consciousness,[10]
employs a similar concept in order to give phenomenological investigation a heightened ability to reveal the fragmentary traces of that
which has not yet come to be, but which is nevertheless present in the
moment. Both Husserl and Bloch want to describe the way specific,
fundamental modes of anticipation and expectation structure human
consciousness.[11]

Protentionality is one of Husserl's technical terms, touched on
in *Ideen zu einer reinen Phänomenologie und phänomenologische
philosophie* (Ideas pertaining to a pure phenomenology and to a phenomenological philosophy) of 1913, and then developed further in the
Vorlesungen zur Phänomenologie des inneren Zeitbewußtseins (Lectures on Internal Time Consciousness). Husserl worked on the topic
from as early as 1904 through the mid 1920s. A condensed form of his
thoughts on internal time consciousness were finally made available to
the reading public at Husserl's own request by Martin Heidegger in
1928, in the *Vorlesungen zur Phänomenologie des inneren Zeitbewußtseins*. It is likely that Bloch became familiar with the idea of
protentionality in the writing of *Ideen*. Despite the polemical and
scattered nature of Bloch's comments on Husserl, close examination
of the structure of his thought reveals that Bloch was a careful and
respectful reader. The power and originality of Husserl's phenomenology left an imprint on Bloch that is apparent across his œuvre, from
Geist der Utopie to *Erbschaft dieser Zeit* to *Experimentum Mundi*.
There is insufficient space here to examine this issue in detail, but it is
worth noting that Husserl's phenomenology is a key event in the
genesis and development of Bloch's thought. His early work is
marked by concern with the problem of futuriality in human consciousness and his concept of the not-yet-conscious, a precursor to the
ontology of not-yet-being, is in part a reworking of ideas that shape
Husserl's phenomenological analyses of consciousness.

As we have seen, Bloch's aesthetics moves outwards from the discovery of the not-yet. It operates with reference to the question: what does art reveal about the structure of being itself? It encompasses within its field of inquiry individual subjectivity, sense perception and human *Dasein* as such. It is, however, simultaneously oriented toward the problem of how the meta-subjective structure of being pre-conditions the individual human subject. Because a focus on the primal ontological ground for human experience informs Bloch's aesthetic, it is a "transcendental" aesthetic. By transcendental here I mean that Bloch claims to offer insight into the true structure of the world and the human by analysing cultural phenomena not just in terms of their formal or sociological characteristics but for evidence of the way in which they reveal the universal structure of being itself. This, the structure of human *Dasein* in relation to the material world, or the being of the objective world, is the realm one must look to in order to understand the "transcendental" preconditions for any given work of art. For Bloch, the structure of being reveals itself in the unfolding of the not-yet. Bloch claims that at the most fundamental level being is incomplete and in a state of development toward something that it has not yet become. Being is future oriented without having an "is" or a settled and finally determinable structure.

The human being is the ultimate reference point for all of Bloch's ontology and for his aesthetic. This, we will find, is true of Hugo Ball's work in the Dada period as well. Once again, Bloch's aesthetic is *simultaneously* oriented toward the human being "as such" and the meta-subjective or transcendental problem of the structure of being. This is one of the sources of Bloch's insistence on the centrality of the problem of the "we" over and against the "I". Given the vast field of human activity, the world of work, Bloch privileges the work of art as a special site where the latent fundamentally incomplete not-yet structure of being reveals itself. For Bloch, the not-yet makes itself more immediately available in the work of art than in other cultural arenas. It is worth underlining again that as early as 1919, before Heidegger began to make a name for himself, Bloch was developing what would come to be an ontology that encompassed the field of the aesthetic and gave the work of art a privileged position within his system as a whole.

The not-yet is the most fundamental ontological category without which Bloch's aesthetic is impossible. In the early works the not-yet, as ontology, is not fully explicit and often difficult to distinguish from a philosophically oriented psychology. Nevertheless the basic structure and ontological implication of the not-yet is present throughout his early philosophical writings. In order to get a better grasp of the ontological structure of the not-yet and its relationship to art, it is instructive to look at his mature work. The following quote contains the basic observation that allows Bloch to join his work on art with his ontology. This, and several of the quotes that follow, are from the section titled "Kunst, die Stoff-Form entbindend" (Art, the delivering of Form from Material) in the closing pages of Bloch's *Das Materialismusproblem, seine Geschichte und Substanz* (The Materialism Problem, its History and Substance). This section of *Das Materialismusproblem* contains the most concise summary of his aesthetic theory available, and is one of the crowning moments in a lifelong preoccupation with aesthetic questions. The structure of the argument here is prefigured as early as 1923 in *Geist der Utopie,* and it contains the essence of his ontology of the avant-garde.

> Human work constantly develops and advances that which is available in existence. It changes its objects insofar as it derails or advances the object according to our purpose. The work of artistic form-giving varies from this only through the nature of its purpose, one primarily for entertainment, for which it develops and advances that which it grasps. (1972: 521)

Bloch sees the work of the artist as developing out of the basic impulse that drives the human being to engage the world, manipulate its raw material, alter and drive forward the processes of change that constitute the world as an always incomplete entity, always on the way toward an indeterminate something.

> The resistant material, this is the material of the "Being-towards-possibility" taken as disruption or inhibition; but the supposed plastic nature, which thinks its picture, that is the material of the "Being-in-Possibility", which is further actualised through the artist. (1972: 521)

The artist actualises the always-latent potential or form-content that resides in the material itself. The artist delivers (*entbindet*) the form out of the substance. The potential for self-realisation resides simultaneously in the material and in the artist as such. Bloch's aesthetic is in this way dialectical and in process, but the form of his dialectic is free of binary polarity. An organic dialectic of self-emergence, where the subject and the object are radically inscribed in one another from the very start, replaces the thesis/antithesis arrangement. On this model the subject and the object remain radically inscribed in one another throughout the process of becoming. This is a reflection of Bloch's larger philosophical project of breaking down the traditional Cartesian model of subjectivity (which depends to a degree on an autonomous notion of the self whose essence stands in binary opposition to the finite material realm), while at the same time retaining a material *a priori*. In other words, Bloch wants to retain a universalisable normative structure to *Dasein*, one that is radically material, a realm where logic exists in and with concrete finite *Dasein* rather than as abstracted from or transcendent of finite *Dasein*. In the following quote, we see Bloch's effort to join the realm of a radical materialism with a normative universalisable realm. Once again, Bloch's aesthetic theory works explicitly to serve the larger philosophical project that I outline above: "[t]he beauty in art brings, creatively through its form, the Dimensions and Norms indicated (embedded) in material nature to completion" (1972: 523).

Bloch's attempt to fuse the particular and the universal into a radical unity is one of the fundamental features of his system. The realm of the aesthetic is privileged as a site where the fusion of the universal and the particular can and does occur. A brief comment on the structure of this system in relation to the aesthetic is worth note here. Bloch's system works against the illusion of completion and independence implied in terms such as "the particular", "the finite", "the universal". In his view, the terms themselves are only possible *via* their interrelationship. His system denies the notion that static, whole, separable units of meaning are possible. The illusion of stasis in meaning comes about because of the presumption that a fixed, static, terminological order is the goal latent in human discourse. For Bloch, the "goal" is intrinsically an abstract form of Utopia, one that he rejects. He privileges the aesthetic as a site where the illusions of static conceptual order, as such, whether linguistic, social or temporal, are most easily punctured. Overcoming, reworking and moving beyond static conceptual orders are the positively charged, productive fruits of the aesthetic. Bloch's drive to get at the philosophical origin, the ground of the new in art, and in being itself, makes it possible for him to break through the static as such. In this sense, Bloch's aesthetic is an aesthetic of emergence. His primary concern is with art and the creative act as moments that mark and instigate the "breaking of ground" that is necessary for processes of change to occur in the aesthetic arena. For Bloch, the not-yet sparks being out of stasis and initiates the process of becoming. He privileges the work of art as a place where this event reveals itself. The following quote illustrates the essential impulse, the drive to move forward and enter into the process mentioned above. It is one of the primary concerns in Bloch's aesthetic.

> The duty of an incomplete entelechy, once placed on its feet, does not end, least of all in aesthetic realism, or in the stupidity of imitation or the lies of amelioration (from which it is markedly distinct). Creative art is one, in which both the typical meaning is marked, and through which Art sparks into movement the not yet complete possibility, encouraging as a pre-forming realistic Ideal. (1972: 524)

From this it is evident, despite his debts to Husserl, that the ultimate locus for Bloch's aesthetic is more fundamental than an analysis of art in terms of a phenomenological analysis of the structure of perception. Bloch's aesthetic operates in a double mode, as phenomenology of the work of art and at the same time an ontological analysis of the preconditions (material and historical) that make the experience of the "phenomenon" itself at all possible. He wants to embed the structures of perception in historical material *Daseinsformen* (forms of being) that are prior to and necessary for the very possibility of perception at all. That is why he emphasises the necessity of turning aesthetics on its feet, divorcing it from the terrain of the purely abstract and turning "entelechy" into an open and "real" ideal. He analyses *Daseinsformen* in terms of their ideologically conditioned nature. Nevertheless, Bloch's aesthetics is not a continuation of Hegelian aesthetics, nor a strictly dialectic materialist position, along the lines of Lukács, a position that reads art works almost exclusively in terms of their social and historical origins. Bloch insists on the necessity of attempting to map the absolute ground, the in-process, unfixable, terrain of becoming that constitutes the universal substrate to all aesthetic experience. Once again, the drive in Blochian aesthetics is a drive toward a material *a priori*. In order to grasp the structure of this curious *a priori* one must grasp its futurial contra-anamentic structure. What makes the ground of Bloch's aesthetics a fragmentary ground, a ground in movement, incompletion and becoming, is the principle of the not-yet. The not-yet works against anamnesis. Bloch wanted to set anamnesis on its feet and rework the history of philosophy according to a forward rather than backward looking structure. The not-yet resides at the start, in the material itself. For Bloch, aesthetic phenomena mark and express this most basic not-yet in a way that is more immediately available to us than all other cultural or conceptual phenomena.

5. Ball and the philosophy in Dada

Zürich Dada, in particular as expressed through the work of Hugo Ball, contains a latent ontologically grounded and systematic aesthetic theory. This claim may appear counter intuitive. Famously Dada, like the name itself, flouted cultural and conceptual norms and tried to break any stranglehold that theory had on art. One of the few things that unified Dadaists such as Hugo Ball, Hans Arp, Marcel Janco and Tristan Tzara was a communal rejection of the title "school" and a deliberate refusal to offer a programme or clear structure for Dada. Dada portrayed itself as anti-theoretical – an arbitrary, anarchistic, chaotic, celebration of art and life that freely incorporated Expressionism, Futurism and Cubism, to name just a few, without holding allegiance to any of them. Dada's manifesto was fragmentation and anti-system. It induced disorientation, shock and chaos. According to Ball, to systematise Dada would be to succumb to the very mechanisms of control (social, artistic, political, conceptual) that Dada endeavours to overthrow. But a closer look at Hugo Ball's work, especially "Das Wort und das Bild" (The Word and the Image) from *Die Flucht aus der Zeit*,[12] reveals that Dada was in part consciously and in part unconsciously guided by a philosophical system; it is however a unique system because it has an open and fluid structure. It is not a system in the traditional sense of unfolding a set of organising principles in a logical and ordered fashion. Dada does not offer arguability. To think of Dada as system, despite itself, means simultaneously to rethink the notion of system itself. It forces a rethinking of what constitutes a valid, explanatory worldview. It means to allow

that the seemingly chaotic, grotesque and unfinished contains more
truth content than the harmonic, ordered and symmetrical. It is possible at this register to interpret Dada, Ball and Bloch in unity. Dada,
at least early Dada, with Ball as its prime motivator, is only very
selectively anti-theoretical. Dada required a theory that does not succumb to the pitfalls of theory as dry, mechanical abstraction. Ball
himself was well aware of this. Ball's training in philosophy made
him alert to the ineluctable but often sublimated relationship between
the realm of the aesthetic and the realm of the conceptual. In a sense,
Dada grew out of the explosive meeting of the conceptual and the
aesthetic in Ball's work. Dada required, and indeed had, a theoretical
coherence and substructure. It is unlikely that an art movement founded on mere dissolute chaos would have garnered the international
attention that Dada achieved. The claim here is that even those cultural events that appear to propagate meaninglessness, chaos and
disorder (perhaps especially those) require in their fundament a guiding logic, and in order to understand what gave Dada its cultural
potency it is necessary to excavate its latent theoretical substructure.
Nevertheless, while Ball was a thinker as well as a poet, and his work,
especially *Die Flucht aus der Zeit,* reveals flashes of Nietzschean
brilliance, he does not attempt to give Dada a coherent philosophical
system. This is why joining Dada with Bloch's ontology is a productive move, and the deep-seated affinities between the two of them are
nowhere more apparent than in Ball's texts, especially *Die Flucht aus
der Zeit.* It is exactly at the juncture of Ball's aphoristic theoretical
work and Bloch's philosophical system that the ontology of the avant-
garde makes itself available. One finds, in Ball's work and in Bloch's
philosophy, a formulation of avant-garde aesthetics as an incomplete,
not-yet ontology.

The notion that Dada has a system becomes less surprising as
one takes into consideration Ball's explicit philosophical position and
his politics. For Ball, as for Bloch, these are not separable fields and
Dada was briefly the place where Ball could most effectively unite
them. The place to go for a picture of "Dada as political philosophy"
is the collection of autobiographical texts, *Die Flucht aus der Zeit,*
which Ball himself carefully edited for publication. The following
quote is indicative of the fundamental aesthetic position that informs
Dadaism, Bloch and Ball simultaneously: "March 12, 1916. The distancing device is the stuff of life. Let us be thoroughly new and in-

ventive. Let us rewrite[13] life every day" (Ball 1974: 56). "Die distanzierende Erfindung ist das Leben selber" ("the distancing device is
the stuff of life") is a deliberately cryptic phrase. Nevertheless it indicates an aesthetic position fundamental to the avant-garde of this
period, a position that informs Bloch's work as well. What Ball indicates here is the aesthetic principle of *Verfremdung*, which during
Dada and at the time of the writing of *Die Flucht aus der Zeit* was an
important emergent aesthetic principle, one that came to hold wide influence among German intelligentsia long before Brecht thematised it
(in a very different way) in the thirties. In the quote above, *Verfremdung* is manifest as the question of "distancing" (distanzierende Erfindung) as "the stuff of life". Ball, like Bloch later in *Geist der Utopie* and the two volumes of *Verfremdungen*, overturns the ordinary
meaning of the word itself, reworks it and gives it a positively charged
significance.

Usually in German *Verfremdung* means something strange or
disconcerting, something distanced from its expected or familiar context. Ball uses the word "distanzierende" in the same sense as Bloch
uses *Verfremdung*, in order to refer to experiences of the "beautiful",
"strange", disconcerting experiences of something "far off", which
produce astonishment and wonder (*Staunen*).[14] In contrast to the alienation of *Entfremdung*, for both Ball and Bloch *Verfremdung* holds out
the not yet realised promise of a new sort of fulfillment. This positively charged model of estrangement has parallels in the work of
Adorno and Benjamin, and in Marx himself insofar as Marx took artistic activity as a model of unalienated human labour. Estrangement is
a mode of aesthetic distancing from the common, the everyday; that
which is expected and reproduced through habit, social dictate and
conceptual hierarchy. *Verfremdung* is meant to overcome both "the
technical cold" ("Die Technische Kälte" in Bloch 1971: 20) or in the
case of Ball the "mechanistic process" that he rails against throughout
Die Flucht aus der Zeit, a process that is the driving force behind reified social relations. Bloch and Ball share an understanding of
Verfremdung, as more than just an abstract aesthetic category, rather it
is a means to rework human experience itself and overcome the wages
of alienation.

As a feature of literary theory, the Russian formalist Viktor
Schlowski gave *Verfremdung* a very thorough formulation in 1916.[15]
Schlowski's treatment of *Verfremdung* fosters the idea that art ought

to operate in opposition to a closed, mimetic understanding of reality. Even the most schematic summary of his work illustrates a basic correspondence with Bloch and Ball, and shows the degree to which even distant branches of the avant-garde operated in accord. The binding concern is with a mode of aesthetic production that offers a new way of seeing; one opposed to the banality and stasis of "realistic" modes of artistic production, and intended to break through reified social order.

Ball, Bloch, and contemporaries such as Benjamin and Lukács were familiar with the theoretical work of the Russian Formalists, Suprematists and Futurists to varying degrees. Here though, the issue is not so much one of measuring direct influence, but rather of assessing the intellectual context and developing a nuanced understanding of the way in which disparate thinkers and artists shared the cultural moment. Avant-garde formalism, understood to include aspects of Futurism and Suprematism, was one of the first and most radical movements to spearhead an aesthetic of "estrangement" (even though formalism was divorced in some respects from the Hegelian and marxist traditions that fostered the most influential analyses of alienation and estrangement). Further, a cross-section of thinkers and artists either directly or peripherally involved in the avant-garde shared the fundamental impulse that shaped the emergence of *Verfremdung* as an aesthetic principle in the early part of the century. For Ball, like many of his contemporaries, the power in the distancing principle, the power of estrangement, is that it breaks open rigid conceptual orders, tradition and hierarchy and offers a path to a genuine authentic "eigentlich" experience of "life". For Ball and Bloch, the creative act is simultaneously a critical principle in that it demonstrates the oppression, dehumanisation and "false consciousness" of modernity. In the following quote, Ball is discussing the simultaneous poems that he performed along with Huelsenbeck, Tzara and Janco at the Cabaret Voltaire in March of 1916:

> The poem tries to elucidate the fact that man is swallowed up in the mechanistic process. In a typically compressed way it shows the conflict of the *vox humana* with a world that threatens, ensnares, and destroys it, a world whose rhythm and noise are ineluctable. (1974: 57)

The concern here, like much of Ball's work during his Dada phase, is how to get at a new experience of "life". This concern is at the same time one of the most fundamental binding features of early twentieth century avant-garde discourse. It is a concern that crosses the boundaries of philosophy, art and literature and is fundamental to the intellectual context of the day. The hope of forging a new openness to "life" as concrete lived experience is simultaneously driven by the hope of making available the fragmentary nature of reality, a reality that is normally covered over and reasoned away through static, totalising social and conceptual hierarchies.

> One thing is certain; art is joyful only as long as it has richness and life. Reciting aloud has become the touchstone of the quality of a poem for me, and I have learned (from the stage) to what extent today's literature is worked out as a problem at the desk and is made for the spectacles of the collector instead of for the ears of living human beings. (1974: 54)

Here, Ball rails against art as contrivance, and elsewhere throughout *Die Flucht aus der Zeit* against the abstract constructs of "theory". Yet he is not against conceptually oriented art, theory or philosophy in principle. Rather, he is opposed to modes of artistic and theoretical discourse that smother and repress the true, fragmentary, broken nature of "life". The social and political implications of his aesthetic stance, and its origins in Marx, are not always foregrounded in Ball's work. Bloch gives the political implications of Ball's aesthetic a more explicit formulation. Beyond the biographical facts of their association, a deep-seated accord as to how avant-garde modes of aesthetic production and experience relate to a spectrum of social, political, epistemological and conceptual issues draws the two together. The term estrangement indicates what unifies them on these questions. For both of them the process of distancing, making strange through art, reveals the fissures in the false totality of mechanised, bourgeois social structures. Both Ball and Bloch, like Marx, wanted art to operate as a model of unalienated labour. This is what justifies their mutual privileging of aesthetic production as a means to overcome alienation in the marxist sense. The overcoming of alienation (*Entfremdung*) through estrangement (*Verfremdung*) lays the path to unalienated life. For Bloch, Ball and the avant-garde in general the aesthetic is the site where this can and does happen. Thus the implicit aesthetic principles that inform Dada are designed to awaken the authentic "essence of the age" and the human being from the slumber induced by an "allgemeine Selbstentseelung", that is a "general self renunciation of the soul" (1926: 97).

6. Dada Time: shifts in the temporal frame

We have seen that Hugo Ball saw Dada as an attempt to liberate the human being from an overly rational social order and its own self-imposed "instrumentalisation". For Ball, Bloch and Dada, what needs to be overcome is the human as an alienated and subjugated being. The liberating impulse that drove Dada was, with a few exceptions, a characteristic fundamental to most contemporary avant-garde movements.[16] The question that allows us to grasp the political significance of Dada is; from what does the liberating impulse want to free itself? What mechanisms empower the processes of alienation and subjugation intrinsic to modernity? Here again the intellectual context that Bloch and Ball shared during and shortly after the First World War was shaped by animosity toward an "instrumentalised rationality"[17] which was seen as dominating European culture. More specifically, Bloch and Ball aim their critique of "the technical cold" (Bloch) and the "mechanistic process" (Ball) at the instrumental linear model of time. This model of time, the time of the clock, dominates and makes possible a closed down, rationalised, manageable social order. Instrumental rationality requires, in order to propagate itself, a rigid rectilinear model of time. The underlying issue is how temporal structure shapes society and reinforces systems of power. The idea here is that the instrumentalised model of time provides the "transcendental" precondition for the possibility of a dangerously mechanised social order. Consequently, much of the early discourse against instrumental rationality aims at the mechanical model of time, the device that drives the technological advance of modernity.

Frequently, Ball's work indicates the centrality of the question of temporal structures for the classical avant-garde. Obvious examples are both the epigraph to the present essay, "The normal clock of an abstract epoch is exploded" (1926: 152), and the title to Ball's own record of his Dada period *Die Flucht aus der Zeit*. Here, Ball shares in the widespread critique of "time as mechanism" that was part of the central European intellectual context. The critique was based on the idea that the instrumental model of time turns it into an empty, infinite, homogenous series of moments, measured and employed to technological ends. The time of the clock institutes an experience of time that is abstract and separate from lived experience. It is the *Verdinglichung* of time. Both Bloch and Ball resist the notion that time is a matter of psychological or empirical fact subject to scientific calculation and measurement. They see aesthetic experience, the realm of art, as the terrain where the linear model of time can be overcome. The effort to reevaluate the significance of "instrumentalised" time is a political and aesthetic event that reverberates across the culture of the Weimar Republic and is integral to Bloch's ontology and Ball's Dadaism.

What makes it possible to read Bloch and Ball together with regards to the question of temporality is encapsulated in Bloch's concept of an "Ästhetik des Vor-scheins". Immediately, the idea of an "Ästhetik des Vor-scheins" resonates distantly with medieval theological traditions that revolved around mystical revelation. Both Bloch and Ball were steeped in the tradition of German mysticism that extended from the medieval period *via* Meister Eckhart, through Angelus Silesius and Jakob Böhme into the seventeenth century. Again, it is not a coincidence that after the Dada period Ball converted to orthodox Catholicism and spent his remaining years steeped in Byzantine and medieval theology. Yet the aesthetic principles at work in Bloch and Ball are very different from a mere falling back on prior models of mystical experience. They share rather a reworking of aspects of the mystical tradition given the intellectual context of the early twentieth century in a way that means to foster originality and openness to the radically new. The groundbreaking and to this day unexhausted inventive spirit of Dada attests to that. The term *Vorschein* plays on a resonance available in the related and more explicitly religious term *Offenbarung* ("Revelation") which was fundamental to the mystical tradition. *Vor-Schein* indicates the fact that many of Bloch's key concepts developed out of his engagement with the mystical tradition, especially Jakob Böhme. Yet the hyphen is a necessity, because it marks the fact that the term is quite distinct from what *der Vorschein* ("revealing") normally signifies. One must translate *Vor-Schein* as something along the lines of "concrete real pre-appearance". Bloch's *Vor-Schein* represents in part a reworking of the common understanding of revelation as a mystical experience that opens up a vertical transcendence of the "concrete" here and now through divine communication with God. In ordinary usage, revelation (and its related theological concepts) carries within it a dualism based on the Christian idea that mystical experience transcends the corrupt, finite this-worldliness of the flesh. Heidegger brought about a radical reversal of the terms of transcendence that informed the western philosophical tradition by refiguring transcendence as horizontal rather than vertical.[18] Premonitions of this reversal are available in Bloch's ontology prior to *Being and Time*. While Bloch did not undo the Cartesian model of the subject and its accompanying vertical structure of transcendence as radically or as rigorously as Heidegger, he problematises a closely related set of conceptual issues. In Bloch, both Cartesian dualism and the dualism that informs the tradition of German mysticism are overcome *via* the "concrete" structure in the "Ästhetik des Vor-Scheins".

It is important here to note again, for the purposes of comparison, that the principles underlying Bloch's *Vor-Schein* are an implicit feature of Ball's work as well. The uniqueness of the aesthetic principle underlying the "ontology" of the avant-garde in Bloch and Ball, that which makes it a radical departure from all prior aesthetics, lies in its emphasis on the concrete, anticipatory nature of the experience made available *via* the work of art. A radical breaking open of "the new" drove Ball's experiments with Dada, and a fundamental concern with the new in being itself drove Bloch's pioneering ontology of the not-yet. The present harbors the new and still not realised; it is, at an ontological level, a pre-existing structural feature of being itself. The pre-appearance of the new in the present (in Bloch's terms the *Novum*) is what allows man to break free from a predictable, linear and static mode of temporality, and thus begin the work of overcoming alienation. Concrete pre-appearance, *Vor-Schein*, is what creates the possibility of a mode of temporality that is radically non-linear and open to its own unforseen possibilities. Two obvious indications of a preoccupation with non-linear modes of temporality in Bloch and in Zürich Dada are evident in Bloch's concepts of non-simultaneity in historical analysis and in the temporally and linguistically destabilising simultaneous poems that Ball,[19] Huelsenbeck, Janco and Tzara read aloud during the initial Dada performances in Zürich.

7. Utopia, community and the politics of hope in Ball and Bloch

Hopefully it is clear by now that the Dada aesthetic, its joy at the unpredictable and accidental, is part of a playful determination to break open the rigid conceptual (and temporal) order that dominates in an entirely rationalised society and awaken the human being to "life". Similarly, Bloch's "Ästhetik des Vor-Scheins" aims to reveal the concrete possibilities that exist in the fundament of the human being. The mode of aesthetic experience valorised on both fronts aims to reveal the true ontologically grounded human content ordinarily forgotten or repressed at the behest of an abstract rationalised social order. Though Ball never explicitly addresses "ontology" as such, the structure of his thought parallels Bloch's ontology. Like Bloch, he sees the human being as by no means closed or finally known. The human being, in the most fundamental sense, is an incomplete project, a creature in process, something on the way toward an unknown not-yet actualised future. On this model, the being of the human being is in a constant state of renewal and rediscovery of its own most fundamental possibilities. The concrete pre-appearance of the new (*der Vor-Schein*) as an aesthetic principle, is both critical and hopeful. It is hopeful in that it wants to reveal and preserve the true, unpredictable and fragile nature of the human being. This effort carries within it a utopian intent, whose socio-political significance will be addressed presently. It is critical in that it works to reveal and overcome the substrate of alienation and domination that reigns in a completely rational and mechanised society. Early on in *Die Flucht aus der Zeit*, Ball indicates the direction of his thinking on some of these issues:

> You know, I would really like to understand, to comprehend. It is the total mass of machinery and the devil himself that has broken loose now. Ideals are only labels that have been stuck on. Everything has been shaken to its very foundations. (1974: 10-11)

This quote, like the emergence of Dada itself, must be seen against the context of shock brought about by the First World War. Ball, Bloch and their contemporaries were witness to the first entirely mechanised war to wreak havoc on a global scale and result in millions of impersonal, faceless casualties. The utopian impulse that underlies Ball's work, like the utopia in Bloch's *Geist der Utopie*, was forged out of the experience of the war. Given this context, the polit-

ical project latent in Dada and explicit in Bloch requires a radical new
form of utopia. Put in overly simplified terms, in order to preserve
hope for a better world and the glimmer of what that better world
might look like, utopia needed reformulation to be made concrete and
immediate. Abstract utopias were more than inadequate; they were
seen as one of the prime instigators of a deadly attachment to false,
abstract ideals. The complete mechanisation of society (the precondition for mechanised warfare) fosters the total subjugation of individuals and the erasure of the human content underlying the machinery. Ball states the threat in dramatic terms as follows:

> The machine gives a kind of sham life to dead matter. It moves
> matter. It is a specter. It joins matter together, and in so doing
> reveals some kind of rationalism. Thus it is death, working sys-
> tematically, counterfeiting life. [...] And what is more, in its
> continuous subconscious influence it destroys human rhythm.
> Anyone who lasts a lifetime near such a machine must be a hero,
> or must be crushed. We cannot expect any spontaneous feelings
> from such a creature. (1974: 4)

Here we can see that Ball, like Bloch and many of their contemporaries, saw alienation, subjugation and repression as the dominant characteristics of an insanely rational society. The forging of a
new utopia was meant to counteract the dangers inherent in the
instrumentalisation and mechanisation of the internal and external life
of the human being. The fear was that without a new "concrete Utopia", hope (the force that drove the anti-war movement in central
Europe) would have to be abandoned for a nihilistic acceptance of
alienation and subjugation. Ball and Bloch also shared a conviction
that the realm of the aesthetic was the place where a more concrete
and immediate form of utopia could be made visible. Here, the connection between the far from obvious political significance of Dada
and Bloch's "Ästhetik des Vor-Scheins" (accompanied by his ontology) becomes apparent. The ontology of the avant-garde carries within it a principle of hope meant to counteract the destructive force of
"instrumentalised reason" as was apparent during the First World War
and the first years of the Weimar Republic.

8. Conclusion

At this point, as way of concluding, I would like to briefly offer a more refined picture of the structure of "concrete Utopia" and comment on the way that it interrelates with the question of community and death in Bloch's thought. Throughout his work, Bloch wants to represent and make thinkable a society in which individual and general well-being are so thoroughly interconnected that anxiety at the thought of one's own end becomes impotent, obsolete. His concept of the "disappearance of the 'lethal nothingness' in socialist Consciousness"[20] stands obviously in the tradition of German Idealism. In the *Encyclopedia of Philosophy*, Hegel reduces the sting of death by seeing that through death the weight of individual existence is finally overcome through the *aufhebung* (supercession) of its intrinsic incapacity for the general (*Allgemeinheit*). In death, the illusion of individuality is overcome in favour of the concept of species (*Gattung*). Feuerbach describes the speculative ground of death in *On Death and Immortality* as follows: "in it (death) infinite Being finally breaks the burden of the Temple of one's own finite being". Bloch's position on death is in some ways structurally similar. In *Das Prinzip Hoffnung* (The Principle of Hope), utopia offers a gathering of the individual into the general (or the universal), which takes the form of the socialist collective. At this register, Bloch's utopianism could be misinterpreted as an abstract metaphysical construct. In simplistic terms, Hegel's Concept, Feuerbach's God and Bloch's socialist collective, are loosely correlate terms that offer a dialectical overcoming of suffering finite existence through death. On this model, death itself is made into a positive in that it negates the negative principle in life. For Bloch in particular, the moments where his eschatological rhetoric becomes most heated are the moments when it appears that death is the threshold to an ideal form of community.

Here once again it is worth repeating that Bloch's utopia marks a radical departure from what is normally understood under the concept utopia. It is in fact the binding agent of human beings, and makes community possible at all. For Bloch, community is only possible because of the impulse toward the ideal community, Utopia, which has to be thought of in terms of something that is not-yet. It is the promise of something that is not yet, and may indeed never be. It cannot be described or named in positive terms. It can only be circumscribed and hinted at in negative terms. Thus, in some ways, Bloch's Utopia resembles a negative theology. Bloch insists that concrete Utopia must be differentiated from the absurd and often dangerous fantasies of abstract utopianism. According to Bloch, fascism to a great degree was a result of ideological attachment to abstract utopias, the utopian propaganda of Nazism being the most prevalent example in the twentieth century. The distinctive feature of Bloch's concrete Utopia is that it is always already present in every lived moment. This form of utopia conditions being-with, in the sense that community is grounded on the latent hope that an ideal community is possible. However, again, the ideal community may never be reached, utopia is not a foregone conclusion, rather a latent hope that spurs the way forward. In *Das Prinzip Hoffnung*, Bloch describes it as follows:

> Utopia presses forward in the will of the subject and in the ten-dency-latency of the process world, beyond the shattered ontology of a supposedly already reached, already settled there. Such is the way of the conscious reality process, exactly that of an increasing loss of a fixed, or even hypostatised static-being, a way of an in-creasingly perceived Nothing, freely also through Utopia. (1959: 363)

Concrete Utopia provides an unconscious normative function to community formation. Without the hope that an ideal community is reachable, as a latent, unconscious goal, even the most poorly functioning actual community would become utterly inoperable. In a sense, concrete Utopia is understood as the ethical substrate to everyday life, the glue that provides for the possibility of community.

Notes

Translations from the German in the text are by the author, unless otherwise acknow-ledged.

[1] Originally, *Kritische Eröterungen über Rickert und das Problem der Modernen Erkenntnistheorie.*

[2] In Munich in 1911/12 Ball came to know Frank Wedekind and helped him stage the piece *Franziska.* In the same period, Ball became friends with Wassily Kandinsky and together they planned an almanac to compliment the Blue Rider work. The project was broken off at the outbreak of the war. Later Kandinsky contributed to Ball's early Dadaist publications.

³ Autobiographical material by Bloch (*Bloch Almanach* 4, 1984 "Gespräche mit Ernst Bloch") and Ball's published letters attest to the fact that they discussed Thomas Münzer in the period 1917–18. Hugo Ball's *Zur Kritik der deutschen Intelligenz* of 1919 (Critique of the German Intelligentsia) includes a long chapter on Münzer titled "Thomas Münzer gegen Martin Luther" ("Thomas Münzer against Martin Luther"). The October Revolution inspired Bloch's *Thomas Münzer als Theologe der Revolution* (Thomas Münzer as Theologian of the Revolution). It was published in 1921. According to Bloch his monograph was the first full-length study of Münzer since 1842. He does not acknowledge Hugo Ball's work on the topic – it is unlikely that Ball was a major influence for Bloch in his work on Münzer. That they shared ideas is clear but the content of the two texts on Münzer are different enough in style and focus to make an argument of direct influence uninteresting. It is more likely that Ernst Bloch drew on Friedrich Engel's book *Der deutsche Bauernkrieg* (The German Peasant War) of 1850. Bloch and Engels read Luther as the theologian of a nascent, repressive bourgeois power structure and Münzer as the genuinely revolutionary theologian for the subjugated classes.

⁴ Some of the implications of this idea for Bloch's concept of time are discussed in section 4.

⁵ Bloch's original articles from the Expressionism debate are reprinted in *Erbschaft dieser Zeit* (Heritage of our Times).

⁶ Bloch's relationship with Benjamin is one of the keys to understanding the genesis of Bloch's aesthetic theory. Though much younger, Benjamin became close friends with both Ball and Bloch while he lived in Switzerland during the First World War. Later on Benjamin was to make important contributions to an aesthetic theory of the avant-garde especially in the short section on the avant-garde in the famous essay "The Work of Art in the Age of Its Technical Reproducibility".

⁷ When applied to Bloch's work the term aesthetics requires a caveat. Bloch was not an aesthetician in a traditional sense. He did not develop a static set of rules for categorising works of art. The role of the aesthetic in Bloch's thought will be addressed in more detail in section 4.

⁸ See Bloch's essay, "Aktualität und Utopie zu Lukács Geschichte und Klassenbewusstsein" (1923) in Philosophische Aufsätze, GA, vol. 10, p. 620.

⁹ See *Gespräche mit Ernst Bloch*, p. 300.

¹⁰ See in particular *Philosophische Aufsätze zur Objektiven Phantasie*.

¹¹ Here the question arises: what is the degree and scope of Freud's influence on Bloch? Despite appearances Bloch's analyses of the "noch nicht Bewusstsein" do not grow out of the prevalence and cultural cache of psychoanalysis in Germany in the early twentieth century. Bloch's engagement with psychology and his education under Theodor Lipps in Munich brought him into closer contact with the phenomenological mode of doing psychological investigation than with Freudian psychoanalysis. Bloch rejected out of hand, in a rash fashion, the preoccupation with bourgeois subjectivity that informed psychoanalytic discourse. His work reveals a concern with consciousness as a meta-subjective and historically preconditioned phenomenon (in spite of, or perhaps exactly in light of, the not-yet). The notion that a nexus of unconscious drives structures the mind, as long as it does not take in the historical and material factors that contribute to the structure of consciousness, contained for him insufficient explanatory power.

---

[12] Quotations are taken from the 1974 English translation, *Flight Out of Time*.

[13] I would suggest that there is no English equivalent for the main verb "umdichten" in the sentence "Dichten wir das Leben täglich um". "Umdichtung" means something along the lines of to refashion, re-poetise and it appears to me that only a distant approximation is possible in English.

[14] I owe features of my treatment of Bloch's aesthetics to Wayne Hudson's excellent study *The Marxist Philosophy of Ernst Bloch* and to Gert Ueding's introduction to the collection of Bloch texts *Ästhetik des Vor-Scheins*.

[15] For a treatment of emergence of *Verfremdung* as an aesthetic principle and its relation to the avant-garde see Hansen-Love's *Der russische Formalisms: methodologishe Rekonstruktion seiner Entwicklung aus dem Prinzip der Verfremdung*.

[16] Marinetti's Futurism, in its valorisation of war and machinery, is perhaps the clearest exception. That Marinetti was included in the first issue of the founding Dada pamphlet *Cabaret Voltaire* is proof of the open and disunified character of Dada. *Cabaret Voltaire* included work by Cubists and Expressionists as well. Nevertheless, even the brand of Futurism that valorised mechanisation in a naïve fashion and later came to lend itself to fascist propaganda was in some respects informed by a drive to rework and fashion a new liberating relation to rational social order, a breaking open of the Dionysian forces within mechanisation and technology.

[17] Aspects of this resonate obviously with the critical work that Adorno and Horkheimer would do later in *Dialectic of the Enlightenment*.

[18] There is no time here to treat the structure and significance of this event in Heidegger's work. I handle the topic in detail in another essay, "Time as Death: Finitude and Heidegger's Thought of Being-With".

[19] See, for example, Ball's poem "Simultan Krippenspiel".

[20] See pages 1378-1384 of *Das Prinzip Hoffnung* (The Principle of Hope).

References

Ball, Hugo
    1926   *Die Flucht aus der Zeit*. Zürich: Limmat (1992).

    1974   *Flight Out of Time: A Dada Diary* (ed. John Elderfield). Ann Raimes (tr.). New York: Viking Press.

Bloch, Ernst
    1964 & 1971   *Geist der Utopie* (1918 & 1923). Frankfurt am Main: Suhrkamp Verlag.

    1959   *Das Prinzip Hoffnung*. Frankfurt am Main: Suhrkamp Verlag.

    1972   *Das Materialismusproblem, seine Geschichte und Substanz*. Frankfurt am Main: Suhrkamp Verlag.

    1974   *Experimentum Mundi*. Frankfurt am Main: Suhrkamp Verlag.

Feuerbach, Ludwig
    1830   *Gedanken über Tod und Unsterblichkeit*. Nürenberg: J. A. Stein.

Hegel, G. W. F.
    1986   *Encyclopädie der Philosophischen Wissenschaften*. Werke 10. Frankfurt am Main: Suhrkamp.

Heidegger, Martin
    1993   *Sein und Zeit* (1927). 17 Aufl. Tübingen: Niemeyer.

Hudson, Wayne
    1982   *The Marxist Philosophy of Ernst Bloch*. New York: St Martins Press.

Husserl, Edmund
    1992   *Ideen zu einer reinen Phänomenologie und phänomenologische philosophie* (1913). Gesammelte Schriften, Bd. 5 Hamburg: Meiner.

    2000   *Vorlesungen zur Phänomenologie des inneren Zeitbewußtseins* (1928). Tübingen: Niemeyer.

Jameson, Fredric
    1977   Afterword to *Aesthetics and Politics: Bloch, Lukács, Brecht, Benjamin, Adorno* (ed. Robert Taylor). London and New York: Verso.

Making an Example of Duchamp:

history, theory, and the question of the avant-garde

David Cunningham

Abstract: In the "Preliminary Remarks" to his classic *Theory of the Avant-Garde*, Peter Bürger states that "the examples from literature and the fine arts to be found here are not to be understood as historical and sociological interpretations but as illustrations of a theory". Debating the Hegelian notions which underpin Bürger's famous account of Dada and early Surrealism – as constituting *the* theory of the avant-garde – and his disputes with Adorno on this basis, this essay seeks to consider the question of what is at stake, more generally, in the attempt to give examples of the avant-garde in critical and theoretical work. The first concrete "illustration" of Bürger's theory to appear in his book is the work of Marcel Duchamp, and it is indeed hard to think of another figure who has been re-presented, so repeatedly, as the object of a demand to exemplify in this way, by both artists and theorists. Offering a critical reading of several accounts of Duchamp's work, the essay goes on to suggest that thinking this peculiar "exemplarity" necessitates a philosophical recognition of the problematic relationship between general and particular inscribed by the concept of an avant-garde itself, insofar as the demand for non-identity (to tradition), which its implicit temporal dynamic articulates, suggests that any example of the avant-garde would have to be marked, not by its repetition of some feature common to all possible examples, but precisely by its lack of any "determinate" commonality. In this way, the essay seeks to ask several questions about what we conventionally mean by "avant-garde", and suggests the limitations inherent within prevailing "art-historical" theorisations of the avant-garde as a collection of period "styles" or "techniques". The essay concludes by arguing that a contemporary response to Duchamp (or to Dada) is not compelled to be a nostalgic mourning for an irrecoverable lost object, but may, in its engagement with the question of an avant-garde, produce (as certain contemporary practices suggest) a repressed futural potential within the present. It is in these terms that the "ex-emplification" of Duchamp should be re-thought: not as the "model" for a repetition of fixed, empirically locatable strategies or techniques, but as "exemplifying" an im-manent logic of non-identity which demands a continual "renewal" of a critical art's relation to social forms and relations other to those with which the category of an avant-garde has previously been confronted.

"The danger remains that he'll get out of the valise we put him in.
So long as he remains locked up." – John Cage

The following essay takes as its central problematic what may seem to
be a more or less abstract, philosophical question. That is: what would
constitute an *example* of the avant-garde? If such a question seeks to
interrogate the theoretical functions of a term most commonly deployed in the discourses of cultural criticism and history, it is nonetheless philosophical in form because it raises the issue of the relation
between particular and universal; the role of the example in mediating
between specific works or practices and the historical generality articulated by the *concept* of an avant-garde. It is in addressing this
question of exemplarity that, in his classic *Theory of the Avant-Garde*,
Peter Bürger, for example, writes:

> A theoretical discussion that wants to avoid becoming abstract
> must also refer to individual works. But such references do not
> have the status of [individual] interpretations. They serve to give
> concreteness to statements that make a more sweeping claim to
> general validity. (1984: 1)

As such, Bürger continues, "the examples from literature and the fine
arts to be found here are not to be understood as historical and sociological interpretations but as *illustrations* of a theory" (1984: xlviii).
Bürger's terminology calls up its own philosophical reference in
Hegel's attempt, in the *Introductory Lectures on Aesthetics*, to mediate between the ahistorical abstractions of aesthetics and the naive
empiricism of art history: theorising proper is not the purpose of the
empirical "study of art, starting from particular and extant works". Yet
it necessarily "furnishes the philosophy of art with the perceptible
illustrations and instances, into the particular historical details of
which philosophy cannot enter" (Hegel 1993: 24-5).

While few have been convinced by Hegel's own reconciliation of "metaphysical universality with the determinateness of real
particularity" (Hegel 1993: 26), this unsatisfactory split between the
torn halves of "empirical method" and "abstract reflection" has continued to trouble all post-Hegelian philosophies of art and culture, and
is one which is hardly resolved in Bürger's account of that being-in-
common which "defines" the avant-garde. Indeed, despite his claim to

have definitively surpassed Adorno's aesthetic theory[1] (a claim which is itself revealing with regard to Bürger's historicist presuppositions), from an Adornian perspective one might well see Bürger here relapsing all too easily into a *pre*-Adornian Hegelianism which, while making the demand that "thought should not proceed from above but rather relinquish itself to the phenomena", ends by reducing particularity only to "the status of exempla" in a way which does violence to the internal non-identity and historicity of the artistic phenomena with which he is concerned (Adorno 1997: 333). I do not have the space here to pursue the complex philosophical issues entailed by this. However, what I do want to consider in this light is what might be *essentially* problematic about the notion of presenting particular works as "illustrations" of *the* avant-garde in general; a problem which, I want to suggest, involves something to do with the *time* of the avant-garde, the distinctive modes of historical temporalisation that its *concept* implies, and which are not reducible to the ultimately homogenous time of (art or literary) historicism.[2]

In an essay from the late 1960s, Maurice Blanchot asserts: "the history of Surrealism is only of scholarly interest, particularly if the conception of Surrealism is not modified by its subject" (1993: 407). What Blanchot states here of Surrealism, I would like to argue, is true of the avant-garde more generally. For, as Susan Buck-Morss has recently reminded us, if the term "avant-garde" originated in a primarily spatial (military) concept, the condition of its familiar metaphorical functioning in political, cultural and artistic discourse, from around the mid-nineteenth century, was its transcription "onto the dimension of historical time" (2000: 61). That is to say, first and foremost – and before any apparent locatability of something called *the* avant-garde within the disputed limits of a socio-historical or art-historical periodisation – the concept of an avant-garde inscribes a particular mode of temporalising history, a particular *politics of time*, in its own right (see Osborne, 1995). It is this that I want to explore further in what follows; not least as a means to rethinking – outside of the characteristic closures of art history – what role the concept of an avant-garde might have to play with respect to the artistic, cultural and political concerns of "today", at the beginning of the twenty-first century.

1. Trying to understand Duchamp

The details of Bürger's account are well enough known not to require much repeating here. Indeed they continue – even for those who would dispute their ultimate conclusions – to cast, some thirty years on, a seemingly inescapable shadow over all debates surrounding the notion of an avant-garde. As this now familiar story would have it, the increasing autonomy of art in its development through the eighteenth and nineteenth centuries provides the historical condition of possibility for the avant-garde's beginning, in revolt against aestheticism and art's institutional separation from social life; the ultimate impossibility of its *telos* of a "sublation of art and life", and the increasing hegemony of the culture industry and the commodity aesthetics of bourgeois society through the latter part of the twentieth century, the conditions of possibility for its end in what Bürger has no hesitation in describing as its failure. As is equally well known, the primary reference points for this heroic avant-garde, which precedes a final and irresistible recuperation in the re-aestheticisation of the so-called "neo-avantgardes" of the post-war era, are the Dada and early Surrealist movements of the 1910s and 1920s. Despite a rather vague footnote suggesting the potential theoretical incorporation of Futurism and Expressionism, as well as the early Soviet movements, it is from these "sources" that Bürger takes all his central examples: Tzara, Heartfield, *Nadja*, *Paris Peasant* (Bürger 1984: 109). Dada, in particular, is situated as "the most radical movement within the European avant-garde"; a radicalism constituted by the fact that it "no longer criticises schools that preceded it, but criticises art as an institution, and the course its development took in bourgeois society". Thus does "the social subsystem that is art enter the stage of self-criticism" (Bürger 1984: 22).

I will return, briefly, to the problems that I think are entailed by Bürger's theory in the final section of this essay, but before doing so I want simply to note that the first actual, concrete "illustration" of it to appear in his book is that of Marcel Duchamp, whose 1917 *Fountain* provides one of the book's few photographic images. And, if the explicit association with Dada that this apparently involves has been disputed by many later critics – and I will return to this also – Bürger is, nonetheless, scarcely unique, in more general terms, in his use of Duchamp in such a way. For it is hard to think of another figure who has been re-presented so repeatedly in aesthetic and art-historical discourse, as the object of a demand to *exemplify*. His work, particularly the readymades, is again and again brought forth, in recent (post-1960s) art and cultural theory, as *the* example of, among others, the attack on institutionality (Bürger), the anarchic herald of a dangerous "anything goes" (Greenberg), the postmodernist turn to the "discourse of the copy" (Krauss), the erosion of the distinction between art and "its own philosophy" (various conceptualists), the destruction of the aura or the frame that divides art from its other, the re-entry of art into the space of the everyday, the revelation that anyone can be an artist and that anything can be art, the fact that art is merely a question of the "name" or of the "context", and so on. This then is the question that I want to ask: what is at stake in this general discursive exemplarity which would seem always to be Duchamp's fate? And what might this have to tell us about the problems involved in theorising the avant-garde in general?

In each case, the imperative would seem to be that Duchamp should be *understood*, that the historical (and theoretical) meaning of this work – its "proposition as to art's nature", as the Conceptual artist Joseph Kosuth puts it – be decided (Kosuth 1991: 18). And of course, more often than not, the attachment of such an imperative to Duchamp's work is, whether positively (Bürger) or negatively (Greenberg), an assertion that in some way "through" it the historical meaning of *the* avant-garde may finally be revealed.[3] If, as Kosuth claims, the "function of art as a question, was first raised by Marcel Duchamp", the imperative is that Duchamp's own questioning be seen to give up some kind of determinate answer (Kosuth 1991: 18). For those, however, who desire such an understanding of Duchamp – and particularly for those, like Kosuth or Danto, who see in his work the culmination of art becoming philosophical or conceptual – there has always been a source of frustration. Despite the famous emphasis on the importance of ideas, one has to contend with the apparent reluctance to divulge explicitly what such ideas might mean, in a substantive conceptual sense, at least as something like propositions about art or what art should be. There is, in other words, the legendary problem of Duchamp's *silence*; a silence which, as the editors of his collected writings assert, "like Rimbaud's exile in Harrar, has weighed heavily on contemporary letters" (Duchamp 1973: 4). Artist Joseph Beuys's frustration is, in its own way, exemplary here: "I criticise him

[Duchamp] because at the very moment when he could have developed a theory on the basis of the work he had accomplished, he kept silent" (Beuys, in De Duve 1996: 285). That theory – the mirror reflection of Greenberg's greatest fears – was the utopian insight that "everyone is an artist"; Duchamp's refusal explicitly to express it, simple enigmatic posturings: "The silence of Marcel Duchamp is overestimated", as the title of a 1964 Beuys television performance has it (Mink 1995: 15).

The directness of Beuys's reproach, representative as it is of the heady rhetoric of its own historical moment, is nonetheless indicative also of a far more general demand inscribed within the according of exemplary status to Duchamp's work: that it tell us, in some way, what the meaning of *the* (true) avant-garde is (or was) in general. And, of course, this just *is*, conventionally, the job of the example: that it should provide the passage of mediation between the particular and the universal; that it stand in, metonymically, for the generality which it exemplifies. The example "is one singularity among others, which, however, stands for each of them and serves for all" (Agamben 1993: 10). Thus, classically, if Duchamp's works are to be taken as examples of the avant-garde, it should be that in their singularity they nonetheless instantiate some universal repeated across all other particulars. It is here, I would suggest, that, philosophically-speaking, matters become rather more complex than is generally acknowledged.

2. Singularity, repetition and the modern

The issue of repetition, and its relation to the singularity of the work, is, it should be noted, one addressed by Duchamp himself at various points in his career. Take the following exchange, for example, from a well-known interview with James John Sweeney:

> MD: You see the danger is to "lead yourself" into a form of *taste...*
> JJS: Taste then for you is repetition of anything that has been accepted; is that what you mean?
> MD: Exactly; it is a habit. Repeat the same thing long enough and it becomes taste. If you interrupt your work, I mean after you have done it, then it becomes, it stays a thing in itself; but if it is repeated a number of times it becomes taste. (Duchamp 1973: 133-4)

If nothing else, such statements rather undermine Duchamp's familiar postmodernist appropriation, and place his work back squarely within that problematic of the avant-garde, which, not so long ago, we were being told was now redundant. Nonetheless, given the influence of this appropriation, at the hands of critics like Rosalind Krauss, it is worth taking a brief digression to explore it further so as to see what it may have to reveal at this point.

The historical and theoretical separation by Krauss of Duchamp from "the avant-garde" connects to her more general argument, shared by other proponents of the postmodern, that "the very notion of the avant-garde can be seen as a function of the discourse of originality" (Krauss 1987: 157), against which "the experience of seriality" engendered by the readymade "factors into this discourse the issue of ... the multiple without original" (De Duve 1991: 179, 36).[4] Simply put, for Krauss, it would be wrong to think of Duchamp as exemplary of the avant-garde, because it would be absurd to think of the ready-mades, in particular, as *original*. It is this observation that for her legitimates, in turn, the theoretical presentation of his work as a kind of proto-postmodernism that prefigures the practices of later artists such as Sherry Levine:

> [...] insofar as Levine's work explicitly deconstructs the modern-ist notion of origin, her effort cannot be seen as an *extension* of modernism. It is, like the discourse of the copy, postmodernist. Which means that it cannot be seen as avant-garde either [...] In deconstructing the sister notions of origin and originality, post-modernism establishes a schism between itself and the conceptual domain of the avant-garde, looking back at it from across a gulf that in turn establishes a historical divide. The historical period that the avant-garde shared with modernism is over. (Krauss 1987: 170)

It is revealing, then, that despite the apparent deconstructive attention to questions of differential temporality and historicity in the essay by Krauss, "history" finally re-appears here in its conventional narrative and epochalising historicist-empiricist form.[5] The deconstruction of the radical break claimed by originality is clearly not to be extended to that radical break thesis which sustains such periodisation. Yet if Levine's foregrounding of reproductive processes – dangerously close to being read as simply a tendentious illustration of Anglo-American poststructuralist theory – is seen within this to deconstruct the avant-garde conception of originality, it is nonetheless unclear how the very *historical* newness of such work is itself to be understood, with any theoretical clarity, outside of the general conceptual domain opened up by the non-identical co-belonging of modernity and tradition, of newness *and* repetition. For, leaving aside the fundamental category confusion that would seem to be entailed by Krauss's argument – a confusion between the demand for the *historically* (rather than merely chronologically or stylistically) new, and originality as a kind of *onto-logical* or *technological* status of particular artistic forms or practices[6] – at the very least one might say, as Eric Cameron does, that "there are a considerable number of statements [...] about [Duchamp's] pro-fessed iconoclasm, about his anti-art, about his desire to wipe the past right out, that have to somehow be accommodated" (De Duve 1991: 36). In this sense, while it is true that the very nature of the ready-mades precludes any conception of them in the terms of a productive originality, at the same time, it is equally impossible *not* to conceive of them in terms of some form of newness, as a non-identity to received taste; the irreducible singularity of "the thing in itself". In this case, it is evident that the concept of newness itself demands not to be abandoned – as Bürger, for rather different reasons, also sug-gests[7] – but to be thought *differently* at this point. It is in this sense that, for Cameron, what is at stake in the debate surrounding post-modernism might be conceived in terms of "a narrower definition of 'modern' versus a much broader definition" (De Duve 1991: 33). And as regards Krauss's own tendencies to reduce modernism to that patently "restricted" version proffered by Clement Greenberg, this is clearly true.[8] Yet arguably, Cameron's response does not itself go quite far enough. For it fails to engage the defining tension – from which the problematic and now waning notion of a "postmodern" ultimately derives – between the modern as used to designate an em-pirical category of art history and, in a more fundamental core sense, "its inherent self-referentiality, whereby it necessarily denotes the time of its utterance, wherever the question of change within the pres-ent is at issue" (Osborne 1995: 4). As such, this is *not*, as Cameron suggests, simply a question of breadth – an eminently classical de-mand for an empirical multiplicity internal to the object – but must be seen to relate to the very nature of that changing object to which the concept of an avant-garde is taken to refer.

Now the crucial point is that, beyond the hold of either Krauss's historicist division of modern and postmodern *or* Bürger's limitation of the avant-garde to a singular and historically-limited social-cultural project, the apparently irreducible interplay of newness *and* repetition that we find manifest in Duchamp's work creates a paradox for the possible exemplarity of any of his particular works; a paradox which has something to do with that temporally dynamic self-referentiality of the modern which he himself implicitly invokes. This is so insofar as their exemplarity would seem to be one which marked, not an identity of a group of works embodied in some repeated feature or style (which could become taste), but their *non-identity*; a non-identity which is, in fact, a facet of that very demand for the historically *new* operative within any affirmative articulation of the modern (in a properly temporalised sense). Everything thus hinges here on the relation between repetition and exemplarity ("[a]lso the exemplary side of the readymade", Duchamp writes at one point).[9] Conventionally, exemplarity and repetition belong together, in the sense that the particularity of that which serves as an example is fractured by the demand that, in itself, in its singularity, it nonetheless gestures beyond itself to others elsewhere where a property or feature is repeated. Thus, to speak philosophically once again, any particular avant-garde work *should*, by the classical logic of the example, serve as an example for the avant-garde in general, to the extent that it opens itself up to a generality in the repetition of a certain property shared by all other members of the class "avant-garde". Yet, as we have seen, this is precisely what Duchamp seems to *disallow* by locating the exemplarity of any particular work, not in its *sameness* to other works, but in its *difference*, its resistance to repetition. The conceptual *aporia* is therefore that a work could, on this basis, only exemplify to the extent that it refused the (conventional) role of the example; its only common property being one of having no-thing-in-common.

If we take Duchamp's own logic seriously then, in its most fundamental conceptual sense, any particular example of the avant-garde could only exemplify a generality of non-identity which, in its singular exemplification, is always non-identical to itself; different from the "time" before. This just *is* the problematic of the new, as Adorno, for one, recognised, as well as the source of its ineliminable "asbtractness" (Adorno 1997: 20-23).[10] Thus, the problem of theorising (and of historicising) the avant-garde is not merely a problem of empirical multiplicity – the apparent variation within the projects of the so-called historical avant-gardes – but the product of something *essential* to the concept of an avant-garde itself. To the extent that the question of, or demand for, the avant-garde is repeated, as of course it must be for any generality to be perceivable, it cannot be thought of as a repetition of the same – the *tradition* of an avant-garde (that oxymoronic phrase we accept too easily) – but as a certain *repetition of the non-identical*.[11] This requires that repetition and singularity be thought as inextricably interlinked. For what opens up the possibility of designating works "avant-garde" is, quite simply, that they involve something like an interruptive *experience* of the non-identical within the cultural present; an interruption of the repetition which leads into a form of taste, as Duchamp himself phrases it. It is this *temporal* structure of experience *alone* (at once always singular and repeated) which provides a certain generality (and thus heterogenous unity) to the aporetic relation of the concept of an avant-garde to particular works or objects, rather than any chronologically-defined period style or project of the type that art history provides.[12]

This requires more theoretical elaboration than can be provided here, but does it not, first of all, offer another way of thinking Duchamp's particular silence, a way which thinks it not (as Beuys suggests) as mere perversity, but as related, very directly, to the *question* of what his work means in fully historical terms? Robert Lebel, who wrote the first monograph on Duchamp in 1959, concluded even then that his works constitute an enigma that "insolently rejects any solution, any key which might be applied" (quoted in Kuenzli and Naumann 1990: 5). Yet, at the same time, any enigma always brings with it a certain temptation to solve the riddle, to read the readymades as some kind of definitive *proposition*, which must be negotiated.[13] Hence, the familiar rhetoric of writings on Duchamp, simultaneously doubting and re-instituting the possibility of a completed historical and theoretical understanding of his work: "We hardly need another magical key to Duchamp, but [...]" (Foster 1996: 240).

Jean-François Lyotard phrases the apparent philosophical and critical dilemma at work here rather well:

> So what will you do? These are the little setbacks of the critic. Is it always hard and irksome? Not always, but it is so here because Monsieur Marcel has the critics in his sights to defy him and poke fun at him. You won't get me, that's his obsession. (1990: 9)

In response to Duchamp's "ruses", Lyotard offers, then, what he calls a "counter-ruse":

> In what you say about Duchamp, the aim would be not to try to understand and to show what you've understood, but rather the opposite, to try not to understand and to show that you haven't understood. (1990: 12)

Of course, Lyotard is aware (as the book which follows his opening statements cannot help but fatally reveal), that the attempt to fail to understand *entirely* could not help but fail itself insofar as we would think on the work of Duchamp at all. Yet, what Lyotard might be seen as articulating is precisely a concern not to give an *answer* to the enigmatic exemplarity of Duchamp's works, with the (always) too hasty determination of a clear theoretical understanding *in the form of a proposition*, but to retain their definitively unfinished status *in the form of a question*. For it is an essential facet of the futural temporality of the question itself that it "inaugurates a type of relation character-ised by openness and free movement; and what it must be satisfied with closes and arrests it" (Blanchot 1993: 14).[14] Moreover, as I will go on to argue in the final section of this essay, in a sense, this quite simply *is* the interruptive and open-ended experience of the non-identical, the explosive capacity to blast apart the historical continuity constructed by tradition (and the institutions which embody it); the temporal structure of experience of which, we may say, defines the avant-garde in its most fundamental and significant conceptual form.

3. An example of exemplification

Before returning to this I want first, however, to explore the revealing issue of exemplification further by looking at one particularly inter-esting attempt at precisely *understanding* Duchamp's work: Francis M. Naumann's essay, "Marcel Duchamp: A Reconciliation of Oppos-ites", which appears in both of what are probably the two most influential collections of critical essays on Duchamp in English.[15] De-spite the customary disavowal of any "attempt to establish a formula, key, or some other type of guiding principle by which to assess or in other ways interpret the artistic production of Marcel Duchamp" (Naumann 1991: 41), it is, in fact, nothing less than something of this order that Naumann begins to outline when he then states: "[w]hether consciously or unconsciously, by the early 1920s he [Duchamp] had already established the major tenets of [a] working method exploring and reexploring themes of opposition that would prevail in his work for the rest of his life" (1991: 42). It is on this basis that Naumann traces the supposed influence of Max Stirner (and through him, knowingly or unknowingly, of Hegel) upon Duchamp from his stay in Munich in 1912 (1991: 65-6). Naumann cites two pieces of evidence for this influence: a conversation with the Swiss artist and critic Serge Stauffer and, more pertinently here, a response to a MoMA questionnaire about the *Three Standard Stoppages*, a work created by Duchamp in 1913–14 consisting of a box containing three pieces of wood whose dimensions were determined by the configurations given by the chance operation of allowing three metre-long pieces of string to fall freely onto a canvas surface. In his conversations with Pierre Cabanne, Duchamp comments on the piece thus:

> For me the number three is important, but simply from the numerical, not the esoteric, point of view: one is unity, two is double, duality, and three is the rest. When you've come to the word three, you have three million – it's the same thing as three […] My *Three Standard Stoppages* is produced by three separate experiments, and the form of each one is slightly different. (Cabanne 1971: 47)

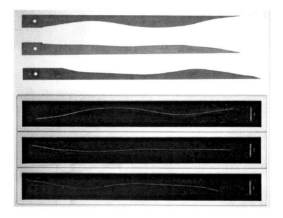

37. Marcel Duchamp, Three Standard Stoppages, *Paris 1913–14*

This significance of three to Duchamp provides the basis for Naumann to cement a relation (although Naumann is careful not to suggest any direct influence) between Duchamp's "working method" and the Hegelian dialectic. I will not dwell here on Naumann's deeply problematic (albeit still all-too-common) rendering of dialectical logic as a progressive movement of thesis-antithesis-synthesis.[16] What does interest me though is the use to which Naumann puts this understanding of the dialectic in reading not only the *Three Standard Stoppages*, but also the readymades:

> [Duchamp's] working method involved a constant search for alternatives – alternatives not only to accepted artistic practice, but also to his own earlier work. It was perhaps with this in mind that in 1913 he asked himself the provocative question: "Can one make works which are not works of 'art'?" – a question he answered within a year by his invention of the Readymade, a "work of art", as he later described it, "without an artist to make it". In strictly Hegelian terms, a work of art could be seen to represent the *thesis*; an object that is not a work of art, its opposite or *antithesis*; while the Readymade succinctly combines these ideas in a single artifact, bringing about their reconciliation, or *synthesis*. (1991: 57)

Though these "Hegelian terms" are not nearly as "strict" as Naumann thinks they are, if nothing else Naumann does usefully lay bare here the system of oppositionality within which Duchamp's work, and the avant-garde in general, is in its "constant search for alternatives" characteristically understood. Thus, customarily, ascertaining what *statement* is embodied in the readymades involves the decision about whether they are a statement of an opposition to art or the aesthetic – whether as anti-art, anti-aesthetics, anti-tradition or anti-art-as-institution – or a call for some kind of extension of the aesthetic itself (rarer, but suggested, for example, by William Camfield, who sees *Fountain* as the intentional selection of a beautiful object; Camfield 1991: 133-178).[17] Naumann's ingenious twist, on the basis of the connection between Duchamp's favouring of the number three and the "Hegelian" dialectic, is to see the readymades as some kind of *reconciliation* of the two.

Yet we should recall Duchamp's precise reasons for asserting the importance of the number three: "one is unity, two is double, duality, and three is the rest". Three is *not*, in fact, an arrival at the final "unity" of art and anti-art – the identity of identity and non-identity – but something *other*, a non-identity which, in its open multiplicity, exceeds the terms of oppositionality: "When you have three, you have three million – it's the same thing as three". In his reading of *Door: 11, rue Larrey*, Naumann asserts:

> This door was located in a corner of the main living room, positioned in such a way as to close the entrance either to the bedroom or to the bathroom, but not to both at the same time. In opposition to the axiom implicit in the common French adage – "Il faut qu'une porte soit ouverte ou fermée" ["A door must be either open or closed"] – Duchamp has ingeniously managed to defy the assumption of mutual exclusivity, uniting these contradictory themes into a compatible totality, or as he might have preferred to describe it, "a reconciliation of opposites". (1991: 59-60)

38. Marcel Duchamp, Door: 11, rue Larrey, *1927*

One may agree that Duchamp's door defies "the assumption of mutual exclusivity" – that is of simple opposition – but does it in fact work to unify "these contradictory themes into a compatible totality"? Rather, does it not turn the French adage into a *question* – "Is the door open or closed?" – a question that itself remains open? One could suggest the same for the *Three Standard Stoppages*. Is it not the case that instead

of resolving the differences between the three in some final "reconciliation of opposites", the piece rather productively provokes the (potentially interruptive) *experience* of an open question or uncertainty about
how their relation is to be understood?[18]

Let us return to the question Duchamp poses himself in 1913:
"Can one make works which are not works of 'art'?" (Duchamp 1973:
74). Naumann is certainly not unique in viewing the readymades as
the answer to this question; a question which, of course, most obviously connects Duchamp to the concerns of Dada. But, like much
Dada work, are the readymades an *answer*, or are they in fact something rather more like a reposing of the *question* in a particular, singular form? For, once again, is this not fundamentally the vertiginous
experience of *Fountain*: not the experience of the comforting achieve-
ment of reconciliation, but rather of the discomforting experience of
uncertainty in the face of a question – "Can one make works which
are not works of 'art'?" – which does not determine in advance an immediately decidable answer? Furthermore, as suggested above, is it
not the case that this just *is*, in singular form, the experience of the
non-identical which defines the general temporality of *the* avant-
garde?

It is of course this dynamic *movement* of non-identity – to
what art has been – that both Bürger and Greenberg, from almost
entirely opposed perspectives, term art's stage of "self-criticism", and
which, for both, determines the historical meaning of the avant-
garde's dialectic of art and anti-art. Yet, in both, this temporal logic of
art's putting-in-question is immediately reduced to the positivised
terms of a singular *project*; the projection of a determinate final
answer to the avant-garde's questioning which may function as an
invariant regulating Idea. As such, what Blanchot terms the question's
"openness and free movement" is closed and arrested; its critical
power enclosed within the completed space of an historical moment
that has now passed. Although not without its own problems, Hal
Foster's objection to Bürger's endgame is revealing:

> [T]he aim of the avant-garde for Bürger is to destroy the insti-
> tution of autonomous art in order to reconnect art and life [...]
> [H]owever, this formulation only seems simple. For what is art
> and what is life here? Already the opposition tends to cede to art
> the autonomy that is in question, and to position life at a point
> beyond reach [...] To make matters more difficult, life is con-

ceived here paradoxically – not only as remote but also as immediate, as if it were simply *there* to rush in like so much air once
the hermetic seal of convention is broken [...] For the most acute
avant-garde artists such as Duchamp, the aim is neither an abstract
negation of art nor a romantic reconciliation with life but a
perpetual testing of the conventions of both. (Foster 1996: 17, 15-
16)

As Foster points out, Bürger does indeed present the readymade "as a
sheer thing-of-the-world", as "transgression pure and simple". Yet
such a presentation is problematic, not only philosophically, but because of the way in which it precisely elides the more complex ways
in which the readymade opens up a *question* concerning the relation of
art and non-art, autonomy and everyday-ness; reducing these, like
Naumann's more hopeful reading of Duchamp, to the terms of simple
opposition. Yet it is precisely through the enigma of his questioning
that Duchamp might – with, as Foster says, exemplary "astuteness" –
be seen to engage the paradoxical *but productive* dilemmas and abstractions of that radical articulation of an anti-art art – the destruction
of art by artistic means, art's putting of itself in question – which
underwrites a certain familiar strain of avant-garde practice from
Dada, at least, onwards; and which reaches, for its own moment, some
kind of knowing linguistic extreme in the delirious paradoxical expression of Tzara's manifestos.

As Ribemont-Dessaignes retrospectively summarises: "Dada
created anti-aesthetic values. So then it created art" (quoted in Nicholls 1995: 227). Yet, this does not have to be read as the tragic
acknowledgement of an inevitable and unsurpassable re-aestheticisation – the final and absolute victory of institutionalisation and the
commodity form – but can be read as affirming that perpetual testing
which the questioning of art must always renew. Moreover, in this
sense, far from being contained by the closure of a particular historical
project, this questioning, I would like to argue, cannot but continue to
make, and re-make, demands upon the art of today, whether or not
such demands are adequately responded to by artists themselves. To
show this, however, requires some further consideration of the historical emergence of the contemporary category of the avant-garde itself.

4. The avant-garde "After Duchamp"

Much of the preceding may well seem insufferably abstract from the perspective of the conventional methodologies of contemporary criticism, which, as Bürger himself puts it, tend still to believe that, all questions about the nature of concepts aside, "one should finally get down to the thing itself, to texts" (Bürger 1984: xlix). Yet to raise such questions, beyond indeed the scope of Bürger's own endeavours, is neither in fact to move away from texts nor from history, but is rather to enquire precisely into the more fundamental modes of historical temporalisation inscribed within those concepts through which, necessarily, the immanent productive logic of certain cultural forms or practices is articulated. For such concepts are not merely an alien imposition upon the individual text but are an ineliminable condition for an understanding of the ways in which they may be said to produce particular possibilities of distinct cultural experience. Moreover it is the case that if in this light any meta-critical account of Duchamp, in particular, takes on a certain historical urgency and significance today, it is precisely because of the high stakes that such over-subscription entails, and what it has to tell us about contemporary problematics in general (hence, what is crucial in the issue of "exemplification"). For there is no doubt much plausibility in the idea – common from Kosuth to Thierry de Duve – that we inhabit an artistic present which may only be historically defined as "After Duchamp". In terms of influence or sheer quantity of critical commentary, the battle for the title of "most significant artist of the twentieth century" seems, from the perspective of the last forty years, long decided; Picasso and Matisse have long since left the field.

Nonetheless, as I am not the first to note, this "After Duchamp" manifests a temporality rather stranger than it may at first appear, insofar as the status of Duchamp is largely "a retroactive effect of countless artistic responses and critical readings" which began around the late 1950s (Foster 1996: 8). Not coincidentally, it is such a retroactive effect that also haunts, as several critics have noted, that recent discourse of the avant-garde for which Bürger's book is in large part responsible. Indeed, a fairly coherent historical narrative of its development could itself be constructed, in which, as Gail Day has noted, such a narrative might find its inaugural moment, not first of all in the now familiar avant-garde/neo-avantgarde distinction, but in that between *Dada* and *Neo-Dada*, as these terms come to be deployed in relation to (and by) Johns and Rauschenberg or the Fluxus artists (Day 2000: 6). Indeed, Bürger's own examples of the neo-avantgarde are almost entirely drawn from this context.

My concern here is not with the justice or otherwise of Bürger's judgement upon these examples – an issue that has been much debated elsewhere – but rather with the role that this renewed historical debate surrounding Dada has to play in the formation of the now hegemonic category of the historical avant-garde, as well as Duchamp's exemplary place within it. Clearly a pivotal moment in the rediscovery of both in the post-war period is the publication of Robert Motherwell's 1951 book, *The Dada Painters and Poets*. Motherwell in fact states that Duchamp himself – who appears in the volume as an "original Dada master" (on the basis of his New York activities)[19] – "examined the dummy of the book on various occasions" (1989: xvii). It is this centrality of Duchamp that Motherwell's book, as well as other texts and exhibitions of the period, assumes, that is then taken for granted by Bürger's theoretical exemplification of the readymades, as regards the avant-garde *in general*. Yet, already by this point, there is elsewhere a certain distancing between Duchamp and Dada taking place. This is very evident in Kosuth's Conceptualist narration of an art "After Duchamp" – which is explicitly *not* in any way equivalent to an "After Dada" – and gains new impetus as the concept of postmodernism develops (alongside a post-Conceptualist practice) in the 1970s. That said, if postmodernism is largely directed against a Greenbergian conception of modernism – centred around the medium-specificity of abstract painting – then the place of the avant-garde, in its newly emergent sense (centred on Dada) is often hard to gauge. For, on the one hand, as historical epoch, postmodernism is also associated with the so-called "death of the avant-garde" – an obituary repeated *ad nauseum* from the 1960s onwards – but, on the other, Bürger's book is often taken up, in an American context at least, as providing essential categories for the understanding of precisely that *contemporary* art which is seen to dismantle the apparently Greenbergian underpinnings of Abstract Expressionism (from Fluxus through to the likes of Hans Haacke, Marcel Broodthaers or Daniel Buren). Leaving aside the fact that this itself involves all sorts of problematic assumptions – most specifically, that an opposition between the historical referents of modernism and avant-garde can simply be assumed here (despite the fact that Greenberg uses the two terms more or less interchangeably and that Bürger nowhere, in *Theory of the Avant-Garde*, opposes one to the other)[20] – the most obvious practical result of this has been an increasing separation of certain individual figures (Duchamp, Bataille, Leiris, and others) from the artistic contexts of Dada or Surrealism with which earlier critics (and Bürger himself) associated them, such that these figures could be presented as proto-postmodernists, while the rest of these movements could be consigned to a kind of historical dead-end – "the death of the avant-garde" – different to, but historically coterminous with, modernism (in its more restricted sense).[21]

The salient point here is fairly simply expressed. While the concept of an avant-garde is an ongoing construction from the mid-nineteenth century onwards, *the* avant-garde – as it is dominantly understood today, as a fixed retrospective category of art or literary history – is a post-war, not a pre-war, phenomenon, deriving, in part, from slightly earlier debates surrounding "Neo-Dada". If nothing else, it is the kind of retroactive effect involved in this that suggests we should be wary of taking Bürger's theory of the avant-garde, and its professedly limited historical referent, as a simple given that now requires no further *conceptual* investigation. Indeed, it is in the light of this issue that Foster, for example, asks whether, "rather than cancel the project of the historical avant-garde, might the [post-war] neo-avant-garde comprehend it for the first time?" (1996: 15). Yet, plausible as it is, Foster's response, too, is not unproblematic. Or at least, we might say, it risks itself accepting rather too easily Bürger's own theoretical limits, to the extent that the so-called neo-avantgarde, for Foster too, essentially consists in the establishment of something akin to a critical *tradition* of the avant-garde – albeit one more positively valued – constituted by the reprisal of "such avant-garde devices of the 1910s and 1920s as collage and assemblage, the readymade and the grid, monochrome painting and constructed sculpture" (1996: 1).

Yet to theorise the avant-garde in these technical or stylistic terms is, once again, to foreclose upon the *questioning* of the avant-garde, to resolve the demand for the non-identical that it articulates back into an empirically-discernible identity in terms of which it can be comfortably encapsulated by historicist theory.[22] It is then a short step from this to the kind of theoretical misrecognition that characteristically underwrites the narration of a "death of the avant-garde";

mistaking, as I suggested in the previous section, the waning of a particular concrete political and technological conjuncture for the end of a temporal logic of questioning or self-criticism *per se*, and, thus, failing to recognise the necessarily changed content of such self-criticism by virtue of that very logic. It is such misrecognition, no doubt, which accounts for the seeming inevitability of the post-war narration of the avant-garde as one of decline or fall. Hence, of course, the dominant contemporary response to Duchamp or to Dada as nostalgic mourning for a now supposedly irrecoverable lost object. Yet, to do so is to miss what is at stake in the promise articulated by the concept of an avant-garde itself, as refracted in the singular work. The social and political defeats of the 1920s and 1930s, of Russia, Weimar or Paris – of totalitarian repression and of the various recuperations of commodity culture – are not the same as the death of that *demand* inscribed within the concept of an avant-garde itself, even if the historical situation within which such a demand is to be heard has (inevitably) altered (Roberts 2000: 26). For, as we have seen, and as Duchamp himself insists, whatever is exemplary in such an untranscendable demand,[23] must promote – if it is not itself to become mere *taste* (tradition) – not a model for the repetition of already given strategies, styles or techniques, or even projective *aims*, but the futurally-open exemplification of an immanent logic of non-identity which demands a continual *renewal* of art's questioning with regard to social forms and relations which are, necessarily, always other to those with which the category of, and demand for, an avant-garde has previously been confronted. If post-war art takes up, as Foster suggests, devices of the 1910s and 1920s, this is not then simply to be explicated through further historicist bifurcations of first and second generation neo-avant-gardes, but requires a properly critical distinction between the stylisation of these devices – the establishment of a continuum that tends towards identity – and their affirmative historical reinscription, in the present, as "living and available for further development", as provocations of non-identity to tradition or institutionality; that is, in terms of their potential to open up a repressed futural potential here and now (Roberts 2002: 378).

It is for this reason – and not simply for the sake of scholarly accuracy – that we should return our attention to the primary (and ineliminable) meaning of "avant-garde" as that of a *present* demand made by, and upon, objects or practices, in a properly historico-

temporal sense. All concrete manifestations of avant-garde-ness practically inscribe a response to and a repetition of the question: what is
avant-garde *now*? It is the temporality of the enunciation of this question itself that conventional histories of the avant-garde actually serve
to elide. To judge something to be avant-garde, whether from the perspective of production or consumption, is, in its core form, to make a
judgement in and about the present; that is, from the standpoint of an
affirmative relating of present to future. A retrospective judgement of
what *was* avant-garde is necessarily secondary to this, in a conceptual
sense, dependent upon the possibility of a present critical reconstruction of some specific historical context; the "delimitation of the received cultural field" within which any particular, practical intervention takes place (Osborne 2000: 59). That such reconstruction might
not be as straightforward as the methodologies of historicism would
tend to suggest, is not, however, to say that it is impossible or that the
concept of an avant-garde can thus *only* be critically employed in relation to the (this) present, to the extent that in order for there to be a
perceivable *general* logic of "vant-garde-ness, repetition of some sort,
and thus critical account of the general relation between non-identical
repetitions, must be possible. This is of course the role of conceptu-
ality itself, as the marker of a certain generality; necessarily abstract
but also a part of social and cultural reality in its practical reciprocal
mediation with concrete forms and practices. Yet thinking what the
avant-garde is clearly cannot, by virtue of its very questioning dynamic, find its answer in the location of some invariant conceptual
denotation in a classical sense; its conceptual unity, such as it is, is of
a quite different order (and as such, its *aporetic* and *abstract* character
is not provisional or contingent – a lack of precision – but necessary
and essential by virtue of the very immanent logic it inscribes). What
has the potential to be cognitively experienced as avant-garde is radically variable (Cunningham 2003a: 62-3). To the extent that the avant-
garde constitutes a specific conceptual domain, it is not so much one
which is filled with the singular, univocal content of a common style
or project, as it is the persistent space – opened up by modernity – in
which an historically and (increasingly) geographically diverse array
of often conflicting and contradictory meanings and possibilities,
forms and practices, are historically and repeatedly put into question
in the present from the perspective of their radical opening onto the
future. As such, in any particular present, the concrete meaning (and

possibilities) of *the* avant-garde is only ever derived from – to use a phrase of Peter Osborne's – "the distributive unity of its specific instances" (Osborne 2000: 59).

It is a recognition of this that should then inform our judgements on the contemporary "reinscription" of Duchamp, or indeed of Dada – and their relation to the demands of the avant-garde – whether in the form of critical and theoretical responses or of artistic practice itself.[24] Let us return then, in this light, finally to Blanchot's assertion that "the history of Surrealism is only of scholarly interest, particularly if the conception of Surrealism is not modified by its subject" (Blanchot 1993: 407). Now, it is not as if there is anything wrong with the claims of "scholarly interest", but we should at least be aware that a scholarly account of something like Dada and its histories – interesting and valid as this may well be – does not, in any way, amount to a wholly adequate theorisation of Dada *as avant-garde*. At the very least, as Paul Mann rightly notes, the "insistent historicism" of art history "fails to consider in the avant-garde a certain resistance to history as such […] an attack on those very encystations of power-knowledge, those inevitably reductive historical narratives in which it perpetually finds itself". And he continues: "Dada in particular demonstrates an anti-historical power that is difficult to confine within any historical account" (Mann 1991: 64). This seems to me correct, but it remains in its own way still too empirical. For what is really at stake here – in the relation between Dada and the avant-garde in general – is, to return to an earlier point, an irreducible (and productive) *tension* between the demands of art history and of that radical mode of historical temporalisation articulated by the *concept* of an avant-garde itself. This goes too for the relation between Dada and Duchamp – the truth of which is too often sought in the so-called scholarly evidence of Duchamp's own shifting assertions (as if we could safely trust these) – and between both and *the* avant-garde. We misunderstand what is of significance in this if we imagine – in exemplary scholarly fashion – that what is required here is some final, completed judgement about how one is to be incorporated (or otherwise) into the historical space of the other, as if each simply marked the more or less extensive chronological span of a period style. Rather, what should be thought through here is the relation that both Duchamp and Dada have to the historical *demands* of the avant-garde – the work to which they put its concept – and, on this basis, their specific negotiations, within their own cultural field, of that dialectics of art and anti-art which constitutes a particular articulation of what I have more generally referred to as the temporal dynamic of art's putting-in-question. (For this, after all, is what allowed the Dadaists and Duchamp to recognise something of themselves in each other.) Thought in this way, we might indeed allow our conventional conception of (art) history to be "modified by its subject". Not only in order to rethink, beyond the closures of scholarship, the avant-garde-ness of Duchamp and Dada – their exemplary non-identity – but also to rethink what it is that lives in them such that may speak to contemporary practices, and thus where today the demands of the avant-garde may continue to be heard.

Notes

[1] "Only because my point of departure was that today the avant-garde movements should be seen as historical could I bracket the value judgements that are essential to the theories of Lukács and Adorno, and hope to pass beyond the theoretical level they attained" (Bürger 1984: lii). This is, of course, an essentially Hegelian point, whereby the avant-garde's end becomes the necessary historical condition of possibility for its theorisation in our time beyond it.

[2] The marginalisation of questions of time in Bürger's text is exemplified by his apparently wholesale (and strikingly counterintuitive) dismissal of "the category of the new" as "not suitable for a description of how things are" as regards the avant-garde (Bürger 1984: 63).

[3] Although this does not of course mean that, as in Kosuth, the readymade must be taken literally as an "analytical proposition".

[4] This particular discussion followed Eric Cameron's paper "Given", at Nova Scotia College of Art in 1987. See De Duve 1991: 1-29.

[5] Krauss uses the term "deconstruction" obviously to associate this position with Derrida's work. However, while it is true that her argument clearly draws upon Derrida's Heideggerian insight into the fact that "the unprecedented is never possible without repetition" (Derrida 1994: 44), the tone of, for example, the writings on Artaud would suggest that this does not somehow mean that we can now safely pass beyond the "conceptual domain" that the concept of an avant-garde articulates (Derrida 1978: 232-250). Moreover, passing from this to a wholesale dismissal of the problem of newness would be to ignore how *important* questions concerning novelty, invention or surprise are in Derrida's work, particularly in his later writings. The same would go, too, for other French thinkers appropriated by Anglo-American post-structuralism, such as Deleuze or Lyotard, and suggests something about what has often been transfigured in the process of translating such writings into the contexts and concerns of Anglo-American art and literary theory.

[6] That this *is* a confusion can be demonstrated, easily enough, by returning to one of the obvious sources for the argument presented by Krauss: Benjamin's essay from the 1930s, "The Work of Art in the Age of Its Technical Reproducibility". For in counter-

posing the ontological multiplicity without origin of film and photography to the uniqueness that constitutes the aura of the painting, Benjamin, very clearly, is making a claim precisely *for* the *avant-garde* character of the former, as against the latter's embeddedness in tradition. This much is evident in Benjamin's notorious (and, admittedly, not unproblematic) linkage between film and Dada; a linkage which, his description of the latter strongly suggests, would have included Duchamp: "The Dadaists attached much less importance to the commercial usefulness of their artworks than to the usefulness of those works as objects of contemplative immersion [...] What they achieved by such means was a ruthless annihilation of the aura in every object they produced" (Benjamin 2003: 266-67). Such destruction is, for Benjamin, nothing other than the mark of the avant-garde in its affirmation of the nonidentity of modernity and tradition. See Cunningham 2003a: 68.
[7] See note 2 above.
[8] It is in this sense that I would argue that the true content of the postmodernism debate must now be seen to have been precisely about the nature of modernism itself. Certainly this makes a good deal more sense than the (counterintuitive) correlate of the postmodernists' exclusive claim upon fragmentation, the body, difference, etc, that various elements of, say, Dada and Surrealism – which don't fit into the customary postmodernist definition of modernism (or the avant-garde) – should now be interpreted as proto-postmodernist.
[9] This is the translation given in Carol P. James, "An Original Revolutionary *Messagerie* Rrose" (De Duve 1991: 281). Sanouillet and Peterson translate the phrase as "also the serial characteristic of the readymade" (Duchamp 1973: 32).
[10] The fact that the abstractness of the new entails modern art working, in a sense, "at the Munchhausean trick of carrying out the identification of the non-identical" (Adorno 1997: 23) is a paradox which postmodernism takes to be decisive, as well as what causes Bürger to reject the new as an unsuitable category for theorising the avant-garde. Yet both these responses miss what Adorno calls the provocation of the new, *as a function of its very abstractness*: "the indeterminateness of what it is and to what purpose it is" (1997: 21). That is to say, what is missed is the provocation of the new as the (open) *form of the question*.
[11] It is on this basis that I concur with the recent comment made by Susan Buck-Morss that it is "misleading to speak of an avant-garde 'tradition' as if such practices could produce their own historical continuum" (2000: 304). As she rightly asserts: "The power of any cultural object to arrest the flow of history, and to open up time for alternative visions, varies with history's changing course [...] No one style, no one medium is [or can be] invariably successful" (2000: 63).
[12] I have explored this point in more detail in Cunningham 2001 and Cunningham 2003a.
[13] I have dealt, at some length, with such a temptation, specifically in relation to Adorno's readings of Beckett, in Cunningham 2002: 125-139.
[14] In a rather different context, I have also discussed this experience of the question, in relation to the writings of Maurice Blanchot, in Cunningham 2003b.
[15] De Duve 1991: 41-67; Kuenzli and Naumann 1990: 20-40. Future references will be to the De Duve.
[16] This formula was actually popularised by H. M. Chalybaeus and was never used by Hegel himself. See Müller 1958: 411-4.

[17] Through the comparisons of *Fountain*, by Louise Norton and Alfred Stieglitz, to, respectively, the Buddha and the Madonna, Camfield constructs an ingenious, if to my mind entirely unconvincing, argument that the urinal is best understood as working within an aesthetics of the beautiful.

[18] Although there is not the space to develop such an argument here, could one not also read the relation between the two halves of Duchamp's *Large Glass* in similar terms? That is, not as harbouring some concealed unity of meaning, but as precisely raising a *question* as to the enigmatic relation of the work's parts?

[19] Duchamp, in 1921, collaborated with Man Ray to produce the single number of *New York Dada*. It should also be said that Duchamp is afforded a central place in all the early histories of Dada (from the 1930s onwards), including those by Georges Ribemont-Dessaignes and Georges Hugnet, and that, as such, Motherwell simply continues this association; not, one must presume, without some (however ambiguous) encouragement from Duchamp himself, given his assistance in putting the book together.

[20] The reception of Bürger's text in America is an issue that deserves further study in itself, most particularly in terms of what is lost in this translation. Two aspects specifically come to mind. First, the fact that Bürger writes, first and foremost, as a literary specialist, yet has been almost entirely rewritten into the terms of the visual arts, in a way which tends to limit the problem of institutionality to the specific concrete spaces of the gallery or museum. Second, that what is in *Theory of the Avant-Garde* largely an argument with Adorno has been rewritten as an argument with Greenberg, who is of course never mentioned.

[21] This is not to say that there is no ambivalence apparent in Duchamp's relation to Dada or in Bataille's relation to Surrealism. There certainly is. But this is not the same as the movement toward some *opposition* between them, as the modernism/ postmodernism divide, pursued by the likes of Krauss, often tends to end up implying. At the very least, the *contexts* of Dada and Surrealism were crucial to Duchamp's and Bataille's own endeavours. Although this is clearly not the intention of postmodernists like Krauss or Foster themselves, to remove Duchamp (or Bataille) from these contexts entirely is to risk the most reactionary reinvention of the category of the individual genius. Such cultural conservatism is, for example, all too obvious in Marjorie Perloff's recent attempt to preserve the "individual talent" of Duchamp from any contamination by Dadaist negation (Perloff 2002).

[22] It is not, in this respect, a question of saying that either Bürger or Greenberg are strictly *wrong* in their theorisations *as such*. No doubt, in fact, both have a certain validity with regard to the practices and self-definitions of particular artists and movements which may indeed be thought to be avant-garde in their abstract temporal structure. Rather, what should be in question is the very idea of ascribing a *singular* historical project *to the avant-garde in general*. In fact, nothing is necessarily lost of Bürger's theory in the kind of rethinking I am suggesting here, only the conception that it in any way constitutes a theory of *the* avant-garde, and that it amounts to an adequate perspective upon contemporary practice.

[23] It is the *myth* of such transcendence – whether tragically or affirmatively inscribed – which sustains a certain version of postmodernism, but, as I am hardly the first to note, one which, as soon as it is articulated, finds itself mired in theoretical contra-

diction (of a generally *unproductive* kind) by virtue of the very "modern" logic of the "post" itself.

[24] One can see, I think, a good example of this is in the role that Dada and Duchamp have played in the recent so-called Philistine Controversy, which followed essays published by Dave Beech and John Roberts in the *New Left Review* and elsewhere. (Various of these pieces, including Beech and Roberts's original essay "Spectres of the Aesthetic", are collected together in Beech and Roberts 2002. For passages of particular relevance to Dada and Duchamp, see Beech and Roberts's "The Philistine and the Logic of Negation" (2002: 290-4), and Esther Leslie's "Philistines and Art Vandals Get Upset" (Beech and Roberts 2002: 201-227). Two things strike me as being of particular importance here. First, that the initial context for the elaboration of the concept of the Philistine was emergent within *contemporary* British art (Roberts 1996), and it is this that underwrites the reinscription of Dada and Duchamp. Second, that while much of the debate is concerned with differing interpretations of Adorno's work – and its appropriation by certain modes of philosophical aestheticism – Beech and Roberts's argument is articulated, so to speak, on the same cultural *terrain* as postmodernism, but without giving up the idea of contemporary art as responding to the demand made by the concept of an avant-garde. (While I share many of his doubts about the so-called young British artists debated, it is this that Julian Stallabrass manifestly fails to appreciate in his critique of Beech and Roberts in *High Art Lite* (Stallabrass 1999: 118-123).) Hence, the importance of Dada which is presented as "a vivid place to examine the logic of anti-art and art, because it throws into relief the burden and trauma of the negation of art under modern art's technologically trans-formed relations of production" (Beech and Roberts 2002: 293-4). However, this is not regarded as an opportunity to mourn the loss of the particular configuration from which Dada emerged, but as an impetus towards "the persistence of the struggle for the violation of art, and art's resistance to art, in an epoch for which anti-art appears to be merely historical or academic" (2002: 293).

References

Adorno, Theodor
    1997   *Aesthetic Theory*. Robert Hullt-Kentor (tr.). London and New
            York: The Athlone Press.

Agamben, Giorgio
    1993   *The Coming Community*. Michael Hardt (tr.). Minneapolis:
            University of Minnesota Press.

Beech, Dave and Roberts, John
    2002   *The Philistine Controversy*. London and New York: Verso.

Benjamin, Walter
    2003   "The Work of Art in the Age of Its Technical Reproducibility"
            (Third Version). In Howard Eiland and Michael W. Jennings (eds)
            and Edmund Jephcott (tr.) *Walter Benjamin: Selected Writings,
            vol. 4, 1938–1940*. Cambridge: Belknap Press.

Blanchot, Maurice
    1993   *The Infinite Conversation*. Susan Hanson (tr.). Minneapolis:
            University of Minnesota Press.

Buck-Morss, Susan
    2000   *Dreamworld and Catastrophe: The Passing of Mass Utopia in
            East and West*. Cambridge: MIT Press.

Bürger, Peter
    1984   *Theory of the Avant-Garde*. Michael Shaw (tr.). Minneapolis:
            University of Minnesota Press.

Cabanne, Pierre
    1971   *Dialogues with Marcel Duchamp*. London: Thames and Hudson.
            Camfield, William. 1991. "Marcel Duchamp's *Fountain*:
            Aesthetic Object, Icon, or Anti-Art?". In De Duve (1991): 133-
            178.

Cunningham, David
    2001   "Architecture, Utopia and the Futures of the Avant Garde". In *The
            Journal of Architecture* 6(2): 169-182.

    2002   "Trying (Not) to Understand: Adorno and the Work of Beckett".
            In Lane, Richard (ed.), *Beckett and Philosophy*. Basingstoke &
            New York: Palgrave: 125-139.

2003a "A Time for Dissonance and Noise: On Adorno, Music and the Concept of Modernism". In *Angelaki: Journal of the Theoretical Humanities* 8(1): 61-74.

2003b "*Ex Minimis*: Greenberg, Modernism and Beckett's *Three Dialogues*". In *Samuel Beckett Today/Aujourd'hui* 13: 29-41.

Day, Gail
2000 "Practices of Negation and False Sublations". Paper presented at *Returns of the Avant-Garde: Post-War Movements* (University of Westminster, London, 24-25 November 2000).

De Duve, Thierry
1996 *Kant After Duchamp*. Cambridge: MIT Press.

De Duve, Thierry (ed.)
1991 *The Definitively Unfinished Marcel Duchamp*. Cambridge: MIT Press.

Derrida, Jacques
1978 "The Theatre of Cruelty and the Closure of Representation" (tr. Alan Bass) in *Writing and Difference*. Chicago: University of Chicago Press: 232-250.

1994 "Nietzsche and the Machine (Interview with Richard Beardsworth)" in *Journal of Nietzsche Studies* 7: 7-66.

Duchamp, Marcel
1973 *Salt Seller: The Writings of Marcel Duchamp* (eds Michel Sanouillet and Elmer Peterson). Oxford: Oxford University Press.

Foster, Hal
1996 *The Return of the Real*. Cambridge: MIT Press.

Hegel, G. W. F.
1993 *Introductory Lectures on Aesthetics*. Bernard Bosanquet (tr.) and Michael Inwood (ed.). Harmondsworth: Penguin.

Kosuth, Joseph
1991 *Art After Philosophy and After*. Cambridge: MIT Press.

Krauss, Rosalind
1987 *The Originality of the Avant-Garde and Other Modernist Myths*. Cambridge: MIT Press.

Kuenzli, Rudolf E. and Francis M. Naumann (eds)
1990 *Marcel Duchamp: Artist of the Century*. Cambridge: MIT Press.

Lyotard, Jean-François
    1990   *Duchamp's TRANS/formers*. Ian McLeod (tr.). Venice: Lapice
           Press.

Mann, Paul
    1991   *The Theory-Death of the Avant-Garde*. Bloomington and
           Indianapolis: Indiana University Press.

Mink, Janis
    1995   *Marcel Duchamp: Art as Anti-Art*. Cologne: Benedikt Taschen.

Müller, G. E.
    1958   "The Hegel Legend of 'Thesis-Antithesis-Synthesis'" in *Journal
           of the History of Ideas* 19: 411-4.

Naumann, Francis M.
    1991   "Marcel Duchamp: A Reconciliation of Opposites". In De Duve
           (1991): 41-67.

Nicholls, Peter
    1995   *Modernisms: A Literary Guide*. Houndmills and London:
           Macmillan.

Osborne, Peter
    1995   *The Politics of Time: Modernity and Avant-Garde*. London and
           New York: Verso.

    2000   *Philosophy in Cultural Theory*. London and New York:
           Routledge.

Perloff, Marjorie
    2002   "Dada Without Duchamp/Duchamp Without Dada: Avant Garde
           Tradition and the Individual Talent".
           Online at: http://wings.buffalo.edu/epc/authors/perloff/dada.html

Roberts, John
    1996   "Mad For It! Philistinism, the Everyday and the New British Art"
           in *Third Text* 35: 29-42.

    2000   "On Autonomy and the Avant-Garde" in *Radical Philosophy* 103:
           25-8.

    2002   "The Labour of Subjectivity/The Subjectivity of Labour:
           Reflections on Contemporary Political Theory and Culture' in
           Third Text 61: 367-386.

Stallabrass, Julian
    1999   *High Art Lite: British Art in the 1990s.* London and New York:
             Verso.

VI. Dada Critical Bibliography

A Decade of Dada Scholarship:
publications on Dada, 1994–2005

Timothy Shipe

Dada Culture appears at a particularly interesting juncture in the history of Dada bibliography. As we begin the ten-year countdown to the centennial of the Cabaret Voltaire, we may anticipate a heightened interest in the Dada movement, to be accompanied no doubt by a massive increase in published scholarship on Dada and the individual Dadaists. Furthermore, it seems likely that events such as the "block-buster" exhibition at the Centre Pompidou and the National Gallery of Art in Washington and the reopening of the original Cabaret Voltaire in Zürich as an innovative gallery and performance space will arouse the interest of the general public, leading to a flurry of publications aimed at the educated layperson.

The year 2005 saw not only the opening of the Centre Pompidou exhibition, but also the completion of the largest single publication project in the history of Dada scholarship, the ten-volume series *Crisis and the Arts: The History of Dada* (1996–2005) edited by Stephen C. Foster. Since that series ended with the promised bibliographic volume by Jörgen Schäfer, and since it began ten years earlier with a volume that included significant bibliographic essays by Rainer Rumold and Michel Sanouillet, it seems fitting to provide here a selective bibliographic survey of the literature of Dada of the decade since the publication of volume 1 of *Crisis and the Arts*. Rumold and Sanouillet surveyed the literature through roughly 1993; therefore, in the following pages I will address the state of the literature from 1994 through the fall of 2005.

During the period under consideration, the study of Dada has been greatly facilitated by the appearance of two major bibliographical tools, both anticipated by Sanouillet in his 1996 essay. Jörgen Schäfer's *Exquisite Dada: A Comprehensive Bibliography* (2005), volume 10 of Foster's series, becomes the definitive and indispensable published bibliography of the movement. Of course, a bibliography in book form is of necessity static, and Sanouillet foresaw the need for an online database to overcome this limitation of the printed bibliography. That database now exists in the form of the *International Online Bibliography of Dada* developed and maintained by the International Dada Archive at the University of Iowa. First made available in 1999, the online bibliography now comprises nearly 55,000 entries. These two comprehensive reference sources have been supplemented by a number of more specialised tools, such as Schäfer's *Dada in Köln: Ein Repertorium* (1995), as well as new or updated bibliographies on individual Dadaists.

Not anticipated in Sanouillet's essay was the proliferation of online resources by means of the World Wide Web (still in its infancy in the early 1990s). As in every field, the number of websites related to the Dada movement is staggering. A Google search on the term "Dada" will retrieve over three million results; "Dadaism" will yield over eighty thousand. Leaving aside misspellings of "data" and false cognates in Indic languages, the vast majority of sites retrieved are the projects of amateur aficionados of the Dada movement or would-be contemporary practitioners of the Dada spirit. Some of these sites are creative endeavours in their own right, aiming to realise a form of Neo-Dada in this most contemporary of media.

Nevertheless, a growing number of institutionally backed websites are providing information vital to scholars of the Dada movement, from bibliographical data and primary documents and images to clearinghouses for research. Among those online resources dealing with the movement as a whole must be counted the website of the International Dada Archive, which, besides hosting the aforementioned online bibliography, has mounted thousands of pages of Dada-era books and journals from its collections. Furthermore, the websites of museums and research institutions (such as the Getty and the Centre Pompidou) with significant holdings of Dada works have become invaluable sources of primary documentation. The Centre

Pompidou, for example, provides online images of virtually its entire collection.

Additionally, a growing number of websites, some of them quite comprehensive and scholarly, provide information on individual Dadaists. Some, like that of the Man Ray Trust, provide comprehensive image databases of an artist's work. Others are more limited and ephemeral. Perhaps it was the ephemeral nature of these sites, which may disappear from one day to the next, which led Schäfer to exclude online resources from his bibliography; but one can only expect the number and usefulness of these scholarly websites to increase in the next decade.

An important trend of the past decade has been the increasing availability of primary sources in published form. The passage of time has lifted some of the barriers to publishing some of the key sources, and a new generation of scholars has arisen to work with the pioneering generation of the sixties and seventies to produce critical editions of the Dadaists' writings. Among the most significant sources now available in print are the extant portions of Aragon's *Projet d'histoire littéraire contemporaine* with its first-hand account of the development of Paris Dada; the massive treasure-trove of Berlin Dada documents buried in Hannah Höch's garden, acquired by the Berlinische Galerie, and finally published in the three two-part volumes of *Hannah Höch: Eine Lebenscollage*; the manuscripts of Breton's and Soupault's groundbreaking *Les Champs magnétiques*; and the definitive version of Ball's *Tenderenda der Fantast*. The monumental critical edition of Ball's works began with a three-volume edition of his letters, including many from the period of Zürich Dada, and the decade saw the completion or continuation of critical editions of Aragon, Breton, Iliazd, Péret, and others.

Similarly, documentation of the visual production of the Dadaists appeared in the form of new or revised *catalogues raisonnés,* from the long-awaited third edition of Arturo Schwarz's *The Complete Works of Marcel Duchamp* to full or partial catalogues of the works of Janco, Man Ray and Schwitters.

In the area of biographical writing, a number of the Dadaists who had not received extensive treatment were the subjects of one or more book-length biographies. Not all of these could be classed as scholarly biographies, and some were sorely lacking in documentation; on the other hand, some of the biographies that were aimed

chiefly at a general readership contained plenty to interest the specialist. Among the subjects of new biographies were Breton, Duchamp,
Hartley, Hennings, Loy, and Tzara.

The output of secondary literature on Dada and the Dadaists
has continued to increase geometrically since 1994. Certain trends remained unchanged. Marcel Duchamp, for example, continued to
receive more scholarly attention than any other figure associated with
the Dada movement. On the other hand, individuals who had received
little or no attention became the focus of an increasing number of
monographs, dissertations, and articles. In particular, the women of
Dada finally began to receive the long-overdue attention of scholars,
with special emphasis on the Baroness Elsa von Freytag-Loringhoven,
Emmy Hennings, Hannah Höch, Mina Loy, and Sophie Taeuber-Arp,
as well as catalogues and essays on the general topic of women and
Dada.

The political changes in Europe between 1989 and 1992 gave
rise to two significant trends. First, the availability of new docu-
mentary sources in central Europe and the former Soviet Union,
together with easier travel for purposes of research and a generally
increased interest in the region led to an increase in western scholarly
activity related to the avant-garde movements of central and eastern
Europe and their relation to Dada. Second, the changes in the region
permitted scholars in Russia and elsewhere to direct their attention to
Dada and to the suppressed Russian avant-garde movements of the
1910s and 1920s. Consequently, there was a dramatic increase in
scholarly publication in Russian and other Slavic and east European
languages. Similarly, increased contacts with the west have led to a
dramatic increase in the number of publications on Dada in Chinese.

The bibliography that follows can only present a sampling of
the most significant publications on Dada during the past ten years.
The scope is limited to monographic publications in the languages
most accessible to anglophone and western European readers. There
was, unfortunately, insufficient space to include articles in journals or
collections, and all but one or two unpublished dissertations had to be
excluded as well. Some periodicals and websites devoted entirely to
the life and work of a particular Dadaist have been included, but only
to the extent that they have significant scholarly content and, in the
case of websites, have an institutional affiliation that makes them
likely to continue to be available in the foreseeable future. In the case

of individuals such as Aragon, Breton, and Evola, whose Dada work constitutes but a small portion of their total careers, only publications with content relevant to the Dada period are included. Because of space limitations, works devoted to two or three individual Dadaists are listed only once, under the name that comes earliest in the alphabetical list.

Timothy Shipe
University of Iowa

BIBLIOGRAPHIES OF DADA

International Dada Archive (University of Iowa). *International Online Bibliography of Dada*. Online at: http://www.lib.uiowa.edu/dada/oasis.html.

Schäfer, Jörgen. 2005. *Exquisite Dada: A Comprehensive Bibliography* (Crisis and the Arts 10). Detroit: G.K. Hall.

GENERAL WORKS ON DADA

Bätzner, Nike (ed.). 2005. *Kunst und Spiel seit Dada: Faites vos jeux!* Ostfildern-Ruit: Hatje Cantz. Catalogue of travelling exhibition.

Béhar, Henri, and Catherine Dufour (eds). 2005. *Dada: Circuit total* (Les Dossiers H). Lausanne: L'Age d'homme.

Brandt, Sylvia. 1995. *Bravo! & bum bum!: Neue Producktions- und Rezeptionsformen im Theater der historischen Avantgarde: Futurismus, Dada und Surrealismus: Eine vergleichende Untersuchung* (Analysen und Dokumente 36). Frankfurt am Main and New York: Peter Lang.

Centre Pompidou. *La Collection du Musée national d'art moderne*. Online at: http://collection.cnac-gp.fr. Database of the museum's collection, including extensive Dada holdings; images available for most works.

Cortenova, Giorgio (ed.). 1997. *Dadaismo, dadaismi: Da Duchamp a Warhol*. Milan: Electa.

Dachy, Marc. 2005. *Archives Dada/chronique*. Paris: Hazan, 2005. Anthology of Dada texts with commentary, followed by a detailed chronology of the movement.

—. 1994. *Dada & les dadaïsmes: Rapport sur l'anéantissement de l'ancienne beauté* (Collection Folio/essais 257). Paris: Gallimard.

Dickerman, Leah. 2005. *Dada: Zurich, Berlin, Hannover, Cologne, New York, Paris*. Washington: National Gallery of Art. Main catalogue of the U.S. venues of the 2005–2006 Dada exhibition.

Dickerman, Leah, and Matthew S. Witkovsky (eds). 2005. *The Dada Seminars* (CASVA Seminar Papers 1). Washington: National Gallery of Art.

Drachline, Pierre. 1995. *Dictionnaire humoristique de A à Z des surréalistes et des dadaïstes* (Collection "Le sens de l'humour"). Paris: Cherche midi. A thematically arranged dictionary of quotations.

Elger, Dietmar. 2004. *Dadaism* (tr. Michael Scuffil). Cologne: Taschen.

Forster, Iris. 2005. *Die Fülle des Nichts: Wie Dada die Kontingenz zur Weltanschauung macht* (Forum europäische Literatur 4). Munich: M Press.

Foster, Stephen C. (ed.). 1996. *Dada: The Coordinates of Cultural Politics* (Crisis and the Arts 1). New York: G.K. Hall.

4 Dada Suicides: Selected Texts of Arthur Cravan, Jacques Rigaut, Julien Torma & Jacques Vaché (tr. Terry Hale et al.) (Anti-classics of Dada) (Atlas Anti-classics). 1995. London: Atlas Press.

Gale, Matthew. 1997. *Dada & Surrealism* (Art & Ideas). London: Phaidon.

Getty Research Institute. *The Getty.* Online at: http://www.getty.edu. Website of the Institute, with databases of library collections and archival finding aids, including extensive holdings on Dada.

Green, Malcolm (ed. and tr.). 1995. *Blago Bung Blago Bung Bosso Fataka!: First Texts of German Dada* (Anti-Classics of Dada) (Atlas Anti-Classics). London: Atlas Press. Translations of *Phantastische Gebete* (Fantastic Prayers) by Richard Huelsenbeck, *Tenderenda der Phantast* (Tenderenda the Fantast) by Hugo Ball, and *Letzte Lockerung* (Last Loosening) by Walter Serner.

Hereth, Hans-Jürgen (ed.). 1998. *Dada-Parodien* (Vergessene Autoren der Moderne 72). Siegen: Universität-Gesamthochschule Siegen. Anthology of parodies of Dada, mostly originally published 1919–1921.

Hopkins, David. 2004. *Dada and Surrealism: A Very Short Introduction* (Very short introductions 105). Oxford and New York: Oxford University Press.

Hunkeler, Thomas, et al. (eds). 1999. *Dada heute (Dada aujourd'hui)* (Dada Today) (Variations 2). Bern and New York: Peter Lang.

Jürgs, Britta (ed.). 1999. *Etwas Wasser in der Seife: Portraits dadaistischer Künstlerinnen und Schriftstellerinnen.* Berlin: Aviva.

Korte, Hermann. 1994, rpt. 2003. *Die Dadaisten.* Reinbek bei Hamburg: Rowohlt.

Kuenzli, Rudolf E. (ed.). *Dada and Surrealist Film.* Cambridge, Mass.: MIT Press.

L'Ecotais, Emmanuelle. 2004. *The Dada Spirit.* New York: Assouline.

Le Bon, Laurent (ed.). 2005. *Dada.* Paris: Éditions du Centre Pompidou. Main catalogue of the Paris venue of the 2005–2006 Dada exhibition.

Lista, Giovanni. 2005. *Dada: Libertin & libertaire.* Paris: L'Insolite.

Pegrum, Mark A. 2000. *Challenging Modernity: Dada Between Modern and Postmodern.* New York: Berghahn Books.

Sawelson-Gorse, Naomi (ed.). 1998. *Women in Dada: Essays on Sex, Gender, and Identity*. Cambridge, Mass: MIT Press.

Schings, Hubert. 1996. *Narrenspiele, oder, Die Erschaffung einer verkehrten Welt: Studien zu Mythos und Mythopoiese im Dadaismus* (Europäische Hochschulschriften: Reihe XXVIII, Kunstgeschichte 232). Frankfurt am Main and New York: Peter Lang.

Schröer, Gregor. 2005. *"L'Art est mort, vive DADA!": Avantgarde, Anti-Kunst und die Tradition der Bilderstürme*. Bielefeld: Aisthesis.

Schrott, Raoul (ed.). 1992, rev. 2004. *Dada 15/25: Dokumentation und chronologischer Überblick zu Tzara & Co*. Cologne: DuMont. First edition published Innsbruck: Haymon.

Sheppard, Richard. 2000. *Modernism-Dada-Postmodernism* (Avant-garde & Modernism Studies). Evanston, Ill.: Northwestern University Press.

Waldberg, Patrick. 1999. *Dada: La Fonction de refus* (Les Essais 8). Paris: La Différence.

Watts, Harriet (ed.). 2004. *Dada and the Press* (Crisis and the Arts 9). New Haven, Conn.: G.K. Hall.

GEOGRAPHIC CENTRES

Berg, Hubert van den. 1999. *Avantgarde und Anarchismus: Dada in Zürich und Berlin* (Beiträge zur neueren Literaturgeschichte 167). Heidelberg: Winter.

—. 1996. *The Import of Nothing: How Dada Came, Saw, and Vanished in the Low Countries (1915–1929)* (Crisis and the Arts 7). New Haven, Conn.: G.K. Hall.

Bergius, Hanne. 2003. *Dada Triumphs!: Dada Berlin, 1917–1923: Artistry of Polarities: Montages, Metamechanics, Manifestations* (tr. Brigitte Pichon) (Crisis and the Arts 5). New Haven, Conn.: G.K. Hall.

—. 2000. *Montage und Metamechanik: Dada Berlin–Artistik von Polaritäten* (Schriftenreihe Burg Giebichenstein Hochschule für Kunst und Design Halle 3). Berlin: Gebr. Mann.

Dachy, Marc. 2002. *Dada au Japon: Segments dadas et néo-dadas dans les avant-gardes japonaises* (Perspectives critiques). Paris: Presses universitaires de France.

Foster, Stephen C. (ed.). 1998. *The Eastern Dada Orbit: Russia, Georgia, Ukraine, Central Europe and Japan* (Crisis and the Arts 4). New York: G.K. Hall. Central and European section ed. Gerald Janecek; Japanese section by Toshiharu Omuka.

Gaughan, Martin Ignatius (ed.). 2003. *Dada New York: New World for Old* (Crisis and the Arts 8). New Haven, Conn.: G.K. Hall.

Goergen, Jeanpaul (ed.). 1994. *Urlaute dadaistischer Poesie: Der Berliner Dada-Abend am 12. April 1918* (Randfiguren der Moderne). Hanover: Postskriptum.

Grazioli, Elio (ed. and tr.). 1998. *Dada a Parigi 1918–1924* (Le Parole dell'arte 4). Cernusco Lomb.: Hestia.

Hackner, Thomas. 2001. *Dada und Futurismus in Japan: Die Rezeption der historischen Avantgarden*. Munich: Iudicium.

Jones, Amelia. 2004. *Irrational Modernism: A Neurasthenic History of New York Dada*. Cambridge, Mass.: MIT Press.

Naumann, Francis M. 1996. *Making Mischief: Dada Invades New York*. New York: Whitney Museum of American Art. Exhibition catalogue.

Nenzel, Reinhard (ed.). 1995. *Dada-Mappe Berlin 1920/21: Fünf Rara, ein Rarissimum und ein Aufsatz zum Thema*. Bonn: Nenzel. Portfolio including facsimiles of *Harakiri!?, Das Bordell,* and *Ein Familiendrama*, by Fried-Hardy Worm, *Die dadaistische Korruption*, by Walter Petry, and *Dass Gewebe reisst, oder, Die Mausfalle*, by Alfred Sauermann, with a booklet, *Walter Petry, Alfred Sauermann, Fried-Hardy Worm: Drei späte Stimmen des Berliner Dadaismus: Versuch einer Lokalisierung*, by Nenzel.

Peterson, Elmer (ed.). 2002. *Paris Dada: The Barbarians Storm the Gates* (Crisis and the Arts 6). Detroit: G.K. Hall.

Pichon, Brigitte, and Karl Riha (eds). 1996. *Dada Zurich: A Clown's Game From Nothing* (Crisis and the Arts 2). New York: G.K. Hall; London: Prentice Hall International.

Riha, Karl, and Jörgen Schäfer (eds). 1995. *Fatagaga-Dada: Max Ernst, Hans Arp, Johannes Theodor Baargeld und der Kölner Dadaismus*. Giessen: Anabas.

Schäfer, Jörgen. 1995. *Dada in Köln: Ein Repertorium* (Bibliographien zur Literatur- und Mediengeschichte 3). Frankfurt am Main and New York: Peter Lang.

Schippers, K. 1974; rev. 2000. *Holland Dada*. Amsterdam: Querido.

Stokes, Charlotte, and Stephen C. Foster. 1997. *Dada Cologne Hanover* (Crisis and the Arts 3). New York: G.K. Hall.

Weisenfeld, Gennifer S. 2002. *Mavo: Japanese Artists and the Avant-garde, 1905–1931* (Twentieth-century Japan 11). Berkeley: University of California Press.

INDIVIDUALS

Louis Aragon

Aragon, Louis. 1998. *Chroniques I: 1918–1932* (ed. Bernard Leuilliot). Paris: Stock. Collected critical articles.

—. 1997. *La Défense de l'infini: Romans* (ed. Lionel Follet) (Les cahiers de la NRF). Paris: Gallimard. Expanded edition incorporating previously unpublished manuscript material.

—. 1997–2003. *Oeuvres romanesques completes* (ed. Daniel Bougnoux) (Bibliothèque de la Pléiade 436, 463, 493). 3 vols. Paris: Gallimard.

—. 2000. *Papiers inédits: De Dada au surréalisme, 1917–1931* (ed. Lionel Follet and Édouard Ruiz) (Les Cahiers de la NRF). Paris: Gallimard.

—. 1994. *Projet d'histoire litteraire contemporaine* (ed. Marc Dachy) (Digraphe). Paris: Gallimard.

Les Annales de la Société des amis de Louis Aragon et Elsa Triolet. 1999 and continuing. Rambouillet: Société des amis de Louis Aragon et Elsa Triolet. Annual publication.

Babilas, Wolfgang. *Études sur Louis Aragon* (Münstersche Beiträge zur romanischen Philologie 20). 2 vols. Münster: Nodus. The author's collected writings on Aragon.

— (ed.). *Louis Aragon Online.* Online at: http://www.uni-muenster.de/Romanistik/ Aragon. A comprehensive website for Aragon research, hosted by the University of Münster.

Barbarant, Olivier. 1997. *Aragon: La Mémoire et l'excès* (Collection "Champ poetique"). Seyssel: Champ Vallon.

Decottignies, Jean. 1994. *L'Invention de la poésie: Breton, Aragon, Duchamp* (Objet). Lille: Presses universitaires de Lille.

Desanti, Dominique. 1997. *Les Aragonautes: Les Cercles du poète disparu.* Paris: Calmann-Lévy.

Gürsel, Nedim. 1997. *Le Mouvement perpétuel d'Aragon: De la Révolte dadaïste au "Monde reel"* (Espaces littéraires). Paris: L'Harmattan.

Halpern, Elisabeth, and Alain Trouvé (eds). 2003. *Une Tornade d'énigmes:* Le Paysan de Paris *de Louis Aragon* (Les Aéronautes de l'esprit). Paris: L'Improviste.

Meyer, Michel. 2001. *Michel Meyer présente* Le Paysan de Paris *d'Aragon* (Foliothèque 93). Paris: Gallimard.

Narjoux, Cécile. 2001. *Le Mythe, ou, La Représentation de l'autre dans l'oeuvre romanesque d'Aragon* (Collection Critiques littéraires). Paris: L'Harmattan.

Piégay-Gros, Nathalie. 1997. *L'Esthétique d'Aragon* (Collection "Esthétique"). Paris: SEDES.

Ristat, Jean (ed.). *Album Aragon* (Album de la Pléiade 36). Paris: Gallimard. A substantial compilation of photographs and facsimiles of source documents.

Vassevière, Maryse. 1998. *Aragon romancier intertextuel, ou, Les Pas de l'étranger* (Collection Critiques littéraires). Paris: L'Harmattan.

Jean Arp

Arp Museum Bahnhof Rolandseck. *Arp Museum Bahnhof Rolandseck.* Online at: http://www.arpmuseum.org. Website of the museum near Bonn.

Casè, Pierre (ed.). 1998. *Arp e l'avanguardia.* Milan: Museo della Permanente and Electa. Exhibition catalogue.

Costermans, Barbara, and Petra Gunst (eds). 2004. *Jean Arp: L'Invention de la forme.* Antwerp: Fonds Mercator; Brussels: Palais des beaux-arts. Exhibition catalogue.

Fischer, Hartwig (ed.). 2004. *Schwitters_Arp.* Ostfildern: Hatje Cantz. Exhibition catalogue, Basel.

Fondation Jean Arp. *Fondation Jean Arp.* Online at: http://www.fondationarp.org. Website of the foundation and museum at Arp's studio in Meudon.

Hopfengart, Christine. 1994. *Hans Arp.* Ostfildern: Hatje. Exhibition catalogue, Nuremberg.

Lulinska, Agnieszka, Brigitte Lucke, and Walburga Krupp. 2003. *Hans Arp, Sophie Taeuber-Arp: Exploracions mútues.* Barcelona: Àmbit; Palma: Fundació "Sa Nostra". Exhibition, Palma de Mallorca.

Rathke, Christian. 1999. *Hans/Jean Arp: Korrespondenz der Formen.* Schleswig: Stiftung Schleswig-Holsteinische Landesmuseen, Schloss Gottorf. Exhibition catalogue.

Stiftung Hans Arp und Sophie Taeuber-Arp. 1997. *Hans Arp, Sophie Taeuber Arp.* Ostfildern-Ruit: Hatje. Catalogue of travelling exhibition.

Winkelmann, Judith. 1995. *Abstraktion als stilbildendes Prinzip in der Lyrik von Hans Arp und Kurt Schwitters* (Bochumer Schriften zur deutschen Literatur 47). Frankfurt am Main and New York: Peter Lang.

Johannes Baader

Baader, Johannes. 1995. *Ich segne die Hölle!: Gedichte 1915–1933* (ed. Dieter Scholz) (Vergessene Autoren der Moderne 64). Siegen: Universität-Gesamthochschule Siegen.

——. 2004. *Konnersreuth: Eine Gesamtbetrachtung*. Munich: Ephemera.

Johannes Baargeld

Baargeld, Johannes. 2001. *Fummelmond & Ferngefimmel: Lyrik und Prosa des Zentrodada* (ed. Walter Vitt). Nördlingen: Steinmeier.

Hugo Ball

Ball, Hugo. 2002. *Ball and Hammer: Hugo Ball's Tenderenda the Fantast* (tr. Jonathan Hammer) (ed. Jeffrey T. Schnapp). New Haven: Yale University Press.

——. 2003. *Briefe 1904–1927* (ed. Gerhard Schaub und Ernst Teubner) (Sämtliche Werke und Briefe 10) (Veröffentlichungen der Deutschen Akademie für Sprache und Dichtung Darmstadt 81). 3 vols. Göttingen: Wallstein.

——. 1996. *Flight Out of Time: A Dada Diary* (tr. Ann Raimes) (ed. John Elderfield) (Documents of 20th-century art). Berkeley: University of California Press. Translation originally published in 1974; new introduction and bibliography.

——. 1995. *Der Henker von Brescia: Drei Akte der Not und Ekstase* (ed. Franz L. Pelgen) (Die Sisyphosse). Leipzig: Faber & Faber.

——. 1996. *Die nichtgesammelten Gedichte* (ed. Franz L. Pelgen) (Die Sisyphosse). Leipzig: Faber & Faber.

——. 1999. *Tenderenda der Phantast* (ed. Raimund Meyer and Julian Schütt). Innsbruck: Haymon. New edition with variants, based on the available manuscripts.

Hesse, Hermann, Emmy Hennings, and Hugo Ball. 2003. *Briefwechsel 1921 bis 1927* (ed. Bärbel Reetz). Frankfurt am Main: Suhrkamp.

Sandqvist, Tom. 1998. *Kärlek och Dada: Hugo Ball och Emmy Hennings*. Stockholm: Brutus Östlings Bokförlag Symposion.

Schmidt, Christoph. 2003. *Die Apokalypse des Subjekts: Ästhetische Subjektivität und politische Theologie bei Hugo Ball*. Bielefeld: Aisthesis.

Steinbrenner, Manfred. 1994. *Dadaismus und Religion: Hugo Balls "Weg zu Gott"*. Egelsbach: Hänsel-Hohenhausen. Microfiche.

Süllwold, Erika. 1999. *Das gezeichnete und ausgezeichnete Subjekt: Kritik der Moderne bei Emmy Hennings und Hugo Ball* (M & P Schriftenreihe für Wissenschaft und Forschung). Stuttgart: Metzler.

Wacker, Bernd (ed.). 1996. *Dionysius DADA Areopagita: Hugo Ball und die Kritik der Moderne.*

White, Erdmute Wenzel. 1998. *The Magic Bishop: Hugo Ball, Dada Poet* (Studies in German Literature, Linguistics, and Culture). Columbia, SC: Camden House.

Zehetner, Cornelius. 2000. *Hugo Ball: Portrait einer Philosophie.* Vienna: Turia + Kant.

Erwin Blumenfeld

Blumenfeld, Erwin. 1999. *Eye to I: The Autobiography of a Photographer* (tr. Mike Mitchell and Brian Murdoch). New York: Thames and Hudson. Translation of *Durch tausendjährige Zeit.*

Blumenfeld, Yorick. 1999. *The Naked and the Veiled: The Photographic Nudes of Erwin Blumenfeld.* New York: Thames and Hudson.

Ewing, William A. 1996. *Blumenfeld Photographs: A Passion for Beauty.* New York: Abrams.

Métayer, Michel. 2004. *Erwin Blumenfeld.* London: Phaidon.

André Breton

Breton, André. 2003. *André Breton: Selections* (ed. Mark Polizzotti) (Poets for the Millennium 1). Berkeley: University of California Press.

—. 1996. *The Lost Steps (Les Pas perdus)* (tr. Mark Polizzotti) (French Modernist Library). Lincoln: University of Nebraska Press.

Béhar, Henri (ed.). 1997. *Chassé-croisé Tzara-Breton: Actes du colloque international Paris-Sorbonne 23-25 mai 1996* (Mélusine 17). Lausanne: L'Age d'homme.

Blachère, Jean-Claude. 1996. *Les Totems d'André Breton: Surréalisme et primitivisme littéraire* (Collection Critiques littéraires). Paris: L'Harmattan.

Dumas, Marie-Claire (ed.). 1996. *André Breton en perspective cavalière* (Les Cahiers de la NRF). Paris: Gallimard.

Graulle, Christophe. 2000. *André Breton et l'humour noir: Une Révolte supérieure de l'esprit* (Collection Critiques littéraires). Paris: L'Harmattan.

Hilke, Manfred. 2002. *L'Écriture automatique: Das Verhältnis von Surrealismus und Parapsychologie in der Lyrik von André Breton* (Europäische Hochschulschriften: Reihe XIII, Französische Sprache und Literatur 264). Frankfurt am Main and New York: Peter Lang.

Polizzotti, Mark. 1995. *Revolution of the Mind: The Life of André Breton*. New York: Farrar, Strauss, and Giroux.

Sebbag, Georges. 2004. *André Breton, l'amour folie: Suzanne, Nadja, Lise, Simone.* Paris: Jean-Michel Place.

—. 1997. *Le Point sublime: André Breton, Arthur Rimbaud, Nelly Kaplan.* Paris: Jean-Michel Place.

Serge Charchounne

Castaño, Antonia (ed.). 2004. *Serge Charchoune, 1889–1975: Entre Dadá y la abstracción.* Madrid: Fundación Cultural MAPFRE Vida. Exhibition catalogue.

Lorenzelli arte. 1996. *Omaggio a Serge Charchoune, 1888–1975.* Milan: Skira. Exhibition catalogue.

Paul Citroen

Bool, Flip, et al. (eds). [1998?]. *Paul Citroen (1896–1983)* (Monografieën van Nederlandse Fotografen (Monographs on Dutch Photographers) 7). Amsterdam: Focus.

Rheeden, Herbert van, Monique Feenstra, and Bettina Rijkschroeff. 1994. *Paul Citroen: Kunstenaar, Docent, Verzamelaar (Künstler, Lehrer, Sammler).* Zwolle: Waanders; Heino/Wijhe: Hannema-de Stuers Fundatie.

John Covert

Mazow, Leo G. 2003. *John Covert Rediscovered.* University Park: Palmer Museum of Art, the Pennsylvania State University. Exhibition catalogue.

Arthur Cravan

Borràs, Maria Lluïsa. 1996. *Arthur Cravan: Une Stratégie du scandale.* Paris: Jean-Michel Place. French version of her *Arthur Cravan: Una Biografía* (Biblioteca menor 8) (Barcelona: Quaderns Crema, 1993).

Charles Demuth

Demuth, Charles. 2000. *Letters of Charles Demuth, American Artist, 1883–1935* (ed. Bruce Kellner). Philadelphia: Temple University Press.

—. 1998. *Three: Georgia O'Keeffe, Florine Stettheimer, Peggy Bacon.* Lancaster, Pa.: All Kinds Blintzes Press.

Demuth Foundation. *Demuth Foundation.* Online at: http://www.demuth.org. Website of the Demuth Foundation and the Charles Demuth Museum in Lancaster, Pennsylvania.

Otto Dix

Beck, Rainer. 2003. *Otto Dix: Die kosmischen Bilder: Zwischen Sehnsucht und Schwangerem Weib.* Dresden: Verlag der Kunst and Philo Fine Arts.

Derouet, Christian (ed.). 2003. *Otto Dix: Dessins d'une guerre à l'autre.* Paris: Gallimard and Centre Pompidou.

Gruber, Sabine. 1999. *Otto Dix.* Ostfildern-Ruit: HatjeCantz. Exhibition catalogue, Stuttgart and Brussels.

Karcher, Eva. 2002. *Otto Dix, 1891–1969: "Entweder ich werde berühmt – oder berüchtigt".* Cologne and New York: Taschen.

Kim, Jung-Hee. 1994. *Frauenbilder von Otto Dix: Wirklichkeit und Selbstbekenntnis.* Münster: Lit.

Knubben, Thomas, and Tilman Osterwold (eds). 2002. *Otto Dix: Aquarelle der 20er Jahre.* Ostfildern-Ruit: Hatje Cantz. Exhibition catalogue, Ravensburg.

Lorenz, Ulrike. 2003. *Otto Dix: Das Werkverzeichnis der Zeichnungen und Pastelle.* Eight volumes. Weimar: Verlag und Datenbank für Geisteswissenschaften.

— (ed.). 2000. *Dix avant Dix: Das Jugend- und Frühwerk 1903–1914.* Gera: Kunstsammlung Gera; Jena: Glaux. Exhibition catalogue.

McGreevy, Linda F. 2001. *Bitter Witness: Otto Dix and the Great War* (German Life and Civilisation 27). New York: Peter Lang.

Otto-Dix-Haus Hemmenhofen. *Otto-Dix-Haus.* Online at: http://www.forq.de/otto-dix-haus. Website of the museum at Dix's home and studio in Hemmenhofen, Germany.

Schönjahn, Claudia, and Ralf Gottschlich. 2001. *Otto Dix: Arbeiten auf Papier: Digitaler Bestandskatalog.* Albstadt: Galerie Albstadt, Städtische Kunstsammlungen. CD-ROM.

Strobl, Andreas. 1996. *Otto Dix: eine Malerkarriere der zwanziger Jahre.* Berlin: Reimer.

Nelly van Doesburg

Moorsel, Wies van. 2000. *Nelly van Doesburg 1899–1975.* Nijmegen: SUN.

Theo van Doesburg

Doesburg, Theo van, and Kurt Schwitters. 1995. *Holland's Bankroet door Dada: Documenten van een Dadaïstische Triomftocht door Nederland* (ed. Hubert van den Berg) (Arsenaal Reeks 2). Amsterdam: Ravijn.

Bakker, Siem, and Emy Thorissen. 1997. *De Dichter Theo van Doesburg/I.K. Bonset: 1882–1931.* Nijmegen: Instituut Nederlands KUN.

Danzker, Jo-Anne Birnie (ed.). 2000. *Theo van Doesburg, Maler-Architekt.* Munich and New York: Prestel.

Hoek, Els (ed.). 2000. *Theo van Doesburg: Oeuvrecatalogus.* Utrecht: Centraal Museum; Otterlo: Kröller-Müller Museum; Bussum: Thoth.

Straaten, Evert van. 1994. *Theo van Doesburg, Constructor of the New Life* (tr. Ruth Koenig). Otterlo: Kröller-Müller Museum.

Arthur Dove

Balken, Debra Bricker. 1997. *Arthur Dove: A Retrospective.* Andover, Mass.: Addison Gallery of American Art; Cambridge, Mass.: MIT Press. Exhibition catalogue.

Marcel Duchamp

Duchamp, Marcel. 2000. *Affectt/Marcel: The Selected Correspondence of Marcel Duchamp* (ed. Francis M. Naumann and Hector Obalk) (tr. Jill Taylor). London: Thames & Hudson.

Ades, Dawn, Neil Cox, and David Hopkins. 1999. *Marcel Duchamp* (World of Art). New York: Thames and Hudson.

Balken, Debra Bricker. 2003. *Debating American Modernism: Stieglitz, Duchamp, and the New York Avant-garde.* New York: American Federation of Arts; D.A.P., Distributed Art Publishers.

Berswordt-Wallrabe, Kornelia von (ed.). 2003. *Marcel Duchamp: Die Schweriner Sammlung.* Schwerin: Staatliches Museum Schwerin.

—. 1995; rev. 1999. *Marcel Duchamp: Respirateur.* Ostfildern: Hatje Cantz.

Bonito Oliva, Achille. 1997. *M.D.* (I Turbamenti dell'arte). Milan: Costa & Nolan.

Buskirk, Martha, and Mignon Nixon (eds). *The Duchamp Effect.* Cambridge, Mass.: MIT Press.

Cabanne, Pierre. 1997. *Duchamp & Co.* (tr. Peter Snowdon). Paris: Terrail.

Chateau, Dominique. 1999. *Duchamp et Duchamp* (L'Art en bref). Paris: L'Harmattan.

Clair, Jean. 2000. *Sur Marcel Duchamp et la fin de l'art* (Art et artistes). Paris: Gallimard.

Dadoun, Roger. 1996. *Duchamp: Ce Mécano qui met à nu* (Coup double). Paris: Hachette.

Darbelley, Odile, and Michel Jacquelin. 2001. *Duchamp Duchamp: Du Lard à l'art* (Actes Sud papiers). Arles: Actes Sud.

Davis, W. Bowdoin. 2002. *Duchamp: Domestic Patterns, Covers, and Threads.* New York: Midmarch Arts Press.

Décimo, Marc. 2005. *Le Duchamp facile* (L'Écart absolu). Dijon: Presses du réel.

De Duve, Thierry. 1996. *Kant after Duchamp.* Cambridge, Mass.: MIT Press.

Eckl, Andreas, Dorothee Kemper, and Ulrich Rehm (eds). 2000. *Marcel Duchamps "Grosses Glass": Beiträge aus Kunstgeschichte und philosophischer Ästhetik* (Kunstwissenschaftliche Bibliothek 16). Cologne: König.

Erfurth, Eric (ed.). 1997. *Marcel Duchamp, Flaschentrockner: Doxographie.* Obernburg am Main: Logo Verlag.

Étant donné. 1999 and continuing. Baby: Association pour l'Étude de Marcel Duchamp. Periodical published approximately annually.

Gervais, André. 2000. *C'est: Marcel Duchamp dans "la fantaisie heureuse de l'histoire"* (Rayon art). Nîmes : Chambon.

Hopkins, David. 1998. *Marcel Duchamp and Max Ernst: The Bride Shared* (Clarendon Studies in the History of Art). Oxford: Clarendon Press.

Jang, Young-Girl. 2001. *L'Objet duchampien* (Collection Ouverture philosophique). Paris: Harmattan.

Joselit, David. 1998. *Infinite Regress: Marcel Duchamp, 1910–1941.* Cambridge, Mass.: MIT Press.

Judovitz, Dalia. 1995. *Unpacking Duchamp: Art in Transit.* Berkeley: University of California Press.

Lartigue, Pierre. 2004. *Rrose Sélavy et cœtera*. Paris: Le Passage.

Le Penven, Françoise. 2003. *L'Art d'écrire de Marcel Duchamp: À Propos de ses notes manuscrites et de ses boîtes* (Rayon art). Nîmes: Chambon.

Marquis, Alice Goldfarb. 2002. *Marcel Duchamp: The Bachelor Stripped Bare: A Biography*. Boston: MFA Publications.

Mink, Janis. 1995. *Marcel Duchamp, 1887–1968: Art as Anti-Art.* Cologne: Taschen.

Moffitt, John F. 2003. *Alchemist of the Avant-garde: The Case of Marcel Duchamp* (SUNY Series in Western Esoteric Traditions). Albany: State University of New York Press.

Müller-Alsbach, Annja, Heinz Stahlhut, and Harald Szeemann (eds). *Marcel Duchamp* (tr. John Brogden et al). Ostfildern-Ruit: Hatje Cantz. Exhibition catalogue, Basel.

Naumann, Francis M. 1999. *Marcel Duchamp: The Art of Making Art in the Age of Mechanical Reproduction*. Ghent: Ludion.

Ottinger, Didier. 2000. *Duchamp sans fins*. Paris: L'Échoppe.

— (ed.). 2001. *Marcel Duchamp dans les collections du Centre Georges Pompidou, Musée national d'art moderne*. Paris: Centre Pompidou.

Oyarzún R., Pablo. 2000. *Anestética del ready-made* (Libros de la invención y la herencia). Santiago de Chile: LOM Ediciones.

Ramírez, Juan Antonio. 1998. *Duchamp: Love and Death, Even* (tr. Alexander R. Tulloch). London: Reaktion Books.

Roth, Moira. 1998. *Difference/Indifference: Musings on Postmodernism, Marcel Duchamp and John Cage* (Critical Voices in Art, Theory and Culture). Amsterdam: G+B Arts International.

Schwarz, Arturo. 1997. *The Complete Works of Marcel Duchamp*. Third edition. Two volumes. New York: Delano Greenidge. Major revision of the *catalogue raisonné*, with new bibliography and exhibition list.

Seigel, Jerrold E. 1995. *The Private Worlds of Marcel Duchamp: Desire, Liberation, and the Self in Modern Culture*. Berkeley: University of California Press.

Suquet, Jean. 2001. *Epanouissement ABC: Le Poëme de Marcel Duchamp*. Paris: L'Échoppe.

Suquet, Jean. 1998. *Marcel Duchamp, ou, L'Éblouissement de l'éclaboussure* (L'Art en bref). Paris: L'Harmattan.

Tabart, Marielle (ed.). 1999. *Brancusi & Duchamp: Regards historiques* (Les Carnets de l'Atelier Brancusi). Paris: Centre Pompidou.

Tomkins, Calvin. 1996. *Duchamp: A Biography*. New York: Holt.

Tout-fait: The Marcel Duchamp Studies Online Journal. 1999 and continuing. New York: CASP/ASRL. Online at: http://www.toutfait.com.

Zeiller, Martin (ed.). 2003. *Marcel Duchamp: Druckgraphik*. Vienna: Universität für Angewandte Kunst.

Viking Eggeling

Werner, Gösta, and Bengt Edlund. 1997. *Viking Eggeling Diagonalsymfonin: Spjutspets i Återvändsgränd*. Lund: Novapress.

Carl Einstein

Baumann, Roland, and Hubert Roland (eds). 2001. *Carl-Einstein-Kolloquium 1998: Carl Einstein in Brüssel: Dialoge über Grenzen (Carl Einstein à Bruxelles: Dialogues par-dessus les frontières)* (Bayreuther Beiträge zur Literaturwissenschaft 22). Frankfurt am Main: Peter Lang.

Carl-Einstein-Gesellschaft. *Carl-Einstein-Gesellschaft*. Online at: http://www.carl einstein.de. Website of the society.

Dahm, Johanna. 2004. *Der Blick des Hermaphroditen: Carl Einstein und die Kunst des 20. Jahrhunderts* (Epistemata: Reihe Literaturwissenschaft 480). Würzburg: Königshausen & Neumann.

Günter, Manuela. 1996. *Anatomie des Anti-Subjekts: Zur Subversion autobiographischen Schreibens bei Siegfried Kracauer, Walter Benjamin und Carl Einstein* (Epistemata: Reihe Literaturwissenschaft 192). Würzburg: Königshausen & Neumann.

Kiefer, Klaus H. 1994. *Diskurswandel im Werk Carl Einsteins: Ein Beitrag zur Theorie und Geschichte der europäischen Avantgarde* (Communicatio 7). Tübingen: Niemeyer.

Kiefer, Klaus H. (ed.). 1996. *Carl-Einstein-Kolloquium, 1994* (Bayreuther Beiträge zur Literaturwissenschaft 16). Frankfurt am Main and New York: Peter Lang.

—. 2003. *Die visuelle Wende der Moderne: Carl Einsteins "Kunst des 20. Jahrhunderts"*. Munich: Fink.

Meffre, Liliane. 2002. *Carl Einstein, 1885–1940: Itinéraires d'une pensée moderne* (Monde germanique). Paris: Presses de l'Université de Paris-Sorbonne.

Neundorfer, German. 2003. *Kritik an Anschauung: Bildbeschreibung im kunst-kritischen Werk Carl Einsteins* (Epistemata: Reihe Literaturwissenschaft 453). Würzburg: Königshausen & Neumann.

Sabel, Johannes. 2002. *Text und Zeit: Versuche zu einer Verhältnisbestimmung, ausgehend von Carl Einsteins Roman* Bebuquin oder die Dilettanten des Wunders (Historisch-kritische Arbeiten zur deutschen Literatur 31). Frankfurt am Main and New York: Peter Lang.

Sorg, Reto. 1998. *Aus den "Gärten der Zeichen": Zu Carl Einsteins* Bebuquin. Munich: Fink.

Wurm, Carsten. 2002. *Carl Einstein, 1885–1940* (Findbuch-Editionen). Berlin: Stiftung Archiv der Akademie der Künste.

Paul Éluard

Éluard, Paul. 1995. *Ombres et soleil (Shadows and Sun): Selected Writings of 1913–1952* (tr. Lloyd Alexander and Cicely Buckley). Durham, N.H.: Oyster River Press. Bilingual edition.

—, and Jean Paulhan. 2003. *Correspondance 1919–1944: "Peut-on changer sans revenir à l'Ancien? changer en avant?"* (ed. Odile Felgine and Claude-Pierre Pérez) (Collection "Correspondances de Jean Paulhan"). Paris: Claire Paulhan.

Gaucheron, Jacques. 1995. *Paul Éluard, ou, La Fidélité à la vie: Essai.* Pantin: Temps des cerises.

Jean, Raymond. 1995. *Éluard* (Écrivains de toujours). Paris: Seuil.

McNab, Robert. 2004. *Ghost Ships: A Surrealist Love Triangle.* New Haven: Yale University Press. On the romantic triangle involving Paul and Gala Éluard and Max Ernst, and their journey to southeast Asia.

Vanoyeke, Violaine. 1995. *Paul Éluard, le poète de la liberté: Biographie.* Paris: Julliard.

Max Ernst

Dering, Peter (ed.). 1994. *Max Ernst und Bonn: Student, Kritiker, Rheinischer Expressionist* (Schriftenreihe Verein August Macke Haus 13). Bonn: Verein August Macke Haus. Exhibition catalogue.

Greschat, Isabel. 1995. *Max Ernst: Text-Bild-Kombinationen 1919 bis 1925* (Internationale Hochschulschriften 133). Münster and New York: Waxmann.

Kaufmann, Susanne. 2003. *Im Spannungsfeld von Fläche und Raum: Studien zur Wechselwirkung von Malerei und Skulptur im Werk von Max Ernst.* Weimar: VDG.

Lindau, Ursula. 1997. *Max Ernst und die Romantik: Unendliches Spiel mit Witz und Ironie.* Cologne: Wienand.

Lücke-David, Susanne. 1994. *Max Ernst "Euclid": Ein mentales Vexierbild.* Recklinghausen: Bongers.

Max Ernst Museum. *Max Ernst Museum.* Online at: http://www.maxernstmuseum.de. Website of the museum in Brühl, Germany.

Spies, Werner, and Sabine Rewald (eds). 2005. *Max Ernst: A Retrospective.* New York: Metropolitan Museum of Art; New Haven: Yale University Press. Exhibition catalogue.

Straus-Ernst, Luise. 2000. *Nomadengut* (ed. Ulrich Krempel) (Irgendsowas: Materialien zur Kunst des 20. Jahrhunderts). Hanover: Sprengel Museum. Memoir by Ernst's first wife.

Ubl, Ralph. 2004. *Prähistorische Zukunft: Max Ernst und die Ungleichzeitigkeit des Bildes.* Munich: Fink.

Warlick, M. E. 2001. *Max Ernst and Alchemy: A Magician in Search of Myth* (The Surrealist Revolution Series). Austin: University of Texas Press.

Julius Evola

Evola, Julius. 1998. *Julius Evola e l'arte delle avanguardie: Tra Futurismo, Dada e alchimia.* Rome: Fondazione Julius Evola.

—. 1994. *Scritti sull'arte d'avanguardia, 1917–1931* (ed. Elisabetta Valento) (Biblioteca evoliana 2). Rome: Fondazione Julius Evola.

Chiantera Stutte, Patricia. 2001. *Julius Evola: Dal Dadaismo alla rivoluzione conservatrice: 1919–1940.* Rome: Aracne.

Echaurren, Pablo. 1994. *Evola in Dada.* Rome: Settimo sigillo.

Studi evoliani. 1999 and continuing. Roma: Europa libreria. Annual publication.

Elsa von Freytag-Loringhoven

Freytag-Loringhoven, Elsa von. 2005. *Mein Mund ist lüstern (I got Lusting Palate): Dada-Verse* (ed. and tr. Irene Gammel). Berlin: Edition Ebersbach. English and German poems; some of the German versions of English poems are by Freytag-Loringhoven, others by Gammel.

Francis M. Naumann Fine Art. 2002. *The Art of Baroness Elsa von Freytag-Loringhoven.* New York. Exhibition catalogue.

Gammel, Irene. 2002. *Baroness Elsa: Gender, Dada, and Everyday Modernity: A Cultural Biography.* Cambridge, Mass.: MIT Press.

Salomo Friedlaender/Mynona

Friedlaender, Salomo. 2003. *Ich (1871–1936): Autobiographische Skizze* (ed. Hartmut Geerken) (Aisthesis Archiv 3). Bielefeld: Aisthesis.

—. 2001. *Das magische Ich: Elemente des kritischen Polarismus* (ed. Hartmut Geerken) (Aisthesis Archiv 2). Bielefeld: Aisthesis.

Exner, Lisbeth. 1996. *Fasching als Logik: Über Salomo Friedlaender/Mynona.* Munich: Belleville.

Hoffmann, Ines. 2001. *Sinnlichkeit und Abstraktion: Versuch, einen expressionistischen Text zu lesen* (Epistemata: Reihe Literaturwissenschaft 347). Würzburg: Königshausen & Neumann.

Otto Gross

Gross, Otto. 2000. *Collected Works 1901–1907: The Graz Years* (ed. and tr. Lois Madison). Hamilton, N.Y.: Mindpiece.

—. 2000. *Von geschlechtlicher Not zur sozialen Katastrophe* (Internationale Bibliothek). Hamburg: Edition Nautilus.

—. 2000. *Werke: Die Grazer Jahre* (ed. Lois Madison). Hamilton, NY: Mindpiece.

Dehmlow, Raimund, and Gottfried Heuer. 1999. *Otto Gross: Werkverzeichnis und Sekundärschrifttum* (Kleine bibliographische Reihe 5). Hanover: Laurentius.

— (eds). 2000. *1. Internationaler Otto Gross Kongress: Bauhaus-Archiv, Berlin 1999.* Marburg: LiteraturWissenschaft.de; Hanover: Laurentius.

—. 2003. *Bohème, Psychoanalyse & Revolution: 3. Internationaler Otto Gross Kongress: Ludwig-Maximilians-Universität, München, 15.-17. März 2002.* Marburg: LiteraturWissenschaft.de.

Dienes, Gerhard, and Ralf Rother (eds). 2003. *Die Gesetze des Vaters: Problematische Identitätsansprüche: Hans und Otto Gross, Sigmund Freud und Franz Kafka.* Vienna: Böhlau.

Goette, Jürgen-Wolfgang et al. (eds). 2000. *Anarchismus und Psychoanalyse zu Beginn des 20. Jahrhunderts: Der Kreis um Erich Mühsam und Otto Gross: Elfte Erich-Mühsam-Tagung in Malente, 2.-4. Juni 2000* (Schriften der Erich-Mühsam-Gesellschaft 19). Lübeck: Erich-Mühsam-Gesellschaft.

Götz von Olenhusen, Albrecht, and Gottfried Heuer (eds). 2005. *Die Gesetze des Vaters 4. Internationaler Otto Gross Kongress: Robert Stolz-Museum, Karl Franzens-Universität Graz 24.-26. Oktober 2003.* Marburg: LiteraturWissenschaft.de.

Gross, Joseph François, and Jérôme François Grosse. 2005. *Le Docteur en droit Hanns Gross, criminologue, et son fils, le docteur Otto Gross, psychanalyste: Identités inconnues entre Lorraine et Habsbourg.* Sarrebourg: Memo Lotharingiae.

Heuer, Gottfried (ed.). 2000. *2. Internationaler Otto Gross Kongress: Burghölzli, Zürich 2000.* Marburg: LiteraturWissenschaft.de.

International Otto Gross Society. *International Otto Gross Society.* Online at: http://www.ottogross.org. Website of the society, with bibliography, documents, news, and other links.

Jung, Christina, and Thomas Anz (eds). 2002. *Der Fall Otto Gross: Eine Pressekampagne deutscher Intellektueller im Winter 1913/14.* Marburg: LiteraturWissenschaft.de.

George Grosz

Grosz, George, and Max Herrmann-Neisse. 2003. *"Ist schon doll das Leben": George Grosz – Max Herrmann-Neisse: Der Briefwechsel* (ed. Klaus Völker). Berlin: Transit.

Fischer-Defoy, Christine (ed.). 2001. *George Grosz am Strand: Ostsee-Skizzen.* Berlin: Transit. Exhibition catalogue.

Goergen, Jeanpaul (ed.). 1994. *George Grosz, die Filmhälfte der Kunst* (Kinemathek 85). Berlin: Freunde der Deutschen Kinemathek.

Jentsch, Ralph. 1997. *George Grosz: The Berlin Years* (tr. Paul Goodrick and John Young). Milan: Electa.

McCloskey, Barbara. 1997. *George Grosz and the Communist Party: Art and Radicalism in Crisis, 1918 to 1936.* Princeton: Princeton University Press.

Schirmer, Lothar, and Sabine Herder. 2001. *George Grosz: Zeichnungen für Buch und Bühne.* Berlin: Henschel.

Whitford, Frank, and Christopher Clark. 1997. *The Berlin of George Grosz: Drawings, Watercolours, and Prints, 1912–1930.* New Haven: Yale University Press. Exhibition catalogue, London.

Marsden Hartley

Hartley, Marsden. 2002. *My dear Stieglitz: Letters of Marsden Hartley and Alfred Stieglitz, 1912–1915* (ed. James Timothy Voorhies). Columbia: University of South Carolina Press.

Hartley, Marsden. 1997. *Somehow a Past: The Autobiography of Marsden Hartley* (ed. Susan Elizabeth Ryan). Cambridge, Mass.: MIT Press.

Cassidy, Donna. 2005. *Marsden Hartley: Race, Region, and Nation* (Revisiting New England). Durham, N.H.: University of New Hampshire; Hanover: University Press of New England.

Kornhauser, Elizabeth Mankin (ed.). 2002. *Marsden Hartley*. New Haven: Yale University. Exhibition catalogue, Hartford, Washington, and Kansas City.

Ludington, Townsend. 1998. *Seeking the Spiritual: The Paintings of Marsden Hartley*. Ithaca: Cornell University Press.

McDonnell, Patricia. 1995. *Dictated by Life: Marsden Hartley's German Paintings and Robert Indiana's Hartley Elegies*. Minneapolis: Frederick R. Weisman Art Museum. Exhibition catalogue, Minneapolis, Chicago, and Miami.

—. 2003. *Painting Berlin Stories: Marsden Hartley, Oscar Bluemner, and the First American Avant-garde in Expressionist Berlin* (American University Studies: Series XX, Fine Arts 30). New York: Peter Lang.

Robertson, Bruce. 1994. *Marsden Hartley* (Library of American Art). New York: Abrams.

Raoul Hausmann

Hausmann, Raoul. 2004. *Courrier Dada* (ed. Marc Dachy). Paris: Éditions Allia. Expanded, annotated edition. Revised version of the text published in Dachy's 1992 edition, with corrections based on the Hausmann papers at the Getty Research Institute.

—. 1998. *Kaléidoscope: Choix de textes poétiques de Raoul Hausmann* (ed. Adelheid Koch-Didier) (Cahiers Raoul Hausmann 2). Rochechouart: Musée départemental de Rochechouart.

—. 2001. *Kurt Schwitters und Raoul Hausmann schreiben im Kino eine Oper* (ed. Eva Züchner). Berlin: Berlinische Galerie. An edition of the original German version of "Die Geschichte von Merz und Gal", a section of the unpublished first part of Hausmann's novel *Hyle*.

—. 1997. *Umbruch* (ed. Adelheid Koch). Innsbruck: Haymon.

Petersen, Jes, Raoul Hausmann, and Franz Jung. 2001. *Strontium: Briefwechsel mit Raoul Hausmannn und Franz Jung* (ed. Andreas Hansen) (Pamphlete 6). Berlin : BasisDruck.

Bartsch, Kurt, and Adelheid Koch (eds). 1996. *Raoul Hausmann* (Dossier 10). Graz: Droschl.

Frenkel, Cornelia. 1996. *Raoul Hausmann: Künstler, Forscher, Philosoph.* St. Ingbert: Röhrig.

Hille, Karoline. 2000. *Hannah Höch und Raoul Hausmann: Eine Berliner Dada-Geschichte* (Paare). Berlin: Rowohlt.

Hübner, Corinna. 2003. *Raoul Hausmann: Grenzgänger zwischen der Künsten: Eine Untersuchung zur Grenzüberschreitung zwischen Kunst und Literatur als künstlerisches Gestaltungsprinzip in Raoul Hausmanns Werk während der Dadaist-ischen Phase.* Bielefeld: Aisthesis.

IVAM Centre Julio González. 1994. *Raoul Hausmann.* Valencia: IVAM Centre Julio Gonzalez. Exhibition catalogue.

Jaunasse, Delphine. 2002. *Raoul Hausmann: L'Isolement d'un dadaïste en Limousin.* Limoges: Pulim.

Koch-Didier, Adelheid. 1994. *Ich bin immerhin der grösste Experimentator Österreichs: Raoul Hausmann, Dada und Neodada.* Innsbruck: Haymon.

—. 1997. *La Poésie a pour objet le mot: Raoul Hausmann, écrivain* (Cahiers Raoul Hausmann 1). Rochechouart: Musée départemental de Rochechouart.

— (ed.). 1997. *"Je suis l'homme de 5000 paroles et de 10000 formes": Écrits de Raoul Hausmann et documents annexes: Inventaire raisonné: Archives Raoul Hausmann, Musée départementale de Rochechouart.* Rochechouart: Musée départementale de Rochechouart.

Musée d'art moderne de Saint-Etienne. 1994. *Raoul Hausmann.* Saint-Étienne: Musée d'art moderne de Saint-Etienne. Exhibition catalogue, Saint-Étienne and Roche-chouart.

Züchner, Eva (ed.). 1998. *Scharfrichter der bürgerlichen Seele: Raoul Hausmann in Berlin 1900–1933: Unveröffentlichte Briefe, Texte, Dokumente aus den Künstler-Archiven der Berlinischen Galerie.* Berlin: Berlinische Galerie; Stuttgart: Hatje.

—. 1995. *Wir wünschen die Welt bewegt und beweglich: Raoul-Hausmann-Sym-posium der Berlinischen Galerie, Landesmuseum für Moderne Kunst, Photographie und Architektur.* Berlin: Berlinische Galerie.

Züchner, Eva, Anna-Carola Krausse, and Kathrin Hatesaul (eds.). 1994. *Der deutsche Spiesser ärgert sich: Raoul Hausmann 1886–1971.* Ostfildern: Hatje. German version of the catalogue of the IVAM exhibition, published for the exhibition venue in Berlin and elsewhere.

Emmy Hennings

Echte, Bernhard (ed.). 1999. *Emmy Ball Hennings 1885–1948: "Ich bin so vielfach-":* *Texte, Bilder, Dokumente* (Roter Stern). Frankfurt am Main: Stroemfeld. Exhibition catalogue, Zurich and Flensburg.

Gass, René. 1998. *Emmy Ball-Hennings: Wege und Umwege zum Paradies: Biographie.* Zurich: Pendo.

Reetz, Bärbel. 2001. *Emmy Ball-Hennings: Leben im Vielleicht: Eine Biographie* (Suhrkamp Taschenbuch 3240). Frankfurt am Main: Suhrkamp.

Hannah Höch

Höch, Hannah. 2004. *Hannah Höch: Album* (ed. Gunda Luyken). Ostfildern-Ruit: Hatje Cantz. Reproduction of an album of photographic images clipped from periodicals, assembled by the artist *c.*1933, now housed in the Berlinische Galerie.

Boswell, Peter, Maria Makela, and Carolyn Lanchner. 1996. *The Photomontages of Hannah Höch.* Minneapolis: Walker Art Center. Exhibition catalogue, Minneapolis and New York.

Dech, Jula. 2002. *Sieben Blicke auf Hannah Höch* (Kleine Bücherei für Hand und Kopf 52). Hamburg: Edition Nautilus.

Maurer, Ellen. 1995. *Hannah Höch: Jenseits fester Grenzen: Das malerische Werk bis 1945.* Berlin: Gebr. Mann.

Museo Nacional Centro de Arte Reina Sofía. 2004. *Hannah Höch.* Madrid: Aldeasa. Exhibition catalogue.

Richard Huelsenbeck

Huelsenbeck, Richard. 1996. *Die Sonne von Black-Point: Ein Liebesroman aus den Tropen* (ed. Herbert Kapfer und Lisbeth Exner). Munich: Belleville.

—. 1996. *Weltdada Huelsenbeck: Eine Biografie in Briefen und Bildern* (ed. Herbert Kapfer und Lisbeth Exner). Innsbruck: Haymon. Edition of Huelsenbeck's letters.

—. 1994. *Wozu Dada: Texte 1916–1936* (ed. Herbert Kapfer). Giessen: Anabas Verlag.

Nenzel, Reinhard. 1994. *Kleinkariete Avantgarde: Zur Neubewertung des deutschen Dadaismus: Der frühe Richard Huelsenbeck: Sein Leben und sein Werk bis 1916 in Darstellung und Interpretation* (Beiträge zur deutschen Literatur des zwanzigsten Jahrhunderts 1). Bonn: Reinhard Nenzel.

Iliazd

Iliazd. 1994 and continuing. *Sobranie sochineni v piati tomakh* (ed. Tatiana Nikolskaia et al.) 2 vols. known as of 2005. Moscow: Gileia; Düsseldorf: Golubo vsadnik. Collected edition.

Marcel Janco

Ilk, Michael. 2001. *Marcel Janco: Das graphische Werk: Catalogue raisonné*. s.l.: Michael Ilk.

Janco Dada Museum. *Janco Dada Museum.* Online at: http://www.jancodada-museum.israel.net. Web site of the museum at the artists' colony founded by Janco in Ein-hod, Israel.

Nocnet, Anca, et al. (eds). 1996. *Marcel Iancu în România interbelic: Arhitect, artist plastic, teoretician.* Bucharest: Editura Simetria, Uniunea Arhitecilor din România and Editura Meridiane.

Franz Jung

Jung, Franz. 1997. *Abschied von der Zeit* (ed. Lutz Schulenburg) (Franz Jung Werke 9/2). Hamburg: Nautilus. Autobiographical documents.

—. 1996. *Briefe, 1913–1963* (ed. Sieglinde and Fritz Mierau) (Franz Jung Werke 9/1). Hamburg: Edition Nautilus.

—. 2000. *Die Verzauberten: Eine Erzählung* (ed. Walter Fähnders) (Pamphlete 1). Berlin : BasisDruck. Posthumous work.

Fähnders, Walter, and Walter Andreas Hansen (eds). 2003. *Vom Trottelbuch zum Torpedokäfer: Franz Jung in der Literaturkritik 1912–1963.* Bielefeld: Aisthesis. Collection of contemporary reviews of Jung's publications and theatrical productions.

Mierau, Fritz. 1998. *Das Verschwinden von Franz Jung: Stationen einer Biographie.* Hamburg: Nautilus.

Schürer, Ernst (ed.). 1994. *Franz Jung: Leben und Werk eines Rebellen* (Studies in Modern German Literature 23). New York: Peter Lang.

Mina Loy

Loy, Mina. 1996. *The Lost Lunar Baedeker: Poems of Mina Loy* (ed. Roger L. Conover). New York: Farrar, Straus, Giroux. Nearly complete edition of the poetry.

Burke, Carolyn. 1996. *Becoming Modern: The Life of Mina Loy.* New York: Farrar, Straus, and Giroux.

Miller, Cristanne. 2005. *Cultures of Modernism: Marianne Moore, Mina Loy, & Else Lasker-Schüler: Gender and Literary Community in New York and Berlin.* Ann Arbor: University of Michigan Press.

Shreiber, Maeera, and Keith Tuma (eds). 1998. *Mina Loy: Woman and Poet.* Orono: National Poetry Foundation.

Walter Mehring

Mehring, Walter. 2001. *Reportagen der Unterweltstädte: Berichte aus Berlin und Paris, 1918 bis 1933* (ed. Georg Schirmers). Oldenburg: Igel.

Weitz, Hans-J. (ed.). 1995. *Drei jüdische Dramen: Mit Dokumenten zur Rezeption* (Veröffentlichungen der Deutschen Akademie für Sprache und Dichtung Darmstadt 69). Göttingen: Wallstein. Includes text of Mehring's play "Der Kaufmann von Berlin" and related documents.

Paul van Ostaijen

Ostaijen, Paul van. 1996. *Der Pleitejazz* (tr. Ida Rook). Berlin: Friedenauer Presse. German translation of "Bankroet-Jazz."

—. 2003. *Le Dada pour cochons* (tr. Jan H. Mysjkin and Pierre Gallissaires). Paris: Textuel.

—. 1996. *Verzamelde Gedichten* (ed. Gerrit Borgers). Amsterdam: Prometheus and Bert Bakker, 1996.

—, and Emma Clément. 1996. *Ik Heb Je Nog Steeds Zeer Lief: Paul van Ostaijen en Emma Clément: Een Liefde in Brieven (1922–1928)* (ed. Marc Reynebeau). Ghent: Poëziecentrum.

Borgers, Gerrit. 1996. *Paul van Ostaijen: Een Documentatie.* Two volumes. Amsterdam: Bert Bakker.

Kötz, Kathrin. 2001. *Die Prosa Paul van Ostaijens: Stilistische, poetologische und philosophische Korrespondenzen mit dem Werk von Mynona (Salomo Friedlaender)* (Niederlande-Studien 24). Münster and New York: Waxmann.

Missinne, Lut, and Loek Geeraedts (eds). 1998. *Paul van Ostaijen, die Avantgarde und Berlin* (Niederlande-Studien: Kleinere Schriften 4). Münster: Lit.

Clément Pensaers

Pansaers, Clément. 2002. *Dada et moi.* Toulouse: Mélanges.

—. 2004. *Orangoutangisme.* Toulouse: Mélanges.

Benjamin Péret

Péret, Benjamin. 1969–1995. *Œuvres complètes*. Seven volumes. Set completed with vol. 7 (Paris: Association des Amis de Benjamin Péret and Librairie José Corti, 1995), including previously uncollected and unpublished writings, correspondence, and a comprehensive bibliography by Masao Suzuki.

Carn, Hervé. 2001. *Benjamin Péret et la Bretagne* (Collection Bretagne, terre écrit). Moëlan-sur-Mer: Blanc Silex.

Prévan, Guy. 1999. *Péret Benjamin, révolutionnaire permanent* (Archipels du surréalisme). Paris: Syllepse.

Trois Cerises et une sardine. 1995 and continuing. Paris: Association des Amis de Benjamin Péret. Periodical published once or twice annually.

Francis Picabia

Picabia, Francis. 2005. *Écrits critiques* (ed. Carole Boulbès). Paris: Mémoire du livre. Second volume of new edition of *Écrits*.

—. 2002. *Poèmes* (ed. Carole Boulbès). Paris: Mémoire du livre. First volume of new edition of *Écrits*.

Bernheim, Cathy. 1995. *Picabia* (Vifs). Paris: Editions du Félin.

Boulbès, Carole. 1998. *Picabia: Le Saint masqué: Essai sur la peinture érotique de Francis Picharabia (sic)*. Paris: Jean-Michel Place.

Felix, Zdenek (ed.). 1998. *Francis Picabia: The Late Works 1933–1953*. Ostfildern-Ruit: Hatje. Exhibition catalogue, Hamburg and Rotterdam.

Galerie Beaubourg. 1998. *Francis Picabia: Classique et merveilleux* (L'État des lieux). Vence: Galerie Beaubourg. Exhibition catalogue.

IVAM Centre Julio Gonzalez, 1995. *Francis Picabia: Máquinas y españolas*. Valencia: IVAM Centre Julio Gonzalez; Barcelona: Fundació Antoni Tàpies. Exhibition catalogue.

Jouffroy, Alain. 2002. *Picabia* (Mémoire de l'art). Paris: Assouline.

Musée d'art moderne de la ville de Paris. 2002. *Francis Picabia: Singulier idéal*. Paris: Paris-Musées. Exhibition catalogue.

Orth, Elke. 1994. *Das dichterische Werk von Francis Picabia (1917–1920)* (Europäische Hochschulschriften: Reihe XIII, Französische Sprache und Literatur 191). Frankfurt am Main and New York: Peter Lang.

Ottinger, Didier (ed.). 2003. *Francis Picabia dans les collections du Centre Pompidou, Musée national d'art moderne*. Paris: Centre Pompidou.

Pierre, Arnauld. 2002. *Francis Picabia: La Peinture sans aura* (Art et artistes). Paris: Gallimard.

Pradel, Jean-Louis. 2002. *Francis Picabia: La Peinture mise à nu* (Découvertes Gallimard: Hors série). Paris: Découvertes Gallimard and Paris musées.

Man Ray

Bouhours, Jean-Michel, and Patrick de Haas (eds). 1997. *Man Ray: Directeur du mauvais movies*. Paris: Centre Georges Pompidou.

Campario, Jean-François. 2003. *Man Ray "avec la lumière meme": Notes sur "Noire et blanche"* (Photogalerie 16). Neuchâtel: Ides et Calendes.

Castant, Alexandre. 2003. *Noire et blanche de Man Ray* (Œuvre choisie). Paris: Scala and SCÉRÉN-CNDP.

L'Écotais, Emmanuelle de. 1997. *Le Fonds photographique de la dation Man Ray: Étude et inventaire*. Four volumes. PhD thesis. Université de la Sorbonne.

—. 2002. *Man Ray: Rayographies*. Paris: L. Scheer.

—, and Alain Sayag (eds). 1998. *Man Ray: Photography and its Double* (tr. Deke Dusinberre and Donna Wiemann). London: Laurence King. Exhibition catalogue, Paris.

Lottman, Herbert R. 2001. *Man Ray's Montparnasse*. New York: Abrams.

Man Ray Trust. *Man Ray Trust*. Online at: http://www.manraytrust.com. Website of the organisation administering reproduction rights to Man Ray's works. Includes a comprehensive image database.

Naumann, Francis M. 2003. *Conversion to Modernism: The Early Work of Man Ray*. New Brunswick, N.J.: Rutgers University Press, c.2003. Exhibition catalogue, Montclair, N.J., Athens, Ga., and Chicago.

Perlein, Gilbert, and Daniela Palazzoli. 1997. *Man Ray: Retrospective 1912–1976*. Nice: Musée d'art moderne et d'art contemporain. Exhibition catalogue.

Schaffner, Ingrid. 2002. *The Essential Man Ray* (The Essential Series). New York: Wonderland Press and Abrams.

Otto van Rees

Blendinger, P. 1994. *Otto van Rees, 1884–1957: 40 opere dalle collezioni in Ticino.* Ascona: Museo comunale d'arte moderna. Exhibition catalogue.

Georges Ribemont-Dessaignes

Ribemont-Dessaignes, Georges. 1994. *Dada: Manifestes, poèmes, nouvelles, articles, projets, théâtre, cinéma, chroniques (1915–1929)* (ed. Jean Pierre Begot). Paris: Ivrea. Revised, expanded editon of the collection originally published in two volumes. (Paris: Champ libre, 1974–1978).

Hans Richter

Foster, Stephen C. (ed.). 1998. *Hans Richter: Activism, Modernism, and the Avant-garde.* Cambridge, Mass.: MIT Press.

Goergen, Jeanpaul, et al. (eds). *Hans Richter: Film ist Rhythmus* (Kinemathek 95). 2003. Berlin: Freunde der Deutschen Kinemathek.

Janser, Andres, and Arthur Rüegg. 2001. *Hans Richter, New Living: Architecture, Film, Space* (tr. Steven Lindberg). Baden, Switzerland: Lars Müller.

Sers, Philippe. 1997. *Sur Dada: Essai sur l'expérience dadaïste de l'image, entretiens avec Hans Richter* (Rayon art). Nîmes: Éditions Jacquelin Chambon.

Christian Schad

Schad, Christian. 1999. *Relative Realitäten: Erinnerungen um Walter Serner* (Die tollen Bücher 11). Augsburg: MaroVerlag.

Lloyd, Jill, and Michael Peppiat (eds). 2003. *Christian Schad and the Neue Sachlichkeit.* New York: Norton.

Richter, Günter A. 2002. *Christian Schad: Die erste umfassende Monographie zu Werk und Leben des Künstlers: Mit einführenden Texten und 120 Legende: Ergänzt um Biographie, Bibliographie und ein Verzeichnis der Einzel- und Themenausstellungen.* Rottach-Egern: Edition G.A. Richter.

— (ed.). 2004. *Christian Schad: Texte, Materialien, Dokumente.* Rottach-Egern: Edition G.A. Richter.

Richter, Marie-Luise, and Theodor Helmert-Corvey (eds). 1997. *Christian Schad: Dokumentation.* Rottach-Egern: Edition G.A. Richter.

Schad, Nikolaus, and Anna Auer (eds). 1999. *Schadographien: Die Kraft des Lichts.* Passau: Klinger.

Kurt Schwitters

Schwitters, Kurt. 2001. *Pppppp: Poems, Performance Pieces, Proses, Plays, Poetics* (ed. and tr. Jerome Rothenburg and Pierre Joris). Cambridge, Mass.: Exact Change.

Centre Georges Pompidou. 1994. *Kurt Schwitters* (Collection Classiques du XXe siècle). Paris: Centre Georges Pompidou and Réunion des musées nationaux. Exhibition catalogue.

Fuchs, Rudi, et al. 2000. *Kurt Schwitters, I is Style.* Amsterdam: Stedelijk Museum; Rotterdam: NAi. Exhibition catalogue, Leipzig and Amsterdam.

Gamard, Elizabeth Burns. 2000. *Kurt Schwitters's Merzbau: The Cathedral of Erotic Misery* (Building 5 Studies). New York: Princeton Architectural Press.

Hereth, Hans-Jürgen. 1996. *Die Rezeptions- und Wirkungsgeschichte von Kurt Schwitters, dargestellt anhand seines Gedichts "An Anna Blume"* (Forschungen zur Literatur- und Kulturgeschichte 53). Frankfurt am Main and New York: Peter Lang.

Krempel, Ulrich, and Karin Orchard. 1996. *Kurt Schwitters: Kurt-Schwitters-Sammlung der NORD/LB in der Niedersächsischen Sparkassenstiftung.* Hanover: Norddeutsche Landesbank and Sprengel Museum Hannover.

Kurt und Ernst Schwitters Stiftung. 2002. *Kurt und Ernst Schwitters Stiftung: der Nachlass von Kurt und Ernst Schwitters* (Patrimonia 222). Hanover: Kulturstiftung der Länder; Kurt und Ernst Schwitters Stiftung.

Meyer-Büser, Susanne, and Karin Orchard (eds). 2000. *In the Beginning was Merz: From Kurt Schwitters to the Present Day* (tr. Fiona Elliott). Ostfildern: Hatje Cantz. Exhibition catalogue, Hanover, Düsseldorf and Munich.

Müller-Alsbach, Anja, and Heinz Stahlhut (eds). 2004. *Kurt Schwitters: MERZ: A Votal Vision of the World* (tr. Caroline Saltzwedel et al.). Bern: Benteli. Exhibition catalogue, Basel.

Orchard, Karin, and Isabel Schulz. 2000–2005. *Catalogue raisonné Kurt Schwitters.* Three volumes. Ostfildern-Ruit: Hatje Cantz.

—. 1998. *Kurt Schwitters: Werke und Dokumente: Verzeichnis der Bestände im Sprengel Museum Hannover (Catalogue of the Works and Documents in the Sprengel Museum Hannover)* (tr. John Brogde). Hanover: Sprengel Museum Hannover.

Riha, Karl. 2000. *Hannover=Kurt-Schwitters-Stadt: Zur Rezeptionsgeschichte des MERZ-Dadaisten.* Siegen: s.n.

Schaub, Gerhard. 1998. *Kurt Schwitters und die "andere" Schweiz: Unveröffentlichte Briefe aus dem Exil.* Berlin: Fannei & Walz.

Sprengel Museum Hannover. *Kurt Schwitters Archive at the Sprengel Museum Hannover*. Online at: http://www.hannover.de/stadtdia_2/sprengel/index_engl.htm. Information on the museum's Schwitters collections, with links to other Schwitters websites.

Stadsgalerij Heerlen. 1997. *Kurt Schwitters in Nederland: Merz, De Stijl & Holland Dada*. Zwolle: Waanders. Exhibition catalogue, Heerlen, Netherlands.

Webster, Gwendolen. 1997. *Kurt Merz Schwitters: A Biographical Study*. Cardiff: University of Wales Press.

Walter Serner

Hackenbruch, Ulrich. 1996. *Sachliche Intensitäten: Walter Serners "erotische Kriminalgeschichten" in ihrer Epoche* (Analysen und Dokumente 37). Frankfurt am Main and New York: Peter Lang.

Peters, Jonas. 1995. *Dem Kosmos einen Tritt!: Die Entwicklung des Werks von Walter Serner und die Konzeption seiner dadaistischen Kulturkritik* (Hamburger Beiträge zur Germanistik 19). Frankfurt am Main and New York: Peter Lang.

Puff-Trojan, Andreas, and Wendelin Schmidt-Dengler (eds). 1998. *Der Pfiff aufs Ganze: Studien zu Walter Serner*. Vienna: Sonderzahl.

Charles Sheeler

Lucic, Karen. 1997. *Charles Sheeler in Doylestown: American Modernism and the Pennsylvania Tradition*. Allentown, Pa.: Allentown Art. Exhibition catalogue.

Stebbins, Theodore E., Jr., Gilles Mora, and Karen E. Haas. 2002. *The Photography of Charles Sheeler: American Modernist*. Boston: Bulfinch Press. Exhibition catalogue, Boston and elsewhere.

Philippe Soupault

Albert-Birot, Arlette, Nathalie Nabert, and Georges Sebbag (eds). 2000. *Philippe Soupault: L'Ombre frissonnante* (Collection Surfaces). Paris: Jean-Michel Place.

Aspley, Keith. 2001. *The Life and Works of Surrealist Philippe Soupault (1897–1990): Parallel Lives* (Studies in French Literature 51). Lewiston, N.Y.: Edwin Mellen Press.

Berne, Mauricette, and Jacqueline Chénieux-Gendron (eds). 1997. *Portrait(s) de Philippe Soupault* (Portrait(s)). Paris: Bibliothèque nationale de France.

Boucharenc, Myriam. 1997. *L'Échec et son double: Philippe Soupault romancier* (Littérature de notre siècle 1). Paris: Champion.

—, and Claude Leroy (eds). 1999. *Présence de Philippe Soupault*. Caen: Presses universitaires de Caen.

Cahiers Philippe Soupault. 1994 and continuing. Villejuif: Association des amis de Philippe Soupault. Occasional periodical.

Cassayre, Sylvie. 1997. *Poétique de l'espace et imaginaire dans l'œuvre de Philippe Soupault* (Bibliothèque des lettres modernes 40). Paris: Lettres modernes.

Chénieux-Gendron, Jacqueline (ed.). 2001. *Patiences et silences de Philippe Soupault* (Collection Arts & sciences de l'art). Paris: L'Harmattan.

Lachenal, Lydie. 1997. *Philippe Soupault: Sa Vie, son œuvre, chronologie*. Paris: Lachenal & Ritter.

Joseph Stella

Haskell, Barbara. 1994. *Joseph Stella*. New York: Whitney Museum of American Art.

Jaffe, Irma B. 1994. *Joseph Stella's Symbolism* (Essential paintings series). San Francisco: Pomegranate Artbooks.

Alfred Stieglitz

Brennan, Marcia. 2001. *Painting Gender, Constructing Theory: The Alfred Stieglitz Circle and American Formalist Aesthetics*. Cambridge, Mass.: MIT Press.

Connor, Celeste. 2001. *Democratic Visions: Art and Theory of the Stieglitz Circle, 1924–1934*. Berkeley: University of California Press.

Hoffman, Katherine. 2004. *Stieglitz: A Beginning Light*. New Haven: Yale University Press.

Greenough, Sarah (ed.). 2000. *Modern Art and America: Alfred Stieglitz and His New York Galleries*. Washington: National Gallery of Art; Boston: Bulfinch Press. Exhibition catalogue.

Whelan, Richard. 1995. *Alfred Stieglitz: A Biography*. Boston: Little, Brown.

Sophie Taeuber-Arp

Fricker, H. R. 1995. *Sophie Taeuber-Arp: Kindheit und Jugend in Trogen*. Zurich: Fink.

Jan Tschichold

McLean, Ruari. 1997. *Jan Tschichold: A Life in Typography*. New York: Princeton Architectural Press.

Tristan Tzara

Tzara, Tristan. 1997. *Dada terminus: Tristan Tzara-E.L.T. Mesens, correspondance choisie, 1923–1926* (ed. Stéphane Massonet). Brussels: Devillez.

Béhar, Henri. 2005. *Tristan Tzara* (Les Étrangers de Paris: Les Roumains de Paris). Paris: Oxus. Biography.

Buot, François. 2002. *Tristan Tzara: L'Homme qui inventa la révolution Dada.* Paris: Grasset. Biography.

Les Cahiers Tristan Tzara (Caietele Tristan Tzara). 1998 and continuing. Bucharest: Editura Vinea. Periodical, published approximately annually.

Ilk, Michael. 1997. *Brancusi, Tzara und die rumänische Avantgarde.* Bochum: Museum Bochum.

Jacques Vaché

Lacarelle, Bertrand. 2005. *Jacques Vaché.* Paris: Grasset. Biography.

Beatrice Wood

Naumann, Francis M. (ed.). 1997. *Beatrice Wood: A Centennial Tribute.* New York: American Craft Museum. Exhibition catalogue.

Marius de Zayas

Zayas, Marius de. 1996. *How, When, and Why Modern Art Came to New York* (ed. Francis M. Naumann). Cambridge, Mass.: MIT Press.

Editorial note: Due to the length, nature and function of the material here presented, the style of entries contained in this critical bibliography differs from the style of entries in the bibliographical reference sections included at the end of each of the individual essays in *Dada Culture*.

List of illustrations

Permission to reproduce the illustrations has been generously granted by several institutions and publishers. We would like to thank copyright holders who have given permission to reproduce their works. Every effort has been made to locate copyright holders for images included in this book, but those we have been unable to reach are invited to contact the publisher so that acknowledgments can be made in subsequent editions. We hope that the parties concerned will see without displeasure the inclusion of the respective works, and accept our thanks.

1. Spiegelgasse 1, Zürich.
2. Lenin, Zürich 1916.
3. Spiegelgasse, Zürich.
4. Spiegelgasse 14, Zürich.
5. Tristan Tzara, "Manifeste Dada 1918", *Dada* no. 3, Zürich, December 1918; International Dada Archive Digital Library, University of Iowa.
6. *Littérature* no. 17, Paris, December 1920; International Dada Archive Digital Library, University of Iowa.
7. *Cravan: Mystery Man of the Twentieth Century*, Dark Horse Publications, Milwaukie, 2005.
8. Tristan Tzara, *Calligramme*, 1920.
9. Walter Serner and Tristan Tzara, Zürich 1919.
10. Christian Schad, *Portrait of Walter Serner*, 1920, typescript and collage, Bibliothèque Littéraire Jacques Doucet, Paris. © Artists Rights Society (ARS)/VG Bildkunst.
11. Marcel Duchamp, *The*, 1915 © Succession Marcel Duchamp/ ADAGP, Paris and DACS, London 2005. Philadelphia Museum of Art: The Louise and Walter Arensberg Collection.
12. Marcel Duchamp, *Erratum Musical*, 1913 © Succession Marcel Duchamp/ADAGP, Paris and DACS, London 2005. Philadelphia Museum of Art: The Louise and Walter Arensberg Collection.
13. Marcel Duchamp, *With Hidden Noise*, 1916 © Succession Marcel Duchamp/ADAGP, Paris and DACS, London 2005. Philadelphia Museum of Art: The Louise and Walter Arensberg Collection, 1950.
14. Marcel Duchamp, *Rendez-vous du Dimanche 6 Février 1916*, 1916 © Succession Marcel Duchamp/ADAGP, Paris and

DACS, London 2005. Philadelphia Museum of Art: The Louise and Walter Arensberg Collection.

15. Marcel Duchamp, *Tonsure* (Duchamp with haircut by George de Zayas, Paris, photo by Man Ray), 1921 © Succession Marcel Duchamp/ADAGP, Paris and DACS, London 2005. Philadelphia Museum of Art: Marcel Duchamp Archive, Gift of Jacqueline, Paul and Peter Matisse in memory of their mother, Alexina Duchamp.

16. Raoul Hausmann, *fmsbw*, poster poem, 1918. © Artists Rights Society (ARS)/ADAGP.

17. Hugo Ball "Karawane" (1916), *Dada Almanach*, Berlin, 1920; International Dada Archive Digital Library, University of Iowa.

18. Otto Dix, *Kartenspieler*, 1920. Ausgewählt für die Schenkung Karsch/Nierendorf, Berlin 1995. © 2004 VG Bildkunst, Bonn.

19. Otto Dix, *Pragerstrasse*, 1920. Stuttgart, Galerie der Stadt. © 2004 VG Bildkunst, Bonn.

20. Otto Dix, *Die Skatspieler*, 1920. Staatliche Museen Preußischer Kulturbesitz, Nationalgalerie. © 2004 VG Bildkunst, Bonn.

21. John Heartfield, *"Arbeiterzeichnungen und Gedichte aus den Betrieben. Die Rationalisierung marschiert!"* ("Workers Drawings and Poems from the Factories. Rationalisation is on the march!"). Photomontage for *Der Knüppel* no. 2, Berlin, February 1927. © Artists Rights Society (ARS)/VG Bildkunst.

22. Kurt Schwitters, *Baum und Kirche (Z 124)*, 1918. Schwitters Estate. Photo: Sprengel Museum, Hanover. © 2006 Artists Rights Society (ARS), New York/VG Bildkunst, Bonn.

23. Kurt Schwitters, *Die Sonne im Hochgebirge (G Expression 2)*, 1918. Photo: Sprengel Museum, Hanover. © 2006 Artists Rights Society (ARS), New York/VG Bildkunst, Bonn.

24. Kurt Schwitters, *Hochgebirgsfriedhof (Abstraktion)*, 1919. Solomon R. Guggenheim Museum, New York. © 2006 Artists Rights Society (ARS), New York/VG Bildkunst, Bonn.

25. Caspar David Friedrich, *Kreuz im Gebirge (Tetschener Altar)*, 1808. Staatliche Kunstsammlungen Dresden, Galerie Neue Meister.

26. Kurt Schwitters, *Das Merzbild*, 1919. Location unknown. Photo: Sprengel Museum, Hanover. © 2006 Artists Rights Society (ARS), New York/VG Bildkunst, Bonn.

27. Kurt Schwitters, *Haus Merz*, 1920. Photo: Sprengel Museum, Hanover. © 2006 Artists Rights Society (ARS), New York/VG Bildkunst, Bonn.
28. Kurt Schwitters, *Merzbau: Blue Window*, c.1930. Photo: Sprengel Museum, Hanover. © 2006 Artists Rights Society (ARS), New York/VG Bildkunst, Bonn.
29. Johannes Baader, *Das ist die Erscheinung des Oberdada in den Wolken des Himmel*, *Der Dada* no. 2, Berlin 1919; International Dada Archive Digital Library, University of Iowa.
30. Johannes Baader, HADO, announcement, Berlin 1919; Getty Research Institute. Photo Estera Milman.
31. Johannes Baader, guest editor, *Die freie Strasse* no. 10, Berlin 1918; Getty Research Institute. Photo Estera Milman.
32. Johannes Baader, "Dadaisten gegen Weimar" broadside manifesto, Berlin 1919; Getty Research Institute. Photo Estera Milman.
33. Johannes Baader, *Dada-Dio-Drama*, 1919–20.
34. Arthur Cravan, "To Be or Not To Be … American", *L'Echo des Sports*, Paris, 10 June 1909.
35. Arthur Cravan, *Maintenant* no. 4, Paris, March-April 1914; International Dada Archive Digital Library, University of Iowa.
36. *Littérature* no. 11/12, Paris, 15 October 1923; International Dada Archive Digital Library, University of Iowa.
37. Marcel Duchamp, *Three Standard Stoppages*, Paris 1913–14. Katherine S. Dreier Bequest. © 2005 Artists Rights Society (ARS), New York/ADAGP, Paris/Estate of Marcel Duchamp.
38. Marcel Duchamp, *Door: 11, rue Larrey*, 1927. © 2005 Artists Rights Society (ARS), New York/ADAGP, Paris/Estate of Marcel Duchamp.

Contributors

David Cunningham teaches at the University of Westminster in London and is an editor of the journal *Radical Philosophy*. He has published widely on modernism, aesthetics and critical theory, and is the co-editor of *Adorno and Literature* (Continuum 2006) and *Photography and Literature in the Twentieth Century* (CSP 2005). He is currently writing a monograph on the concept of an avant-garde.

T. J. Demos is lecturer in the Department of History of Art, University College London. A member of *Art Journal*'s editorial board, he writes widely on modern and contemporary art, and his articles have appeared in magazines including *Artforum*, *Grey Room*, and *October*. His book entitled *The Exile of Marcel Duchamp* is forthcoming from MIT Press. He is currently working on a book-length study of contemporary art and globalisation.

Stephen C. Foster is professor emeritus of art history at The University of Iowa and was director of the Fine Arts Dada Archive and Research Centre from 1979 until 2001. He was also the Director of the Programme for Modern Studies from 1988 until 1997. Concentrating on European art of the First World War era, Professor Foster's publications include *"Event" Arts and Art Events* (1988), *The World According to Dada* (1988), *Franz Kline: Art and the Structure of Identity* (1994), *Dada: The Coordinates of Cultural Politics* (1996), *Dada Cologne Hanover*, with Charlotte Stokes (1997), *Hans Richter: Activism, Modernism and the Avant-Garde* (1998), and *An American Odyssey, 1945/1980: Debating Modernism* (2004). Professor Foster served as general editor for *Crisis and the Arts: The History of Dada* (ten volumes) between 1996 and 2004. He is currently preparing a two volume monograph and catalogue on the work of Franz Kline and a comprehensive monograph on Berlin Dadaist Johannes Baader.

Joel Freeman is assistant professor at the University of California, Berkeley. His research work addresses the interrelationship of death and time in Ernst Bloch, Martin Heidegger and Thomas Mann. He has worked extensively on the novel, the theory of the novel and in particular the high modernists, Thomas Mann, Alfred Döblin, Robert

Musil and Hermann Broch, and in his work engages aesthetic theory from Alexander Baumgarten to the "classical" avant-garde of the early twentieth century.

Martin Ignatius Gaughan, formerly director of the history and theory of art degree programmes at the University of Wales Institute, Cardiff. He has contributed chapters to the series *Crisis and the Arts*, and edited volume 8, *Dada New York: New World for Old* (2003). His most recent contribution to Dada studies is "Narrating the Dada game plan" in *Art of the Avant-Gardes* (Yale University Press and the Open University, 2004). His book *German Visual Culture: Modernism and Modernisation 1907–1937* (Peter Lang) is due for publication in early 2006.

Curt Germundson is assistant professor of art history at the Minnesota State University at Mankato. He received his PhD at the University of Iowa and his dissertation is entitled *Kurt Schwitters in Hanover: Investigation of a Cultural Environment*. He is the author of "Kurt Schwitters and the Alternative Art Community in Hanover", in *Crisis and the Arts* (1997); "Kurt Schwitters's collage *Hindenburg-Merzzeichnung 157*" in *Collecting Modernism: European Masterworks from the Munson-Williams-Proctor Arts Institute* (2005); and "Alexander Dorner's Atmosphere Room: The Museum as Experience" in *Visual Resources* (2005).

Dafydd Jones has written and published on Dada within the *Crisis and the Arts* series, presenting work on the avant-garde in the field of critical theory, most recently to the Avant-Garde Project's *Mapping the Neo-Avantgarde* conference at the University of Edinburgh (2005). He was among the speakers at the first English-language conference devoted to the work of French philosopher Alain Badiou, at Cardiff University in 2002, with ongoing research work into the category of subject evasion. He lectures in twentieth century and contemporary art practice at Cardiff, working in text broadcast, and is the editor of the University of Wales Press.

Cornelius Partsch is assistant professor of German at Western Washington University in Bellingham, Washington. His publications include a book on jazz and popular music in the Weimar Republic, entitled *Schräge Töne* (2000), and various articles in the area of popular culture studies. He is currently preparing a book on German spy fiction.

Anna Katharina Schaffner completed her PhD on language dissection in historical avant-garde and concrete poetry at the University of Edinburgh. She is working as post-doctoral research assistant in the AHRC sponsored avant-garde research project at the University of Edinburgh and the University of Glasgow, and teaches courses on the short story and on avant-garde art, literature and film.

Timothy Shipe is curator of the International Dada Archive at the University of Iowa Libraries. He completed his PhD in Comparative Literature at the University of Iowa. In addition to his work on the bibliography of the Dada movement, he has written on artists' books and twentieth-century German literature, among other topics.

John Wall has written and published several articles on the relation between language and body as it is expressed in the novels of Samuel Beckett. For several years he has read Beckett's work as an expression of the "corporeal imagination", a concept theorised with the aid of Merleau-Ponty's notions of embodied space and time. It is anticipated that this research project will be prepared for publication in 2007. He is currently editing a volume of essays on music and culture, and teaches at Eastern Mediterranean University in Cyprus.